THE
FOURTH
MAN

THE
FOURTH
MAN

THE HUNT FOR A KGB SPY
AT THE TOP OF THE CIA
AND THE RISE OF
PUTIN'S RUSSIA

ROBERT BAER

 hachette
BOOKS

NEW YORK

Copyright © 2022 by Robert Baer

Jacket design by Amanda Kain

Jacket photograph by Mike Boese

Jacket copyright © 2022 by Hachette Book Group, Inc.

Hachette Book Group supports the right to free expression and the value of copyright. The purpose of copyright is to encourage writers and artists to produce the creative works that enrich our culture.

The scanning, uploading, and distribution of this book without permission is a theft of the author's intellectual property. If you would like permission to use material from the book (other than for review purposes), please contact permissions@hbgusa.com. Thank you for your support of the author's rights.

Hachette Books
Hachette Book Group
1290 Avenue of the Americas
New York, NY 10104
HachetteBooks.com
Twitter.com/HachetteBooks
Instagram.com/HachetteBooks

First Edition: May 2022

Published by Hachette Books, an imprint of Perseus Books, LLC, a subsidiary of Hachette Book Group, Inc. The Hachette Books name and logo is a trademark of the Hachette Book Group.

The Hachette Speakers Bureau provides a wide range of authors for speaking events. To find out more, go to www.hachettespeakersbureau.com or call (866) 376-6591.

The publisher is not responsible for websites (or their content) that are not owned by the publisher.

Print book interior design by Six Red Marbles

Library of Congress Control Number: 2022933333

ISBNs: 9780306925610 (hardcover), 9780306925603 (ebook)

Printed in the United States of America

LSC-C

10 9 8 7 6 5 4 3 2 1

CONTENTS

CONTENTS

AUTHOR'S NOTE

IN 1991, THE KGB was broken up into several agencies. Most important, its foreign intelligence apparatus was separated from counterintelligence. But for simplicity's sake, I'll often slip into calling the KGB successor organizations simply the KGB, as many Russians do. The KGB is a way of thinking as much as it is an organization. It's just as I'll toggle between Russians and Soviets, as this story jumps back and forth chronologically across the fall of the USSR. In the same spirit, I'll do my best to avoid the usual bureaucratic alphabet soup that comes with spy books. As for references, two books about the KGB and American mole hunting were indispensable for keeping the facts and dates straight in my head: Milt Bearden and Jim Risen's *The Main Enemy* and Sandy Grimes and Jeanne Vertefeuille's *Circle of Treason*. As for my sources, many prefer to remain anonymous, if for no other reason than the Fourth Man is still the subject of an ongoing criminal espionage investigation. I tried to reach all the main players; though, as I'll get into, many refused to talk about it. For every nonpublic piece of information, I did my best to get at least two corroborating sources. Finally, this story is about the CIA's hunt for the Fourth Man rather than the FBI's—though I will scratch the surface of the latter. It's a story I hope someone else can someday reveal in full.

AUTHOR'S NOTE

As the Fourth Man hunt is still an active investigation, in the course of writing this book I offered both the CIA and the FBI the opportunity to remove any information that would impede either organization's investigation. The CIA did ask for minimal redactions, which I've gladly made. None of them in the slightest changed the narrative or my conclusions about the investigation.

ONE

coun·ter·in·tel·li·gence /ˌkaʊn tər ɪnˈtɛl ɪ dʒəns/ *n.* The practice of keeping enemies outside your walls and catching the ones inside.

Moscow; 1992

THE PROBLEM WAS how to find a KGB operative in Moscow who didn't want to be found. He deliberately hadn't given the CIA his Moscow phone number or address. He wasn't listed in any Moscow directory the CIA possessed. And there was no way any-one from the CIA was about to knock on the KGB's door to ask for him: The CIA wanted to have a word with the man in private, not give the KGB cause to arrest him for espionage.

Since KGB surveillance and counterintelligence were all over the CIA in Moscow, it was going to make running him to ground all the harder. Even after the Soviet Union came crashing down in 1991, the Cold War declared over and Russia now aligned with the West (on paper, that is), it's not the way the KGB saw things. It never for a moment stopped looking at the United States as Rus-sia's sworn enemy and at the CIA as primed to sabotage Russia any way it could. With CIA operatives tailed around Moscow, trying to buttonhole any Russian, let alone an intelligence officer, was highly risky if not impossible.

The KGB operative the CIA wanted to talk to was a tall, gaunt, mustached ethnic Georgian by the name of Alexander Ivanovich Zaporozhsky. He joined the KGB in 1975 and since then worked in the counterintelligence directorate of its foreign intelligence service, the First Chief Directorate. After Yeltsin broke up the KGB in 1991, his service was renamed the SVR.

Although Zaporozhsky in his dealings with the CIA always considered himself more accomplice than spy—an agent, as the CIA calls them—he'd started to drop intriguing hints about KGB double agents in American intelligence. To the handful of people who knew about him inside the CIA and FBI, Zaporozhsky was known as Max.

The first time the CIA ran across Max was in 1988 in East Africa. The occasion was Max's heavy-handed recruitment attempt of an American official assigned to the embassy there. After the embassy official informed the CIA about Max's suspicious overtures, the CIA decided the best course was to let Max know face-to-face that it would be best to back off. As choreographed in advance, a CIA operative—a case officer, in CIA parlance—by the name of Mark Sparkman crashed a dinner between Max and the official. The official quickly stood up and excused himself, leaving Max and Sparkman to continue with dinner. Without missing a beat, Max said he knew exactly where Sparkman worked, the CIA. But Max wasn't put off; rather, he found the turn of events amusing. Why spoil the evening by bolting?

It wasn't a surprise Max knew Sparkman was CIA. The East

African country he was assigned to in those days was an obedient Soviet ally that kept the KGB informed about American officials assigned there. Nor were the circumstances of the first meeting between Max and Sparkman all that unusual. In Africa, the rules of engagement between the KGB and the CIA were pretty much made up as you went along. While fraternizing was mostly borne out of sheer boredom, one unintended consequence was to turn Africa into a happy hunting ground for both the CIA and the KGB. Any Russian who wanted to defect or volunteer to spy for the CIA knew exactly whose door to knock on, and vice versa.

Max and Sparkman weren't alone at their first encounter. One of Max's duties was to train the local intelligence service in spy tradecraft. As part of an exercise, Max that night tasked an undercover team to spread out around the restaurant and discreetly observe his dinner with the American embassy official. Who knows what they thought about an uninvited American showing up, but since Max didn't seem to mind, neither did they.

Sparkman suspected he might have a fish on the line for the very reason Max hadn't bolted, which should have been standard protocol for a KGB officer ambushed in this fashion. Instead, they sat for the next couple of hours ironically running through tired Cold War talking points. Sparkman's easygoing Southern charm helped blunt the awkwardness of the first meeting and polish the night. At the end of dinner, they agreed to keep in touch. When Max peeled out of the parking lot, Sparkman knew he was dealing with a conflicted man. He definitely wasn't your usual tight-lipped, ramrod-serious KGB apparatchik.

After a series of CIA case officers met Max, there came a point when he started to drop hints about his service's possessing two double agents in American intelligence. He didn't know the true name of either, but he heard one was in the CIA and the other in the FBI. He'd seen one of their files on a colleague's desk, he said. He even knew which safe it was kept in. But he wasn't in a position to get his hands on it. In the KGB's world, curiosity kills the cat. But what Max was absolutely certain about is that both double agents were still in place and, from what he'd gleaned, spilling their guts. Max also provided the KGB code names for the two agents in American intelligence. (I would have noted them here, but the CIA has asked me not to.)

Keep in mind, Max's allegations about double agents in American intelligence were made years before CIA and FBI spy catchers concluded there in fact were any. There'd been devastating, unexplained losses of CIA Russian agents in 1985 and 1986. And there certainly were those who suspected the problem was a mole. But there was nothing in the way of airtight evidence to support the theory.

Sparkman's station chief in East Africa, a man I once served with, wasn't convinced Max was the real thing. Or at least not in the beginning. An old-school cold warrior, he had been at the receiving end of enough KGB disinformation campaigns to be wary of Max. His position was that until Max turned a corner and started to provide hard intelligence about the double agents, he'd treat him as what the CIA calls a "dangle"—a triple agent programmed by Russian intelligence to drive the CIA into a paranoid frenzy about the enemy within. There's little the KGB takes more joy in than muddying the water and fouling the air at Langley.

In fairness to Max, the CIA didn't exactly handle him with finesse. One case officer sent out to the East African country to meet him had a well-deserved reputation for being an unapologetic prick. Max took an immediate dislike to him and made up stuff out of pure spite. Needless to say, it didn't improve the station chief's opinion of Max. Nor Langley's: The Langley desk officer who handled Max's file agreed, telling me she never knew when to trust him. Nor did it help that when Max was transferred back to Moscow, he flat-out turned down contact there. And the CIA didn't much care. It's risky enough meeting a Russian agent in Moscow, let alone one who can't be counted on to submit to the rigors and discipline of what the CIA calls "denied area operations"—Moscow Rules, as they've come to be popularly called—spy tradecraft tactics meticulously crafted to operate under the KGB's eagle eye and not get caught.

Another reason doubts about Max's credibility weren't entirely his fault is that he was never sat down for a proper debriefing, one at which he would have been pressed to describe the exact circumstances of his learning about the two American double agents. Debriefing an agent on the fly, and especially a KGB officer as gun-shy as Max, inevitably leads to misunderstandings and miscues. Also, Max's eccentricities aren't unique when it comes to agents, especially the better ones, who often are psychologically flawed. While a case officer would prefer an agent show up at every meeting with a briefcase of top secret documents, then quietly disappear into the night, in practice they're often erratic and untrustworthy.

Then there's this: If Max truly believed his service had penetrated the CIA, he had every reason in the world to keep the CIA at arm's length. With hindsight learned the hard way, he'd one day realize he should have ridden away from the CIA at a full gallop. At least he had enough common sense not to meet the CIA in Moscow when reassigned there from East Africa.

Max likely would have stayed on the back burner, eventually consigned to the archives, had the FBI and CIA not come around to concluding there indeed was a double agent in CIA Russian operations. Between the two agencies, in 1992 they'd pieced together enough evidence to draw up a list of suspects. But there was one name in particular that best matched the double agent's profile, a CIA case officer by the name of Aldrich "Rick" Ames. While Ames had access to the files of the Russian agents the CIA and FBI lost in the 1985–86 time frame, what really drew the investigators' interest was that he'd bought an expensive house with cash. But the problem was that Ames was one of more than two hundred suspects. And although the CIA spy catchers thought the case against Ames was solid thanks to the house and doubts about Ames's character, before the FBI could initiate a full-scale investigation, it needed proof he was in fact in contact with Russian intelligence. Since catching Ames meeting his Russian handler in Washington was a long shot, the hope was Max might be able to help. The FBI bluntly informed the CIA that if it couldn't run Max to ground in Moscow, the FBI would.

With the CIA at a complete loss as to how to reconnect with Max, it had no other choice but to wait for luck to knock on its door. And miraculously, it did. It occurred at a "liaison" meeting between the chief of station in Moscow, Dave Rolph, and his Russian intelligence counterparts. The venue was a gloomy Moscow mansion once inhabited by Stalin's psychopathic, mass-murdering ex–security chief, Lavrentiy Beria. These occasional get-togethers were never not an utter waste of time, with the Russians declining to hand over anything that could be described as worthwhile intelligence. The CIA wasn't much more generous. But pretenses had to be kept up after the Cold War, and the charade continued.

One time at Beria House, Rolph was astonished to find Max there as a notetaker. As soon as Rolph got back to the station, he cabled Langley for instructions. Langley shot back, instructing him to unobtrusively slip Max a note at the next meeting proposing they meet away from Beria House, at some out-of-the-way site in Moscow. Taking the risk of passing a note to a Russian intelligence operative in the presence of his colleagues was, to say the least, highly unorthodox. It was all the odder for Rolph because no one would tell him why it was so important for Langley to talk to Max away from his colleagues. Normally a chief is informed about everything Langley does in his backyard. But Rolph, who'd been in the Army special forces and spent enough time in the CIA to no longer be surprised by its bizarre ways, didn't ask and saluted. He was now left to puzzle over how he'd pull off this sleight of hand.

At the next meeting at Beria House, when Rolph and Max fortuitously happened to ride up alone in an ancient, rickety elevator, Rolph stuck the note in Max's hand. Max didn't say anything, only pocketing it.

Max never took him up on the offer.

With the FBI still on its back, in early 1993 Langley decided to invite its Russian intelligence counterparts to Washington for a conference. In those early, optimistic days after the collapse of the Soviet Union, visits like these were fairly standard. But for this one, Langley's extravagant hope was that the Russians would include Max on the invite list. To everyone's surprise, lightning did strike twice, and Max's name was right there on the list.

Of the case officers Max met in East Africa, he particularly got along with Dick Corbin, an old Soviet hand now assigned to counterintelligence at Langley. A compact, athletic man, Corbin was a straight shooter, roundly liked by everyone who knew him, and especially Russians. He'd learned fluent Russian when he worked for the National Security Agency, the eavesdropping arm of the Pentagon. But more important for Langley, he was among maybe a dozen or so in the CIA and FBI fully read into the CIA mole hunt, thus one of the few who knew exactly why such elaborate plans had been made to bring Max to Washington.

Most attendees on the American side, including Rolph, had no clue why Corbin was there. Considering Corbin wasn't working on Russia at the time, it made little sense. On the other hand, they knew not to ask. When it came to Russian operations, the rules of the road were as categorical as they come: No talking. No questions. It was only years later that Rolph found out he was an unwitting player in the Ames hunt.

Now, with the Russian intelligence delegation in Washington, the problem was getting Max away from his colleagues. In spite of perestroika and the end of the Soviet Union, Russian intelligence officers on trips abroad kept a close eye on one another, sometimes at night even posting a security officer in the corridor of the hotel where they were staying. Often they were forced to share rooms to make sure one didn't slip out in the middle of the night. The CIA attendees saw a lot of Max around conference tables and social events, but there was no opportunity to pull him aside for a one-on-one. They had to settle for snatches of conversation with him in hallways and stairwells. The lead CIA investigator on the mole-hunting team, Jeanne Vertefeuille, got a couple of words with Max when the meetings moved from the DC area to the stately Greenbrier, a luxury resort in White Sulphur Springs, West Virginia. But he said nothing about the two KGB double agents in American intelligence.

It wasn't until Corbin took Max fishing very early one rainy, cold morning that Max dropped his bombshell: A Russian intelligence colleague by the name of Yuri Karetkin had traveled to Caracas to meet a CIA double agent. Corbin couldn't believe his ears. Max, for the first time, was providing a usable piece of intelligence that possibly could be corroborated. Although Max still didn't know the double agent's true name, the Caracas lead was enough for the FBI to match the dates of Karetkin's travel with those of Ames. It also was enough for a judge to authorize the FBI to secretly break into Ames's house and search it. Finding incontrovertible evidence he was a Russian double agent, the FBI arrested Ames on February 21, 1994, and quickly extracted a confession of espionage from him. He copped to betraying in 1985 nearly a dozen CIA and FBI Soviet agents. He'd done it for money, banally fencing the CIA's crown jewels to treat himself to a new Jaguar and suburban spread. It was an act of treason from which the CIA would never completely recover, to this day.

One takeaway from Max's story is that there's some truth to the old espionage piece of wisdom that it takes a spy to catch a spy. The FBI and CIA have never publicly owned up to it, but Max's Caracas lead was critical in putting Ames behind bars. But what counted for any future mole hunts is that, in a moment, Max went from suspected dangle to the best counterintelligence agent the CIA and FBI have ever had, bar none. Anything going forward he had to say about Russian double agents, whether FBI or CIA, had to be taken with the utmost seriousness. And he did have more to say.

No one I've talked to can remember exactly when, but at one point Max made an even more sensational claim: There was another KGB double agent in the CIA, one more senior and better placed than Ames. Factoring in a series of unexplained compromises to the KGB that couldn't be accounted for by Ames, the CIA and FBI launched a nearly three-decade hunt for a new KGB penetration of the CIA in its top ranks.

The spy catchers initially called Max's new CIA double agent "the big case." Eventually some came to call him the Fourth Man, after three other notorious double agents in Russian operations— Ames, CIA case officer Edward Lee Howard, and FBI special agent Robert Hanssen. Howard defected to Russia in 1984, and Hanssen was arrested in 2001. All three met bad ends: Ames and Hanssen are now in federal penitentiaries for life. Howard somehow broke his neck in Moscow.

The Fourth Man, on the other hand, has never been publicly named, let alone charged with espionage, and to this day remains the Holy Grail of American counterintelligence. The FBI remains sufficiently convinced to continue investigating. It's just that they were up against someone who knew how to play the game to win.

TWO

need-to-know /nid tʊ noʊ/ *adj.* Limiting a secret to the absolute fewest people possible.

Langley, Virginia; 1996

I GOT A glimmer of what was going on a few years later, in March 1996, when my boss, Bill Lofgren, and I were called down to the White House about something I now can't remember.

At that time, Lofgren headed Langley's operations division responsible for field stations in the former Soviet Union and Eastern Europe. I oversaw his stations in Central Asia and the Caucasus. In those days, our job was mostly trying to charm the new intelligence services spun off from the KGB, convince them we weren't the enemy anymore. The CIA not being much of a charm school, I can't say we were all that successful.

Both Lofgren and I would have preferred to be in the field running agents, but we tried to make the most of our stints at Langley. We were both from Colorado, and he appreciated my saying exactly what was on my mind rather than putting aside the time to kiss his ass. We'd taken a long trip halfway around the world on the director's Gulfstream, a trip that came with lots of late-night, diplomatic-like meetings. I must have acquitted myself okay, as I earned some measure of trust. Or at least to the degree spies ever trust each other. Another thing we had in common was tilting at windmills. Although we never put it in these terms, we both were after the unvarnished truth, even within Langley's closed precincts where it wasn't always easy to find.

Driving up the George Washington Parkway back to Langley, Lofgren announced out of nowhere that he'd had enough and was about to retire. As he explained it to me, because he was married with a second set of children, he needed both his retirement and a new job to get his kids through school.

"But there's some unfinished business I feel bad about," he said, almost to himself. I waited for him to tell me, but he'd gone quiet, evidently weighing how much he should say.

As he started to pull into a parking space in front of headquarters, he said, "We've got another one."

"Another what?"

"The KGB's running an asset in the building. Up there."

Lofgren pointed up at the seventh floor of the main headquarters building, where CIA management resides. Overlooking the Potomac, it unsurprisingly has the best view in the house.

I stupidly looked up, expecting to see what, another Ames looking down at us?

Of course I was curious to know what in hell he was talking about, but asking too many Russia-related questions in the post-Ames CIA was a good way to find yourself in hot water. So I didn't ask. When Lofgren retired as promised, I was convinced this was the last I'd ever hear about it.

It wasn't until twenty-three years later, in March 2019, that the seventh-floor mole would come waltzing back into my life. To be more precise: hijack it.

By now I was twenty years resigned from the CIA, and had been writing books since. In one way or another, they all had to do with my time in the CIA. But having said what I had to say about espionage, I'd made the firm decision to find something else to write about.

Lofgren and I kept up over the years, usually over a one-beer lunch with a few long-retired old-timers. He now had early-onset Lewy body dementia, which meant I did the driving.

It was after one of these lunches, just as we were turning down his street, when Lofgren said, apropos of nothing, "I think I know who the KGB mole is."

I could only assume he was talking about our conversation in the CIA parking lot that afternoon in 1996. Knowing he was touching upon a sensitive subject, to say the least, I let him talk rather than probe.

"I have to wonder if I'd only hung on whether we'd have caught him," he said.

He paused a beat, like a man with a troubled conscience about to confess to a horrific crime, then dropped a name on me.

Surprise doesn't come easy to me these days, but I considered pulling off the road to demand Lofgren tell me how in hell he came to such an outlandish, conspiratorial conclusion like that. I couldn't imagine a universe in which the man he'd just named would come to the dark decision to volunteer to spy for the KGB. Nor could I imagine what his motivation could have been, or for that matter how he could have gotten away with it all these years.

I was sure Lofgren had to be wrong. But then again, Lofgren has never had the time of day for conspiracy theories or baseless calumny. And it isn't like he'd been out of the loop: Lofgren was a key player in seeing Ames into a jail cell.

I'd seen passing references in books and the press to a KGB mole in CIA Russia operations beyond Ames. Milt Bearden, Lofgren's predecessor as division chief overseeing Russia once removed, wrote an op-ed in the *Los Angeles Times* in which he raised the possibility there'd indeed been one. Although he didn't offer a name, he was the first to publicly assign the mole the sobriquet the Fourth Man.

As we drove along in silence, the implications of the man's possible treachery ricocheted around my skull like popcorn. He would have been in a position to inflict more damage on our national security than any spy in American history, many orders beyond Ames, Hanssen, and Howard combined. He had access to almost every secret the CIA possessed, including the identities of all its agents and undercover case officers. He also was in position to give up most of the National Security Agency's secrets, as well as those of the State Department and Pentagon. The KGB couldn't have done better short of breaking American codes.

But then it occurred to me that there'd been no evidence of the man's treachery I was aware of. In espionage, like journalism, an extraordinary claim demands extraordinary proof. I'd have been quicker to believe in this man's guilt had I seen with my own eyes Russian news photos of his victims shackled and marched into a Moscow courtroom. With Howard, Ames, and Hanssen, we'd seen all the evidence we needed attesting to their treason: dozens of CIA and FBI Russian agents executed. Then again, who was I to say how exactly the story of the Fourth Man might have played out.

It wouldn't happen until a couple of meetings down the road, but Lofgren would come around to proposing I blow the dust off the Fourth Man investigation and see what I could do to restore it to life. He didn't think I'd solve it, let alone put the Fourth Man in jail; the FBI had tried its best and failed. But Lofgren's hope was that in my poking through the ashes, it would come to the Fourth Man's attention and make him pay the piper in the currency of sleepless nights. That's of course if the man indeed were guilty; if not, he'd ridicule the whole enterprise as conspiratorial bullshit and not give it a second thought. Either way, spend as much time as I did in the Cold War CIA, and as quixotic as Lofgren's challenge sounded, there was only one answer.

The CIA wasn't done with me yet; so much for finding something else to write about.

In all my time in the CIA, I rarely worked against what the CIA called the "Soviet target" and instead did my street time in the wreckage of one empire or another—Sarajevo, Beirut, Khartoum, and so on. Soft targets, as they were called. But I did work alongside many who devoted their entire careers to watching the Soviet Union. They'd help me make sense of the Fourth Man hunt, I was sure.

When I started to call around to my ex-colleagues to ask about the Fourth Man and the KGB, things usually started out with a hearty "Great to hear from you." However, the moment they understood what I was after, some switch in their head flipped, turning them as tight-lipped and sullen as any Soviet apparatchik. They evidently thought I had absolutely no need to know about the Fourth Man, the hunt, or anything remotely connected to him. Ergo, I could take a hike. Some flat-out lied to me, with a few even pretending they'd never heard of the Fourth Man when I knew for a fact they had. Frankly, I was astonished by the pointlessness of their lies so many years later, sort of like denying we'd ever worked together in the CIA.

I'm not sure why, but early on I was naive enough to believe resurrecting the Fourth Man investigation would be a matter of simply getting the band back together. I'd rewarm our bygone camaraderie, appeal to their innate curiosity, and together we'd bring some measure of clarity to this old mystery. I stupidly assumed the fog of suspicion and paranoia trailing in the wake of the Fourth Man should have thinned out by now. After all, it's been more than a quarter of a century since the CIA ordered the investigation. But my sincere entreaties about water under the bridge fell on cold, deaf ears. Did these people possess some deep dark secret they'd never let pass their lips? Maybe. But my guess is they're embarrassed for an organization they devoted their lives to. No one in retirement wants to believe it was all for naught.

Time certainly did nothing to temper Hugh "Ted" Price's vows of omertà. He'd been the CIA deputy director of operations who ordered the hunt for the Fourth Man. I called him hoping at least he'd be curious about where the investigation had gone after he retired in 1995. But he quickly cut me off in the clipped accent of his caste, telling me he wasn't interested in talking about the past. He'd put it all far behind him, he said; and that's that. He died during the writing of this book. I got the same cold shoulder from his predecessor, Tom Twetten, the deputy director of operations who'd had the misfortune to occupy Price's job when Ames was first unearthed. I'd worked for Twetten in an overseas posting, but it did nothing to melt the ice. Ames was the problem, he said, and the only one. Which meant there was no point in talking about it. Mike Sulick, another former deputy director of operations and chief in Moscow, said he didn't believe there'd been a Fourth Man. There'd been an investigation into a CIA code clerk, he said, but it went nowhere. Former director of national intelligence James Clapper and former CIA director Mike Hayden both told me they'd never heard of the Fourth Man. I wondered how it was possible considering that, at least from what I'd learned about it, the Fourth Man hunt is arguably the most important spy mystery in American history.

I called up the former chief of station in East Africa who'd been so skeptical of Max in the beginning. But he told me in no uncertain terms that while he was there, the station had no KGB agents or KGB "developmentals"—people a case officer attempts to recruit as an agent. I considered asking him what use it was covering up for Max, since Max was no longer active and more or less safely out of reach of the KGB. And not to mention that by now I knew Max's story better than he did. But it was a question I could tell he wasn't inclined to answer.

Those further down the ranks I talked to didn't exactly warm to the subject, either. A former head of Russian operations was shocked I'd even heard there'd been a concerted search for the Fourth Man. But then he conceded, yes, there'd been a hugely damaging Russian double agent post-Ames. "You wouldn't believe the names on the short list," he said. He threw me a sop that the Russians sometimes referred to him as *Siem*, seven in Russian. He then went on to say that the Fourth Man was somehow connected to an investigation into the suspicious death of an MI6 officer in London working in Russian operations. The unfortunate man had been killed in a still-unsolved hit-and-run in downtown London one Saturday night. I asked him if there was a possibility the Russians might have murdered him because of something he'd learned about the Fourth Man. But at this point, he apparently decided he'd already gone too far and said he had to run. He never picked up my follow-up calls.

Another former chief of Russian operations corrected me that the Russian double agent was never called the Fourth Man but rather the Third Man. He came by that number by subtracting Howard, who strictly speaking was a defector rather than a double agent. Numbering aside, he had no doubts there had been a high-level Russian penetration of the CIA, one much more senior than Ames. "There were too many indicators to come to any other conclusion," he said. "The trail went all the way to the seventh floor," he added without elaborating. As this Russia chief told me, the Third Man was so well positioned, he'd done more damage than Ames by many magnitudes. Along with a lot of sensitive secrets, he'd passed the Russians memoranda of conversations between Yeltsin and Clinton. The KGB, he explained, then weaponized the memoranda by waving them in front of Yeltsin's nose as a warning that he'd better not get too cozy with the Americans or they'd find out about it and he would pay the price. But here my former colleague drew a line, refusing to tell me who he thought the Third Man was or why he knew about what the Third Man gave up to the KGB. When I asked why this story was so hard to get at, he ominously left it with "The Russians will do anything to protect the Third Man."

I mentioned to Sandy Grimes, one of the main investigators in the Ames hunt, the sort of allergic reaction I was getting. My naivete amused her. She said even as the evidence against Ames piled up, no one on the seventh floor wanted to hear that the KGB could possibly have a mole in CIA Soviet operations. They also definitely didn't want to contemplate the possibility that a mole was about to be arrested on their watch. Why would it be any different today? The Russia chief who told me about the Third Man ran into the same brick wall, as he told me. When he was a rookie case officer and early on tried to make the case that a double agent was responsible for the '85–'86 hemorrhaging of Russian agents, his boss, the Soviet division chief Burton Gerber, scoffed at the whole thing, writing him off as a wing nut wasting everyone's time with his "dark side" conspiracy theories. His career then promptly took a nosedive. He was forced out of operations and into the Directorate of Intelligence. Purgatory for a case officer. Lofgren was the one who brought him back into operations.

Fortunately, there were a few directly involved in the Fourth Man hunt who talked to me on record. As best they could, they laid out for me the evidence against him. Considering it was the most disturbing thing that occurred in their professional lives, how raw power is able to crush a truth of this consequence, they remember best the investigation's aftermath. There also were a dozen or so accommodating souls who agreed to talk to me about the Fourth Man on deep background, including a recent CIA director who'd been briefed on the Fourth Man.

No surprise, after all these years and memory being what it is, there were more than a few discrepancies in their stories. For instance, memories differed over whether or not there'd been a plan for Max to break into the safe where the Fourth Man's file was kept. I also could never completely confirm the story about Corbin's taking Max out on a fishing trip. The head of the division that oversaw Russian operations, John MacGaffin, remembered the fishing outing. But others at Greenbrier were certain it never happened. And while Corbin remembers Max tipping him off to Ames meeting his KGB handler in Caracas, others were certain it was Bogotá. There were other small details for which I would have liked corroboration, but could never get it. There are also numerous problems with chronology, which at times I've had to do my best to make sense of. Incidentally, if it's not already obvious, unlike almost every single book about contemporary spy scandals, I got no help from the CIA. In the end, though, I believe I arrived at a satisfactory composite picture of the Fourth Man investigation, or at least the inaugural stages of it. Even with all sorts of caveats and adjustments for gaps in my sources' recollections, a story this big is worth telling.

At times, the story can feel dizzying in its depth and complexity. I met most of the suspects on the Fourth Man short list, but in my occasional dealings with them I saw in none the markings of a traitor. As far as I was concerned, they were all above reproach. Also, through it all I've constantly reminded myself I have only a slice of the story, but at the same time it's of a piece with a bigger story spanning empires and decades, continuing today. Finally, one of the main suspects is still alive and the subject of a very active FBI investigation. After this book hits the presses, some new, sensational revelations very well could occur, putting the narrative in a new light. Who knows what might emerge. It's inevitable that my telling meant navigating holes in a tangled web, leaving me to constantly straddle the gap between suspicion and evidence.

The only firm conclusion I walk away from it all with is that the Fourth Man, a high-level mole in the CIA, wasn't an urban myth. There are too many trustworthy insiders who are certain there was another mole to believe otherwise. But what I'm absolutely not equipped to do is come down on his identity, and I can only pass on the story as I've reported it. And whether the spy catchers flagged the right man and he's indeed the greatest traitor in American history, or whether he was an ingenious fabrication on the part of Russian intelligence designed to lure the CIA and FBI into a witch hunt, the story of the Fourth Man hunt nonetheless goes a long way in explaining America, Russia, and the state of the world today.

THREE

mole /moʊl/ *n.* The layman's term for a double agent recruited or inserted in an intelligence service's ranks. Called a "penetration" in intelligence circles.

•

Langley, Virginia; 1991

ONE REASON IT took nine years to catch the arch traitor Ames—from the time he first started spying for the KGB in 1985 until his arrest in February 1994—is because the CIA had pretty much given up on looking for KGB moles. When the Berlin Wall came down in 1989, history started to move too fast to give them much thought. Then, with the collapse of the Soviet Union in 1991, the world was flipped on its head, as was the CIA. In a moment, KGB mole hunting went out of vogue.

Milt Bearden, chief of the CIA division overseeing spying on Russia (Central Eurasia Division), declared the Cold War's battles fought, the bodies buried, and Russia the abject loser. As we heard it in the field, Bearden had started to go around saying Russian dicks were dragging in the dirt, and what's left of the country was now nothing more than Upper Volta with nukes. According

ction. A big-picture man, he was
more statesman than spymaster, someone who could fast-talk and
charm his way into the corridors of power. His talents really paid
off when he was chief in Islamabad, where he oversaw the arming
of the Afghan mujahideen, a ragtag guerrilla force that helped put
an early end to the Soviet Empire. Incidentally, in terms of caring
about his people, Bearden was one of the best bosses I've ever had.

At the same time, I can see why none of this impressed the
dour, die-hard cold warriors in his division. And all the more so
when Bearden bluntly informed them that he considered Russia
no more of an espionage threat to the United States than tradi-
tional allies like Germany or Denmark. Which meant it was time
to play nice with what was left of the KGB. To the cold warriors,
it was pure heresy, but there was nothing they could do about it.

Bearden ordered a to-the-bone culling of the CIA's Russian
agents in Moscow. The rumor went around that he was thinking
about having case officers show up at their Moscow apartments to
inform them they'd been fired. Even more alarming, another rumor

had it he even thought about outing them to Russian intelligence. None of it happened, but Bearden summarily stopped targeting Russian intelligence officers and turned away nearly every Russian volunteering to spy for the CIA. Among them was Vasili Mitrokhin, a KGB archivist who'd smuggled out of Russia a treasure trove of secrets. Adding insult to injury, Bearden ordered the destruction of the Russian counterintelligence database. Bearden's thinking was that not only was it no longer needed, but if Russians were to catch wind of the CIA still keeping tabs on them, they would take it amiss.

No one dared challenge Bearden because, when it came to questions of strategy, he'd made it clear Russia was his chasse gardée. Anyone brazen enough to try would have been run out of his division and exiled to some sinecure like the Luxembourg desk. The rank and file could only watch in mute disapproval as Bearden and the CIA fell head over heels for America's new best friend, Russia.

Never taking his eye off history, Bearden's one concession to CIA spying on Russia was Kremlin politics. He openly and often complained how the CIA had failed to predict the fall of the Berlin Wall and the August 1991 coup attempt by KGB and Communist hard-liners against Gorbachev. Unforgivable lapses, he'd do his best to make sure something similar didn't happen on his watch. Bearden thought recruiting a spy inside Boris Yeltsin's cabinet might be worth the risk, or maybe even a senior general to keep a finger on the pulse on Russia's military. But otherwise, Bearden was done with Cold War cloak-and-dagger skulduggery: The KGB was a spent force, and there was no point in arguing about it.

It's not that the cold warriors completely disagreed with Bearden. The CIA indeed had failed to predict the August 1991 coup. But their comeback was that they missed it because the CIA had no worthwhile Russian agents in Moscow at the time, largely thanks to the '85–'86 losses. Their argument boiled down to what they thought should have been obvious to Bearden: The CIA couldn't hope to recruit a source in the Kremlin without first cleaning its own house of Russian moles, and the only sure way to accomplish that would be to recruit a Russian spy who knew about them. Things became so acrimonious that Bearden's deputy Paul Redmond challenged him to a debate about the merits of spying on the KGB. Redmond even put up flyers around Bearden's division, advertising it. Bearden soon shuffled Redmond off to counterintelligence, where he could do all the rooting around for Russian moles he liked and no one would be much bothered.

Redmond had a different take on the story, telling me it was actually Tom Twetten, the deputy director of operations, who made the decision to move him out of the division responsible for Russian operations. Twetten, he said, called him up to the seventh floor one day, and without even allowing him to take a seat told him he was "too Angletonian" for the job, referring to James Jesus Angleton, the former head of counterintelligence who tangled the CIA up in knots looking for KGB moles. Redmond says at one point Twetten even tried to shunt him off to Bangkok, but he refused. Whether it was Bearden or Twetten, the bottom line is that counterintelligence veterans like Redmond knew something their bosses refused to see, as would become very clear after Ames's arrest.

What worried the unreconstructed cold warriors in Bearden's division was just how little the CIA knew about Russian intelligence, mainly thanks to the sheer size and sprawl of it. At its peak in 1988, the KGB employed 480,000 officers and troops. Add to it hundreds of thousands of KGB informants and co-optees, and the KGB was a leviathan difficult for even Russians to get their minds around. No doubt, like the rest of the Soviet Union, the KGB suffered its bureaucratic inefficiencies and unforced errors, but it had more than enough smart, dedicated officers prepared to loyally serve the Soviet Union, to include running high-level moles like the Fourth Man without getting caught. The KGB was very good when it needed to be. Who could know who spied for it and who didn't.

When in October 1991 Gorbachev decided to break up the KGB, his intention was to defang it. The most radical change was the severing of counterintelligence (Second Chief Director-ate) from foreign intelligence (First Chief Directorate). The Second would eventually be renamed the FSB, and the First the SVR. On paper, the KGB should have been cut down to size, a shadow of its former self. But it's not the way things turned out. Putin's banking on the FSB to seize power in 1999 is evidence enough of that. As for the SVR, it never lost a step recruiting and running agents around the world. Only now, with the oligarchs and their hundreds of billions of dollars roped in to finance high-end operations, there's a good argument that it's even more effective today. Russian intelligence's getting a toehold in the 2016 Trump campaign tells that story.

Yeltsin could press glasnost on the KGB all he liked, but apart from releasing some old historical files and prattling on about how the Stalinist security state was finished, the KGB revanchists continued on as if the Soviet Union had never come apart. At no point did they ever consider permitting the Kremlin to tutor them on how to operate, or more importantly to cough up the identities of its sources or the kompromat it had collected on foreigners and Russians. They openly ignored Yeltsin's handpicked KGB chairman, Vadim Bakatin, not even bothering to keep their defiance out of the press. The 1991 coup may have failed on paper, but not in the eyes of the hard-line KGB operatives. They held ranks and continued to do what they did best—spy on Russia's enemies.

For those paying attention at the CIA, there was more than enough evidence the KGB had made only a tactical retreat to plot its comeback. Aside from the name changes and no longer executing and sending millions to the gulags, the KGB successor organizations are basically the same outfit Lenin set up on December 5, 1917, a ruthless secret police with an iron grip on Russia. It never stopped acting with lawlessness and violence. Russian intelligence's recent spate of assassinations, "active measures" (political and economic sabotage), and blowing up stuff in the Czech Republic are evidence enough of that. Unlike American intelligence, it is still able to protect its secrets. To describe the KGB as a black hole is short of precise because the term implies a certain optimism that one day someone might come along with a flashlight and offer us a look around. Yeltsin did seem to try his best, but in the end the KGB proved itself to be a bona fide black hole stubbornly impervious to light. A cult by any other name. (And it's why I'll slip into calling it the KGB even at points in the story after it was broken up.)

None of this is to deny that the CIA and other Western intelligence services had successes against the KGB, but those were mainly against the First Chief Directorate, its foreign intelligence apparat, and the GRU, military intelligence. They knew next to nothing about the many other KGB directorates. For instance, when the CIA found out that the Third Directorate, the one tasked with keeping tabs on the Soviet military, had started to target Americans in Europe for recruitment, it had no idea how the Third operated or how successful it had been. The same went for KGB codes, which the CIA spared no effort in attempting to break.

But it was counterintelligence, the KGB's Second Chief Directorate, that represented the CIA's most tenacious and opaque opponent. Not only was it the most powerful and efficient part of the KGB, it was staffed by some of its most trusted officers. It rarely suffered defectors and was never penetrated by the CIA or any other intelligence service the CIA knew about. It regularly operated independently, to include running agents outside Soviet borders without informing other directorates, which is normally outside the purview of counterintelligence. In a sense, it was a KGB within the KGB, an inner sanctum where very few were allowed entry.

One reason for Second Chief Directorate's privileged status was that the Soviet regime never forgot it had come to power thanks to exiles plotting from abroad. Almost worse, it was with the connivance of an enemy—Germany, who smuggled Lenin back into Russia in April 1917 in a closed boxcar. Determined not to let itself succumb to the same fate, the Soviet regime was unstinting in its support of the Second. For its most important work it enlisted the best and the brightest, true believers who'd never consider betraying the Soviet Union. For Russia watchers, it's no surprise that under Putin, the Second's successor, the Federal Security Service (FSB), has held on to the same preeminent status and today is effectively Putin's Praetorian Guard. It also has started to conduct more and more foreign spying operations.

During the Cold War, what no one at the CIA had any doubt about was the sort of real and persistent threat the Second was. CIA case officers operating in the Soviet Union were under unrelenting, round-the-clock surveillance. Their phones were tapped, their offices bugged, and their apartments and cars subject to constant break-ins. Running agents meant months of preparation for a single meeting, then the case officer disappearing into Moscow and perfectly oiling every move before making contact with an agent. And to be sure, there couldn't be any bullshit Hollywood moves, like looking over your shoulder or into a shop window checking for a tail. Any small mistake on the part of a case officer, and their agent would end up on the gallows. Max, then, was absolutely in his rights refusing to meet the CIA in Moscow.

It didn't help that the CIA knew next to nothing about the workings of the Second Chief Directorate. The one source the CIA briefly lucked into was a Moscow street cop seconded to it. He knew little about its internal organization, but he did find out the KGB was sprinkling radioactive "spy dust" on the clothes of CIA officers, which left an invisible bread-crumb trail for surveillance teams to follow. The cop provided a sample of the spy dust, leaving no doubt in the CIA's mind that KGB counterintelligence would go to any length to track its case officers. When the cop was betrayed by Ames, arrested, and executed, the CIA was back in the dark.

Another telling advantage the Second had over the CIA was unlimited police powers, from spot arrests to warrantless wiretaps. It could stop a suspect on the street and haul him in for questioning without probable cause. The KGB was able to conduct trials in private, with judges, prosecutors, and defense attorneys under ironclad gag orders. On the other hand, every time the CIA and FBI took an espionage case to court, they leaked extremely sensitive secrets to the press. One book by a *New York Times* journalist published a year after Ames's arrest even alluded to Max's role in nailing Ames. But Max was still in Moscow spying for the CIA. Although the book didn't identify Max by name, if the Russians hadn't known beforehand they had a double agent problem on their hands, they certainly did now.

Other suspicions about the KGB's reach and talents ran to the darkest corners of the CIA's imagination. It couldn't ignore the possibility, as remote as it was, that the KGB had broken American encryption. In the sixties and seventies, CIA counterintelligence suspected the Second Chief Directorate had recruited a CIA code clerk and continued to run him when he was reassigned to Langley. It was a worst-case scenario, but with a back door into CIA encryption, there wouldn't be an internal secret Russian intelligence wouldn't be privy to. While in the end there was no good evidence that CIA codes had indeed been broken, the possibility couldn't be dismissed out of hand.

A more plausible explanation was that the Second had bugged the CIA's premises in Moscow. At one point, there was some evidence for it. From 1945 to 1952, the Soviets had a bug in the American ambassador's study, hanging over his desk inside a wood carving of the Great Seal of the United States that was given as a gift by a Soviet youth organization. Then in the mid-eighties, the Second cultivated two embassy Marine security guards thanks to sexual entrapment. Honey traps, as they're popularly called. The suspicion was the two had let KGB break-in teams into the embassy. It was eventually determined they hadn't, but it offered up the possibility that other ruses might have gone unnoticed. In that case, the Second would have been in a position to eavesdrop on everything that went on in the station, from conversations to cable traffic. When the United States finally negotiated for a new Moscow embassy and began building it in 1979, the Soviets bugged it so thoroughly (and obviously), it wasn't usable until 2000. In short, it was a miracle the CIA managed to come up with a way to securely run agents in the Soviet Union.

Equally alarming, with the Second's blanket coverage of the CIA and other American officials, it had more than enough opportunities to run up the score in terms of recruitments. The Second devoted a limitless amount of resources and manpower to snooping on the private lives of Americans. Nothing could be kept private from the Second, which took full advantage of the tiny Moscow fishbowl the Americans were forced to swim in. It was a snap identifying personal vulnerabilities or financial problems. Every time an American called home to check in with family, the Second was listening in. If a marriage was on the rocks, the Second knew all about it, in all its ugly and lurid detail. It had beautiful young Russian girls and handsome Russian men standing in the wings, shoulders to cry on. The deeper I investigated the Fourth Man hunt, the more I heard stories about Moscow station officers tripped up on polygraphs thanks to Russian flings. Many were with translators put in their paths by the Second. As one former KGB operative told me, everyone in the KGB knew the extension where a prostitute could be ordered up for a honeypot recruitment. Most American dalliances, or at least the ones the CIA and FBI got to the bottom of, didn't go beyond pillow talk, but it was enough to derail their careers.

A few years after the collapse of the Soviet Union, an intelligence service in the Caucasus demonstrated for me how sexual kompromat works. They sat me down to show me a film clip shot from a camera concealed in a ceiling heating vent. The black-and-white film's resolution was grainy but good enough to see a man and woman on a bed in acrobatic congress. Out of the camera's view, there's the sound of shattering wood as the door to their room is broken down. A half-dozen thugs pour into view. They handcuff the man, who squeals like a stuck pig, pleading for mercy. As I was told, he was a radical Muslim cleric who agreed to work as an agent rather than let the film be broadcast. When the film stopped, my host turned to me and said, "See, my friend, how a proper recruitment works."

In the event of a financial approach, a former Russian intelligence officer told me, a Russian operative would invite himself to sit down next to his American target in a café or restaurant and flash a briefcase with a million dollars cash in it. It's yours for signing on the dotted line, they'd be told. The money staring back at the target for recruitment represented a promise of instant, lifelong financial reprieve. And it was made clear the first million wouldn't be the end of it: The Russian operative would point to another table where a colleague would be sitting with an identical briefcase, presumably with another million.

In the early days of the Soviet Union, the recruitment of foreign spies was mostly a matter of finding someone who'd fallen for Marx's utopian dreaming. It worked wonderfully, with the Soviets placing agents just about everywhere they needed them. With the tarnishing of Communism, the pace of recruiting slowed, but the Russians retook ground by switching from recruitment pitches leveraged by ideology to ones baited with money. Russia being no stranger to the workings of greed, they quickly adapted.

It's no wonder, then, that what kept the CIA's spy catchers awake at night wasn't what they knew about the KGB, but what they didn't. They could only speculate on how many Second honeypot and million-dollar pitches had worked. With the thousands of American officials rotating in and out of Moscow and the rest of the Soviet Union over the years, the Second could have recruited dozens of well-placed agents in American national security for all they knew. When I told a former head of CIA Russian operations that there was some speculation the Fourth Man might have worked for the Second Chief Directorate, his immediate reaction was "It makes sense the Second recruited him in Moscow."

The CIA had this habit of whistling by the cemetery, telling itself the Russians aren't ten feet tall, but the truth was, the United States had been dealt a losing hand when it came to playing the Great Game against Russian intelligence. The KGB and its successor organizations never lost their touch for recruiting moles in the ranks of its adversaries, then running them for years without getting caught. As the former head of CIA operations Mike Sulick told me, "It's just a reality the Russians make better spies."

In fairness to Bearden and his fellow Russian defenders, they were only riding a wave of blind optimism washing over all of Washington in the years after the Soviet collapse. The White House's laser-focused objective was to prop up Yeltsin and Russian democracy by ramming aid packages through Congress. As

Bearden's successor John MacGaffin told me, "It's almost impossible today to understand the mood back then." One day, a senior Clinton adviser on Russia called MacGaffin to ask permission to pass a sensitive CIA report on Russian politics to the Russian foreign minister. MacGaffin was at a loss for words wondering just how far the Russian mania had gone. When he regained his composure, he said no, explaining that it would be a felony.

For part-time Russia watchers like me, it was easy to fall for the hype. When I'd pass through Moscow, I couldn't miss how fast and badly things were coming apart. It was impossible to keep track of all the mob assassinations, but there seemed to be about one a day. I went to my share of funerals of gunned-down Russians. When Yeltsin shelled the Duma during a constitutional crisis in 1993, which left more than a hundred Russians dead, as far as I could tell it was pretty much greeted with a shrug of the shoulders. As for Russian intelligence, it looked to me like they'd given up the ghost. I saw no sign of agents lurking in Moscow hotel lobbies and airports or sitting in parked Zhigulis on street corners like they used to. For all appearances, just as Bearden proclaimed, they indeed looked like a spent force. If they were planning a comeback, I saw no evidence of it.

One time, in transit to Central Asia, a few of us stopped in Moscow for a few days, and we were eager to try out a new satellite communications system, basically a cell phone–sized transceiver that allowed us to tap into the American telephone system via a low-flying US Navy satellite. We were supposed to wait till we got to Central Asia before trying it out, but instead we picked the lock on the door leading to our hotel's roof and gave it a try. In Soviet times, pulling a stunt with what looked like a piece of spy equipment would have earned you a quick arrest and a lifetime expulsion from Russia. Now no one seemed to notice. On another trip through Moscow's domestic airport, we set off a metal detector because we were carrying sidearms. We sheepishly confessed, and the guard manning the metal detector simply motioned for us to walk around it.

Washington's political class worked hard at selling the line that the Soviet Union's fall was on par with the defeat of Nazi Germany. It obviously wasn't—as became all too clear with the seemingly miraculous ascension of Putin and the rebirth of Russia's police state—but it was a lie the Clinton White House was forced to pay some obeisance to, mainly because Republican national security hard-liners and evangelicals were crowing about how their patron saint Reagan single-handedly brought down the "evil empire." Langley duly went along for the ride, turning a deaf ear to its unreconstructed cold warriors who wouldn't shut up about how they saw no evidence the Russians had changed their stripes, or even their tune.

By the late eighties, veteran cold warriors at the CIA were all but certain the Russians possessed at least one double agent in the CIA. It was the only reasonable explanation left for the '85–'86 losses. The smart money—even before Paul Redmond suspected him—was on Ames. In early 1992 the head of Russia Group started warning his people to steer clear of Ames and not let a word slip about ongoing Russian operations. Further supporting their case against the KGB, in spite of the ballyhooed thaw between Russia and the United States, it was clear the KGB was still working hard at trying to recruit Americans, almost as aggressively as it had during the Cold War. It never let up on tailing the CIA around Moscow. The bottom line was that Bearden and the other Russia apologists could go on all they wanted about Russian intelligence being the CIA's new best friend, but the stark reality was that the Cold War was still very much on as far as Russia was concerned. In the Langley cold warriors' eyes, Bearden was a narcissist who harbored grandiose delusions. Bearden returned the sentiment, dismissing them as "the haters behind the green door"—a reference to his division's back room from which Russian internal and counterintelligence operations were run.

Unshaken in their conviction, the CIA's spy catchers ignored Bearden, certain that in giving Russian intelligence a pass, the CIA didn't stand a chance at clearing up the long-standing mystery of who betrayed its Russian agents between 1985 and 1986. The only way to figure out who the double agent was would be to give every KGB officer who approached the CIA a hearing rather than turn them away, and especially those who'd been in American operations in the early to mid-eighties when the losses first started to occur. Retired or not, any one of these KGB operatives might possess a crucial piece of the puzzle.

But they didn't blame Bearden alone. The spy catchers knew chapter and verse how the mole hunt from day one had been too halfhearted to even put together a manageable suspect list. Among many egregious lapses, the CIA never bothered with spot background investigations on officers who'd had access to the identities of the compromised Russian agents. They knew that the longer the CIA continued to sweep the '85–'86 losses under the carpet, the more precious time was being lost, the mole's trail going cold.

And although it should have been the ideal time to conduct a mole hunt, something very strange was happening. After the fall of the Berlin Wall and—two years later—the Soviet Union, the CIA should have been in the catbird seat, a flood of Russian and East Europeans knocking on its door volunteering to spy for it, motivated by either money or a change of heart about Communism. There should have been all sorts of demoralized KGB and Kremlin officials looking for back channels to Washington, hoping to shore up their political positions or make some money on the side. It's what normally happens when any country turns chaotic and disintegrates. But the flood never showed up. Contrary to all expectations, it turned out to be exactly the opposite, not even a trickle. Something was clearly wrong.

Left with the *New York Times* and CNN to keep it up to speed on Russia, the CIA in the 1990s could only speculate what was going on deep inside the country. All it knew was that the KGB ghost had somehow snuck into the machine, was everywhere and nowhere, robbing the CIA blind of its Russian secrets, and there was no evicting it. The KGB not only brought CIA Russian operations to its knees, but did major damage to American national security as well. As I'll keep coming back to, the CIA failed to foresee how an ex-KGB operative named Vladimir Putin, backed by KGB cronies, would insinuate himself into power and restore Russia's security state in all its hideousness. As time would tell, the CIA's unreconstructed cold warriors were right about the KGB lying in wait to strike at an opportune time. But without Russian agents, that's as deep as their forecasting could go.

We can only speculate what the Fourth Man must have thought about it all. I can only imagine he must have considered it a stroke of extraordinarily good luck that his CIA comrades were a seraglio of eunuchs who felt most comfortable with their heads stuck in the sand. There couldn't be a better time to get away with high treason.

FOUR

treach·er·y /ˈtrɛtʃ ə ri/ *n.* An action that betrays the confidence of a person or group.

Washington, DC; February 1994

THE FOURTH MAN investigation didn't formally get under way until June 1994, about three months after Ames's arrest. But for CIA and FBI spy catchers, as a point of fact it dates back to June 13, 1985. Two disasters—"flaps," as the CIA euphemistically calls them—occurred on that day, marking the gutting of CIA spying on Russia. One flap the CIA wouldn't find out about for another nine years; the other it did right away. Discrepancies surrounding the two would become the foundation of the Fourth Man investigation.

The disaster the CIA took years to discover took place over a quiet lunch at Chadwicks, a Georgetown hamburger joint. In the shadow of the Whitehurst Freeway and facing a dismal parking lot along the Potomac, it's not the sort of place where you'd expect the single greatest known act of treason in American history to occur, but it's where Rick Ames decided to betray nearly every CIA spying operation against Russia he knew about, including outing nearly a dozen agents who'd been vital in helping the United States understand the Soviet Union and the power behind the Kremlin throne, the KGB.

The lunch crowd midweek at Chadwicks was always thin, not a bad place for a romantic rendezvous or a quick hamburger at the bar. But it wasn't as if Ames cared who saw him there with his KGB go-between, a Russian diplomat acting under KGB direction. When Ames came to the decision to sell out his country, he'd been cunning enough to insinuate himself into a joint CIA-FBI unit targeting Russian officials in Washington for recruitment. It gave him the perfect alibi to meet Russians when and where he wanted. Had the FBI tailed his Russian contact to Chadwicks, it would have assumed Ames was there on its behalf.

At some point during the lunch, Ames discreetly kicked under the table a shopping bag reportedly containing seven pounds of secret documents. As Ames would describe its contents after his arrest, there was more than enough evidence for the KGB to arrest nearly a dozen Russian agents and send them shivering to a filthy grave. Who knows how Ames or anyone else arrived at that fairly precise weight of seven pounds. But there's no doubt about the magnitude of the damage he did.

One agent he betrayed was Major General Dmitri Fyodorovich Polyakov, who'd spent a long, successful career in military intelligence, the GRU. Among many critical pieces of intelligence he'd passed the CIA was a heads-up on the Sino-Soviet split. It reportedly helped convince Nixon to take the risk of visiting Beijing and as a consequence driving the wedge deeper between the Soviet Union and China, cracking open the Communist monolith.

But of more current interest, some of the other agents Ames betrayed ran in the same KGB circles as Vladimir Putin, whom the

CIA knew virtually nothing about before he took power in 1999. Had it not been for Ames, there's a not bad chance one of them would have been in a position to alert the CIA to Putin's machinations on his way to seizing power and to what he intended to do as Russia's new czar. For instance, one of the agents Ames betrayed was at the KGB training academy and would have had access to Putin's file, or at the very least would have been in a circle to query KGB colleagues close to Putin as he made his move to power. The United States may never have been in a position to stop Putin's rise, but even a secondhand understanding of the man's character and bloody vision would have at least braced us for what was to come.

One thing for certain was that the arrest of Rick Ames on February 21, 1994, took the wind out of the CIA's sails. Any pretense of being an elite espionage service equipped to protect its secrets was shown to be a patent joke. The humiliation was all the worse when it came out that Ames had been a bumbling, greedy alcoholic and a problem for the CIA from day one. His picture in the papers—handcuffed by the FBI next to his new Jaguar—was the perfect metaphor for a broken CIA. Even those who couldn't care less about espionage scratched their heads wondering what in God's name possessed the CIA to ever trust Ames with a secret, let alone the identities of its irreplaceable Russian agents.

The answer to that question is complicated, but it basically goes back to Ames's having been a CIA brat, a legacy hire who wasn't subjected to the normal vetting procedures. Although his father was a lackluster case officer who'd served a lackluster tour in Burma, then been brought back to Langley to push paper until he could retire, it was enough for his son to be treated as a trusted member of the tribe. In the CIA, like in most places, blood's thicker than common sense.

In high school, Ames worked summers at the CIA in menial clerical jobs. He got into the University of Chicago but promptly flunked out. After knocking around in the theater in Chicago, he ended up back in Washington attending George Washington University at night while working days at the CIA thanks to his father. With a degree in hand, in 1962 he segued into a two-year CIA apprenticeship preparing junior officers to work overseas as undercover case officers in the Directorate of Operations. The CIA is basically made up of two directorates: operations, which handles "the collection of intelligence acquired by human sources," and analysis, which "provides timely, accurate, and objective intelligence analysis." During Ames's days, Directorate of Operations case officers were considered the CIA's elite, with several of them ending up heading the CIA.

After training, Ames married a colleague, a Directorate of Intelligence analyst. The two served unremarkable tours in Ankara, Turkey, and New York. Notoriously lazy, Ames never recruited a single agent, which is precisely what case officers assigned overseas are meant to do. After separating from his wife, Ames took a bachelor assignment in Mexico City in 1981, and they divorced the following year. As far as I know, Ames's first wife has never publicly offered her side of the story.

Ames never put the brakes on his drinking. He'd routinely stagger back from lunch drunk as a boiled owl, even when assigned to Langley. One time, CIA security had to drive him home after a Langley office party. During a tour in Rome, the police fished him out of a gutter and returned him to the embassy. Even his KGB handlers were worried about his drinking, which is saying a lot considering how much the Russians drink. But there was nothing the Russians could do about it; they weren't trained AA counselors.

Ames also was a notoriously sloppy case officer. He was caught in a CIA safe house bedding his fiancée, a vivacious and well-educated Colombian diplomat he'd taken up with in Mexico City. Just as blatantly against the rules, he introduced her to a Soviet defector. Ames also once left a briefcase of secrets on a train. Any one of these offenses should've been grounds to fire him or at the very least send him off to some bureaucratic pasture where he couldn't do any real harm. But the CIA, as was its wont, swept the mess under the rug and in 1983 gave him one of the most sensitive jobs at Langley, the head of Soviet counterintelligence.

It didn't help Ames's state of mind that counterintelligence was a dead end for a case officer with even modest ambitions. The way the CIA operations directorate was run in those days, promotions largely came thanks to serving overseas and recruiting agents. Or, if you were more senior, holding a position that oversaw case officers recruiting agents. But serving as a counterintelligence analyst stuck in a dreary cubicle thumbing through stale files did nothing for a career other than doom it. They'd be lucky to retire as a GS-14, approximately the rank of a lieutenant colonel in the military. In terms of prestige and power, CIA counterintelligence didn't hold a candle to the KGB's Second Chief Directorate. It ate away at Ames.

According to some who worked with him, Ames wasn't as complete a loser as many have portrayed him. He had a reputation for being a good debriefer, thorough and with an ability to put Russian defectors at ease. He also had an easy personality. His main character flaw, though, was ego. Sandy Grimes, who carpooled with him years before serving on the mole hunt that caught him, told me she of course had seen no sign Ames one day would commit treason. But on the other hand she got the impression he was deeply resentful he hadn't got all he thought he deserved, his career topping out too soon and his true talents unappreciated. He saw himself eventually shuffled out the door like his father and forced to live on a retirement inadequate for his wants. Fueled by a cocktail of resentment, financial precarity, and alcohol, Ames was a train wreck looking for a place to happen.

Ames brought his Colombian girlfriend back to Washington intending to marry her. Divorce was par for the course in the CIA, but marrying a foreigner was strongly discouraged, if not grounds to force a resignation. The CIA's entirely reasonable point of view was that a foreign spouse opens the door to divided loyalties. Moreover, it's nearly impossible to conduct a thorough background investigation on a foreign fiancée. It's not as if CIA security could show up in a foreign country and start asking questions about one of its nationals.

There's no evidence Ames's Colombian wife drew him into selling out to the Russians. But coming from a well-educated, well-off family, she wasn't delighted about the prospect of living in the Washington, DC, area on her husband's modest paycheck. It must have been all the more unsettling for her because in Mexico City it seemed Ames was doing just fine. But that would be to overlook his foreign living allowance, an apartment and car paid for by the CIA, and a nearly limitless entertainment allowance. Now in Washington, the wolves were starting to scratch at the door. As these things so often go, Ames's decision to appeal to the Russians for a handout came piecemeal, not unlike someone broke deciding to apply for a onetime "payday" loan to tide things over.

Ames was savvy enough to know he couldn't just drop in on the Russians out of the blue. The risk was too high that an FBI observation post across from their embassy would spot and identify him.

That's when he persuaded his bosses to let him work on the joint FBI-CIA unit tasked with recruiting Soviet officials in Washington. It worked like a charm: Ames meeting Russian officials, filing reports with the FBI and the CIA, and no one the wiser. At one point he even walked into the Russian embassy to meet the KGB face-to-face, indifferent to the FBI observation post clocking him in and out. On that occasion, Ames asked for $50,000 in return for revealing the names of what the CIA thought were Russian dangles—fake volunteers dished up by the Russians to mislead American intelligence. In Ames's mind, if they were fake rather than actual Russian agents, it wasn't a real betrayal. But it then occurred to him that word of his approach to the KGB might get around the Washington KGB rezidentura and then back to the FBI. Ames knew the FBI had recruited two KGB operatives serving there, and it dawned on him that he'd better out them to his handler to save his own skin.

At some point—it's hard to know precisely when and how with a drunk—he decided to go all in and give up the names of every CIA and FBI KGB agent he knew about. The Russians would eventually pay Ames nearly $4 million for his efforts. Ames never bothered trying to hide the money, paying for his half-million-dollar house in cash. The CIA fell for the lie that it was his wife's money until Paul Redmond and his spy catchers Sandy Grimes, Jeanne Vertefeuille, Diana Worthen, and Dan Payne figured out he'd been making layered cash deposits into his checking account soon after his meetings with the Russians. Then, with Max's 1993 Caracas tip, it all came together.

When all the ugly details came out in the press and congressional hearings, Ames looked like a mole only the willfully blind could miss. The inevitable question was how the CIA could've overlooked a modestly paid bureaucrat splurging on a new Jaguar and an all-cash half-million-dollar house, designer clothes, and cosmetic dental work. Not to mention a wife always expensively and elegantly dressed, her new life one long shopping spree. Ames's claim that the money came from his wife's family was easily demonstrated to be a transparent lie. If CIA security had bothered to ask colleagues who knew her and her story from Mexico City, it would have seen through Ames's claim right from the beginning. In the end, the CIA never could come up with a plausible explanation as to why Ames had been let into Ali Baba's cave of secrets.

In the cold light of day, the CIA also was forced to come to terms with how easy it had been for Ames to get away with high treason for nine years, let alone its hiring him in the first place. It also belatedly recognized that management's failure to order a serious, comprehensive counterintelligence investigation after the '85–'86 losses was a case of unforgivable bureaucratic negligence. It was all the more so considering the system that should have prevented it was already in place when Ames volunteered to the KGB in 1985. Polygraphs and a rigorous background investigation early on should have spotted him as a problem and led to either firing him or at the very least preventing him from taking a sensitive job like head of Soviet counterintelligence. The fact that it took an on-again, off-again agent like Max rubbing the CIA's nose in it—a matter of sheer luck—didn't put things in a better light.

What made it all the worse was that CIA counterintelligence had utterly failed at its core mission: spotting traitors in its ranks. The only reasonable course of action after the '85–'86 losses should have been an all-hands-on-deck beating of the bushes on the entirely justified assumption that a double agent in Russian operations was behind the losses. For a start, they should have polygraphed everyone who'd had access to the Russian files with a single-issue polygraph: *Are you a KGB agent?* From there, the investigation would have moved to credit checks, pulling up bank and telephone records, a search for unexplained international travel, and so on. Finally, if CIA counterintelligence had factored in everyone who'd had contact with the Russians, it could have easily come up with a very short list of double agent suspects. Ames would have been right at the top of it, in the company of maybe four or five others. It's the systematic, rigorous work counterintelligence is designed to do.

It came as no surprise to anyone that Ames's arrest was a publicity nightmare for the CIA, exploding in all its hideousness across the world's press, followed by a slew of books that did the CIA no favors. It laid bare the CIA's problems for the whole world to see. Now no Russian in their right mind would consider volunteering to the CIA, considering it could very well be riddled with KGB spies. There would, of course, be the slow to catch on, but those definitely wouldn't be the pick of the litter. And certainly no one in a position of power would ever risk talking out of school to the CIA. Its aura now gone like an old breeze, the CIA could no longer count on a regular flow of Russians knocking on its door volunteering to spy for it. When Hanssen was arrested in 2001, it was all the worse. So no wonder Russia went back to the blank slate it had been for its entire history, a place where a palace coup can occur without the rest of the world knowing until it's over. Or where, one day, without warning, the Kremlin would meddle in American and European elections.

With its dismal track record hunting moles, the CIA now couldn't help but wonder how many more there were in its ranks and, most troubling, how many there were who knew how to get away with it.

For instance, moles who didn't take money and knew better than to leave correspondence with the KGB lying around the house. The realists at the CIA and FBI knew that catching a terrible spy like Ames wasn't all that extraordinary an accomplishment. After all, Ames had more or less been hiding in the open. But a traitor who knew what they were doing would be a bird of another feather.

Some heads did roll after Ames's arrest, and while it may have slaked the bloodlust of an outraged Congress and White House, as well as a CIA-hating press, it did nothing to repair the soil Ames sprouted out of, a tired bureaucracy that had lost its sense of direction in the waning years of the Cold War. With the rot reaching its very head, no one knew where to even start looking for a fix. Calls for turning intelligence over to the State Department were made in all seriousness.

There was a time when the CIA used to pat itself on the back that it would never suffer the British disease of public-school boys betraying their country out of misguided idealism, recalling how a KGB predecessor, the NKVD, had thoroughly penetrated British intelligence in the thirties and forties. The infamous Cambridge Spy Ring, which counted among its members MI6's head of counteres-pionage operations, Kim Philby, was the most notorious spy cluster, but the NKVD seemed to have sources everywhere that counted. At one point, some were convinced Britain's head of MI5—the equiva-lent of the FBI—was an NKVD mole. But now, with the CIA's head of Soviet counterintelligence having sold his soul for a Jaguar and straight teeth, the smirk was wiped off the CIA's face. And for those raking through the ashes left behind by Ames, it was looking more and more like the CIA had another problem, one that would make Philby and Ames look like garden-variety snitches.

FIVE

par·a·noi·a /pær ə'nɔɪ ə/ *n.* A vague or baseless fear.

Moscow; June 13, 1985

PUTTING AMES BEHIND bars was cold comfort for the CIA. He wasn't going to do any more damage, but there was nothing the CIA could do to repair its tattered reputation. That is, other than try to write Ames off as a lone rotten apple, never to be replicated. The CIA's seventh floor tried to convince itself Ames was the only problem and there was no point in digging any deeper. But as happens all too often with counterintelligence, the devil's in the detail.

The second disaster to befall the CIA on June 13, 1985, the same day Ames dropped seven pounds of secrets on his Russian handler, took place on the other side of the world, on a deserted Moscow street a little after eight in the evening. There, KGB muscle tackled a Moscow CIA case officer by the name of Paul Stombaugh and arrested him. A former FBI special agent, Stombaugh was on his way to meet a Russian agent named Adolf Georgievich Tolkachev. Stombaugh was certain he hadn't picked up a KGB tail, but what he didn't know was that Tolkachev had already been arrested and subjected to brutal KGB interrogation. Little doubt it was during one of these sessions Tolkachev gave up details of his meeting arrangements with Stombaugh. From there, it was a simple matter of the KGB unobtrusively lying in wait, with cameras poised to document Stombaugh's arrest and the CIA's humiliation. Stombaugh was released thanks to diplomatic immunity and expelled from the Soviet Union. Tolkachev was tried and executed.

Tolkachev, an electronics engineer, was one of the best agents the CIA has ever possessed, Russian or otherwise. Over the course of seven years, he provided reams of extremely sensitive Soviet military documents mainly related to advances in missiles and radar. The secrets Tolkachev supplied helped give the United States air superiority over the Soviet Union and were one reason American fighters outfought Iraq's Soviet-built planes during the 1990–91 Gulf War. Without a substitute for Tolkachev, the Pentagon was in the dark about important Russian military developments. A *Washington Post* journalist would write a riveting best seller about Tolkachev's time spying for the CIA, marking it as a great Cold War intelligence victory.

Tolkachev's arrest rattled the CIA. Not only was he irreplaceable, but the CIA had no idea how the KGB had caught on to him. Forced to speculate in a vacuum, it considered one possibility that the KGB had discovered Tolkachev thanks to a mistake on Stombaugh's part. For instance, Stombaugh might have failed to spot a KGB tail on his way to an earlier meeting with Tolkachev. It then would have been as simple as the KGB following Tolkachev home and arresting him. No one withstands a KGB interrogation for long.

If the KGB made Tolkachev thanks to surveillance, it wouldn't be much of a surprise. The Soviet Union was one of the most efficiently and thoroughly surveilled societies in the world, with no Russian or foreigner allowed to slip off the KGB's radar. Moscow swarmed with KGB mobile and fixed surveillance teams, plus tens of thousands of KGB informants supporting them. According to a former Russian intelligence officer, one in ten Russians secretly reported to the KGB. There were bugs and cameras everywhere. The police were also at the KGB's beck and call. Surveillance on the CIA was all the more suffocating because the bulk of its attention was directed at a handful of its undercover case officers whose true affiliation couldn't be kept secret from the KGB. MI6 caught the same heat. Add to all this a population under the heavy thumb of fine-tuned suspicion and xenophobia, and there was no place in Moscow an operative could be certain of escaping the KGB's vigilant eye.

There also was the possibility Tolkachev himself had made an error. He might, for instance, have confessed to his wife, who panicked, then ran to the KGB to denounce him. It wouldn't be the first time a family member gave up the game. Or it could have been a coworker who spotted Tolkachev photographing documents at work and reported him. Another possibility is that the KGB might have stumbled across Tolkachev during a routine security investigation, something in his past catching its attention. Still, the likeliest scenario is that the KGB found out Tolkachev had been living far beyond his means. It's the dread of every case officer that in handing an agent a stack of cash, the agent won't be able to resist the temptation to freely spend it and draw attention to himself. That's what first tipped off the spy catchers to Ames.

ROBERT BAER

However, the mystery of Tolkachev's arrest was apparently cleared up on August 1, 1985, when a KGB colonel, soon to be promoted to general, named Vitaly Sergeyevich Yurchenko defected to the CIA in Rome. As a deputy head of the Americas department in the KGB's foreign intelligence directorate, Yurchenko had a lot to say, but of immediate interest was what he knew about two American intelligence officers who'd spied for the KGB. Yurchenko didn't know the names of either, but said one had worked for the National Security Agency and the other for the CIA.

Yurchenko's description of the CIA officer nicely matched Ed Lee Howard. A newly minted CIA case officer, Howard had been in the pipeline to Moscow, where he was supposed to take over the handling of Tolkachev. But having failed a series of polygraphs, he was fired in May 1983 before he made it to Moscow. As I heard it from someone in the Office of Security, the CIA decided to fire him after he confessed that he stole money out of a woman's bag on an airplane to "test his nerves" for his upcoming Moscow assignment. After Howard was out on the street and stewing about his lot in life, he confided to a CIA psychologist that he'd thought about volunteering to the KGB out of revenge. But no one thought to pass that little nugget to the FBI in time.

Howard deserved to be fired, but on the other hand, firing him on the spot when he had a head full of sensitive Russian secrets was a dereliction of duty no one in management would ever be held accountable for. That is, other than blackening the CIA's reputation. When Howard found out the FBI was onto him, he fled to Russia. Safely under KGB protection in Moscow, Howard denied having betrayed Tolkachev. But at this point few at Langley were in a frame of mind to believe anything he had to say.

The NSA spy that Yurchenko didn't have a name for turned out to be Ronald Pelton, who'd volunteered to the KGB in 1980. Fired from the NSA, he'd run into serious financial problems and turned to the KGB for a handout. Yurchenko, assigned to the Washington rezidentura at the time, had been one of the first to meet Pelton. As the FBI would determine, Pelton had given up everything he knew about the NSA, among other things betraying an NSA/CIA tap on a Soviet military cable under the Sea of Okhotsk. The KGB's only regret was that Pelton wasn't with the NSA anymore.

In fingering both Howard and Pelton, Yurchenko was toasted around Washington and in the press as an intelligence bonanza. For the CIA, he was in-the-flesh proof it could on its own clean up in-house messes like Howard. I was back at Langley at the time and couldn't miss how thick the place was with glee and chest pounding. Although it would turn out not to be entirely warranted, for the moment it came down to the wishful thinking that if a colonel from the KGB's Americas department had crossed the lines and defected, the KGB had to be in serious trouble. And so had to be the Soviet Union. In the numbering system this book follows, Howard is the first man. The CIA couldn't bring itself to believe he wouldn't be the last.

Yurchenko's credibility took a broadside, though, when he re-defected to Russia in October 1985. His change of heart was partly thanks to unrequited love, partly to a bout of homesickness. His love interest, the wife of a Soviet diplomat, rejected him when he paid her a visit in Canada. Now heartbroken and depressed, Yurchenko decided to try his luck back home. Never arrested or paying the usual penalty for treachery other than being forced to resign from the KGB, his instincts proved correct. Yurchenko was spotted from time to time freely walking Moscow's streets, apparently doing just fine. Some reports even said that he never lost his KGB job. But since the CIA didn't understand KGB upper management's thinking, no one at Langley was exactly sure how Yurchenko had managed to find his way out of the woods. It led the morbidly suspicious to consider that he could have been a plant from the beginning, a faux defector sent on a mission to throw the CIA off the scent of something. Maybe another double agent other than Howard. But as they admitted, there was no sound basis for the suspicion.

Yurchenko skeptics were quick to point out that his slap on the wrist was the polar opposite of the brutal way the KGB normally treats traitors—namely, a speedy trial followed by, as the KGB charmingly puts it, a "control shot" in the back of the head. But their skepticism was based on more than that. Most telling, Yurchenko hadn't given up a single active American agent spying for the KGB. For those convinced the KGB was indeed running bona fide active American agents, it made little sense Yurchenko would know nothing about them.

One explanation Yurchenko apologists came up with was that he hadn't been in the job long enough to read the American files. Another was that there were all sorts of KGB senior officers never read into the sensitive cases. Either way, to the skeptics it all sounded a little too convenient. As for outing Howard and Pelton, it looked to them like they were throwaways—agents of no use other than as sacrificial lambs to protect more valuable agents. Both were gone from their respective agencies and would never have access to new information. While Yurchenko's giving them up burnished his credentials, in reality they were no real loss to the KGB. After Ames's arrest, the die-hard Yurchenko skeptics were all the more convinced he was a provocateur "run into" the CIA. How could he possibly not have heard something about Ames, even the thinnest rumor? they asked. But CIA management scoffed at the possibility Yurchenko was some sort of Trojan horse, arguing that the KGB would never dare put one of its senior officers in jeopardy like this.

Paul Redmond, the head of the USSR Branch at the time of Yurchenko's defection, privately told a colleague he had his own doubts about Yurchenko's bona fides. There was nothing specific Redmond could put his finger on, but he thought it fishy Yurchenko appeared so soon after Tolkachev's arrest. There might have been nothing to it, but he couldn't rule out the possibility that Yurchenko was a red herring, used to throw the CIA off the scent of the traitor who truly had betrayed Tolkachev. Redmond also didn't like that while Yurchenko had served in the Washington, DC, rezidentura for five years, he had little of real value to say about KGB modus operandi and agents. It was akin to the Pink Panther breaking into Tiffany's and emerging with only a worthless silver pendant.

Langley's spy catchers would never stop wondering how it was that Yurchenko knew nothing about Ames. Surely by the time of Yurchenko's defection in August 1985, Ames must have been a subject of gossip around KGB headquarters. The KGB was a place notorious for its "wall talkers"—KGB desk officers gossiping about their cases at the urinals under the assumption that running water defeats mics. More junior than Yurchenko, Max found out about the two double agents in American intelligence, so there was the legitimate question of why Yurchenko hadn't known about Ames. At the very least, Yurchenko should have heard something about the ongoing investigations into the colleagues Ames had betrayed a month and a half before his August 1 defection. It just didn't seem plausible that someone as high up as Yurchenko, the number two in the Americas department, wouldn't have caught wind of them, however secondhand. Not to mention Yurchenko had nothing to say about the Fourth Man, who, as it would turn out, was likely on the KGB's books by August 1985, when Yurchenko defected.

For the CIA spy catchers obsessed with detail, one small anomaly that caught their attention was that Howard knew Tolkachev only by his cryptonym rather than his true name. Nor was Howard informed of Tolkachev's exact position at his institute. There was always the possibility he'd inadvertently found out about it while he was on Langley's USSR Branch waiting to go to Moscow, but there's no evidence for it. If in fact Howard was only able to give his KGB handlers a vague description of Tolkachev, the question then became whether it would have been enough time for KGB counterintelligence to narrow down the scores of potential suspects between when Howard first brought up Tolkachev at a meeting with the KGB in November 1984 and Tolkachev's arrest, which the CIA knew had to have been well before June 13, 1985, the day his case officer was detained in Moscow. For some spy catchers, the timing was way too tight.

The deeper the spy catchers looked into Tolkachev's compromise, the more questions they had. In April 1983, Tolkachev told the CIA about the Second Chief Directorate's investigation of a leak of classified information from his institute. The Second didn't have a name for him, but from what Tolkachev was told it was certain there was a spy somewhere in the institute. The significance of it is that this investigation occurred long before Howard made contact with the KGB. Then there came a point where Tolkachev's reporting started to encounter odd problems. On one occasion, his photos of secret documents were uncustomarily blurred and unreadable. Some pages were also out of sequence and sections missing. It could have been a coincidence or an indication he'd been caught and put under KGB control. There was no way to pin down a date when this might have occurred, but again it threw into question when and who first betrayed Tolkachev.

A former Russian intelligence officer told me that when he went through training, Tolkachev had been the subject of a counterintelligence case study. It was described as an "under the cap" investigation, meaning it was long-running and involved. Among other things, his class was told that Tolkachev was put under discreet 24/7 surveillance, had his apartment bugged, and was secretly photographed at work. The KGB's objective was to make sure Tolkachev didn't have accomplices. Standard practice in any complex counterintelligence investigation, it would have taken months to put in motion and many more to allow it to run its course. It adds to the suspicion the KGB was onto Tolkachev earlier than first suspected. Possibly before Howard outed him.

Another intriguing thing about Tolkachev's roll-up is that his family never paid the usual penalty for an immediate relative caught spying. Normally a spy's family is assigned what the KGB calls a "wolf ticket"—its version of a scarlet letter. Among other things, the entire family is rusticated to some godforsaken part of the Soviet Union and barred from important jobs. But that's not what happened in Tolkachev's case. His family was never evicted from their

Ploshchad Vosstaniya district apartment, a prime piece of Moscow real estate. And Tolkachev's son Oleg was allowed to continue with his architectural career. According to my former Russian intelligence source, the only reason the family could have avoided a wolf ticket is because Tolkachev had fully cooperated with the KGB as soon as he was caught. This also lends credence to the hypothesis that someone had outed Tolkachev before Howard did.

Finally, one discrepancy that particularly bothered the FBI about Howard is that he had told his wife he was under the distinct impression that the KGB already knew about Tolkachev. According to what her husband told her, his KGB handlers showed little interest in what he had to say about Tolkachev—for instance, how he was met in Moscow or what he'd produced over the years. Instead, they impatiently nodded as Howard tried to tell them about him. But since Howard's wife was complicit in her husband's treason, anything she had to say was taken with a grain of salt. There's also the possibility Howard had lied to her about the KGB's indifference, hoping to lighten the burden of guilt for his role in the murder of a man who'd put his life in the CIA's hands. In the end, there was nothing more to be done with all this other than to put it down as one more anomaly that plagues the Tolkachev case still today.

What to make, then, of the possibility that Howard wasn't the first to betray Tolkachev, as has become the accepted explanation? The first, most obvious question is whether Ames could have done it. If he had, it obviously wasn't at his June 13, 1985, meeting at Chadwicks because Tolkachev had long been arrested by then. There's a remote possibility Ames dropped Tolkachev's name at an earlier contact with the Russians, possibly in April or May 1985, but even then the timing would have been much too tight for Tolkachev's arrest. Not to mention Ames hadn't been formally read into the Tolkachev case. When a case officer is read into a case, it means they're given access to an agent's "201" file, which contains all relevant information known about the agent. With no counterintelligence angle to it, Tolkachev's 201 was held by the USSR Branch rather than Soviet counterintelligence, which Ames headed. Ames certainly knew about Tolkachev and did eventually pass his name to the KGB, but most believe Tolkachev's name wouldn't have been foremost on his mind to bait the KGB in his early meetings with them.

That aside, the CIA and FBI investigators who questioned Ames after his arrest uniformly concluded that he gave a full and frank confession. He'd done so in exchange for the Department of Justice going easy on his wife. For instance, when an FBI agent told him that a British agent in the KGB whom he'd compromised had been recalled to Moscow and interrogated a month before his June 13 lunch, and that the chances were good that someone else first outed the British agent, Ames was visibly shocked. He even seemed a bit envious that he'd been beaten to the punch. It didn't appear to be an act.

Everyone I talked to agrees that Ames also had a remarkable memory for operational detail, including the ability to recall exactly what he'd handed over to the KGB at the June 13 meeting. He knew which copies of which files he'd stuffed in his shopping bag. He even remembered the Russian agents' true names, along with their positions and their CIA-assigned cryptonyms. As you'd expect of a sociopath indifferent to sending so many people to an early grave, he was proud that in selling out his country, he had been as efficient and thorough as he could arrange it. But then again, the word of a drunk and a traitor can't be completely trusted.

Another anomaly that would bother the spy catchers about Yurchenko was his claim that Howard had informed his KGB handlers about a Soviet intelligence officer in Budapest spying for the CIA. As Yurchenko heard it, Howard knew him only as "the angry KGB colonel," who apparently was unhappy about the way the CIA had been handling him. The CIA had no doubt that the colonel Yurchenko referred to was a Budapest-based agent, Colonel Vladimir Mikhailovich Vasilyev. But rather than the KGB, he worked for Soviet military intelligence, the GRU. As for anger issues, Vasilyev would have preferred to have been run by a military officer rather than a civilian. The spy catchers didn't completely discount the possibility that Howard had told his handlers about the "angry KGB colonel," but there were doubts about whether this was enough for the KGB to pinpoint Vasilyev's identity and arrest him.

Not long after Yurchenko's defection, in the fall of 1985, Vasilyev returned to Moscow from Budapest on routine reassignment. Throwing caution to the wind, the CIA decided that in spite of Howard's possible outing of him to the KGB, it would go ahead and make contact with him in Moscow. The thinking was, the KGB didn't have enough to identify Vasilyev, if for no other reason than there were too many intelligence colonels assigned to Budapest to sort through them all. But that turned out to be tragically mistaken. The last contact with Vasilyev would be on December 11, 1985, via dead drop. (A dead drop is when an agent leaves documents in a concealed location for his case officer to retrieve, or vice versa.) At some point after that, he was arrested, tried, and executed for espionage. Justified or not, Howard immediately got the rap, with zero inclination on the part of management to dig any deeper. Nor did management want to entertain the possibility that Vasilyev's December 11 contact might have occurred under KGB control. The KGB very well could have had its reasons to make it appear like Vasilyev was doing fine through December 11, despite his having been outed many months earlier, and likely by someone other than Howard. Someone who, unlike Howard, knew Vasilyev worked for the GRU, not the KGB.

The spy catchers also factored in the fact that Vasilyev's file had been held in East European operations, not the USSR Branch where Howard sat. Because Russian internal and external operations were strictly compartmented—siloed, as it's sometimes called—Howard had never been read into the Vasilyev case. The same went for Ames, who as a matter of routine didn't have access to Soviet cases run in Eastern Europe. Nor did anyone recall their talking to Howard about it. No one could be absolutely certain that Howard or Ames hadn't overheard something about a Soviet agent in Budapest, but without evidence it couldn't be taken as a given. (Incidentally, Hanssen didn't know about Vasilyev, either.)

Questions about what Howard compromised didn't stop there. Around the time he made contact with the KGB, agents reported that certain CIA documents or summaries of them had found their way to Moscow. Yurchenko thought Howard might have provided them. But according to the records, Howard had never had access to the documents. Moreover, there was no evidence Howard had walked out the door with any classified documents. But again, the CIA's seventh floor was content to accuse Howard of passing the documents to the KGB, though it remained a question mark for the ever-suspicious counterintelligence analysts.

It's forgivable for the reader to wonder why any of this still matters, why these inconsistencies and lingering questions are more than minute details in stories that seemingly no longer matter. And while these anomalies and discrepancies, even put in the worst light, don't amount to proof of another double agent in the CIA who betrayed Tolkachev before Howard or who was responsible for the other compromises to the KGB, they do represent the first hints that there might have been a problem beyond Howard. Not that the CIA's seventh floor wanted to hear it. It took the unimaginative Occam's razor approach to the evidence, blaming every discrepancy and unexplained compromise it possibly could on Howard. As for Yurchenko, with no concrete evidence surfacing that he was a faux defector, his word was taken as writ. Nonetheless, Langley's spy catchers filed it all away in the back of their minds, hoping one day new evidence would surface that would make better sense of the discrepancies.

Indeed, Ames's February 1994 arrest would account for most of them, but not all. FBI agent Bob Hanssen, who was arrested in 2001 as a Russian spy, would account for many of the rest. But these two traitors combined, along with Howard, can't explain all the losses. Which makes proof of the Fourth Man's existence a matter of math. As one investigator still on the case put it to me, "Subtract the compromises assignable to Howard, Ames, and Hanssen from the total number of compromises to the Russians, and the only conclusion you can come to is there was another KGB double agent in CIA-Russian operations."

SIX

prod·i·gal son /ˈprɒd ɪ gəl sʌn/ *n.* A disgraced figure who
returns home to be forgiven.

South America; April 1994

AT A LITTLE past seven in the morning, Laine Bannerman was
walking down a deserted Langley hallway when she spotted her
boss, Paul Redmond, now the number two in counterintelligence,
rounding a corner at a brisk trot. When Redmond caught sight of
her, he started to wave a piece of paper in her direction. Redmond
was more agitated than she'd ever seen him. As soon as he got to
her, he turned the paper around so she could read it.

"That's him, right?" Redmond asked Bannerman. She now
understood Redmond's problem.

It was a routine classified cable from a South American station informing Langley that a Russian intelligence officer by the
name of Alexander Zaporozhsky had approached the station and
asked to meet as soon as possible with his regular CIA contact,
Dick Corbin. Zaporozhsky claimed to possess an urgent piece of
intelligence.

The South American station had no idea who Zaporozhsky was, that at Langley he was called Max, or that he was the agent ultimately responsible for catching Ames. It also had no idea the nature of the urgency he wanted to convey. But to make sure Langley had no confusion about his identity, Max told the South American station the nickname his case officers used with him. (Along with not mentioning the country Max showed up in, the CIA requested that neither Max's nickname nor cryptonym be mentioned.)

Normally, agents aren't supposed to be told their cryptonyms, but along the way some transgressive case officer must have thought letting Max in on this little secret would help build rapport. But right now, that was the least of it. As Bannerman instantly knew, the problem was that the cable had been sent to Langley via routine channels, which meant it was now widely distributed. For a case that was now deemed so sensitive that it had been taken out of cable traffic and digital databases altogether, it was a potential nightmare. If there was another Russian double agent in the CIA, as Max himself had started to hint at, the chances of his learning about Max resurfacing in South America were good.

Before Bannerman could read to the end of the cable, Redmond ordered her to move as fast as her feet would carry her and run down every last copy of the cable, no matter where they'd been distributed, and personally shred them all. She was also to ask the IT people to de-index Max's name from Agency digital databases. When done, she was to find Corbin and get him on the next plane to South America to meet Max. Bannerman said she thought Corbin was on leave hiking somewhere in the mountains. Redmond didn't give a damn. "Just find him," he barked.

As Bannerman went around the building hunting down copies of the cable, she now read to the end of it. When she came to the part where Max said he'd been in South America on assignment for more than a month, her first thought was *Typical Max, always deciding when and where to meet us.* Always the accomplice rather than the agent.

Bannerman knew as well as anyone involved how difficult Max had been to handle: how he'd disappear for months at a time; how Max, priding himself on being a smart operator, never wanted to hear a word from the CIA about operational security. He'd do things his way, which as it turned out wasn't the best. For instance, Max should have known better than to make a cold approach to a station that had no idea who he was. There were all sorts of ways things could have gone sideways, like the local counterintelligence service spotting his meeting with American officials, then a Russian double agent in that service informing the Russians. Chance sightings like that happen all the time.

Even after Greenbrier, Max still refused to give the CIA fall-back contact coordinates to reach him in Moscow. He wouldn't even agree to the CIA's signaling him with time-tested methods like a chalk mark on a wall or a flowerpot moved in a window. Nor for that matter would he commit to any predictable meeting arrangements outside Russia. Nothing the CIA could say would change his mind.

Normally an agent as erratic and unpredictable as Max would have been cut loose. "Terminated," as the CIA puts it. But his grand-slam Caracas tip-off definitely ruled that out. With the best KGB sources lost in the eighties, the CIA didn't have another spy in Russian counterintelligence nearly as good as Max. With no way to control him, it was left with a silent prayer that he wouldn't disappear for good, but rather one day would show up with a new double agent lead. It was like betting all you have on a rigged roulette wheel.

Corbin flew down to South America to meet Max. Redmond's faith in Max wasn't misplaced. Time has blurred memories, but it was either at Corbin's meeting with Max in South America or another in the same time frame that Max delivered a tip nearly as important as Ames's Caracas trip: details about another Russian double agent in the CIA beyond Ames and Howard. But what my sources have no doubt about is that Max delivered two key details about this agent. First, the new double agent attended CIA Directorate of Operations division chief meetings. Two, this new double agent at one point had access to the files cataloguing meeting sites in Moscow where officers could meet agents. The double agent described to his handler how the main files for the sites were kept in a four-drawer safe in the USSR/Russian Branch at Langley, but that the summaries of them were jotted down on handwritten 3×5 cards for quick reference. Again memories vary, but some recall Max having claimed the new double agent passed at least some copies of cards to his KGB handler. Max even claimed to have seen a copy of a meeting-site 3×5 card on his boss's desk.

Needless to say, these new revelations grabbed everyone's undivided and panicked attention. Ames never attended Directorate of Operations division chief meetings—only about a dozen officers did, all very senior. Nor of course did Howard. But if Max was right, he was talking about an officer who had a bird's-eye view of American intelligence operations worldwide. If the National Security Agency were to break a code it never had before, he'd hear about it at one of these meetings. If the president were to order some ultra-secret covert action plan, he would hear about that, too. Then there was the danger to America's military. For instance, for decades the CIA spared no effort to steal Soviet and later Russian military technology manuals, allowing the Pentagon to redesign its armament accordingly. But if this new double agent in the CIA had tipped off the Russians to what had been stolen, they would have been in a position to redesign their weaponry. Little doubt it's what they did after they learned about the Tolkachev breach.

It was bad enough the new double agent might have sat in Directorate of Operations division chief meetings, but the possibility that the 3×5 cards had been compromised to the Russians was equally alarming. Both Ames and Howard knew that intelligence from sensitive Soviet sources was recorded on 3×5 cards, but neither knew anything about Moscow meeting-site cards because this system wasn't in place in their dealings with the USSR Branch. Only about a half-dozen people on the branch had access to these cards. If Max was right about the 3×5 cards, the KGB had been or was still running a mole in Soviet operations, one almost certainly better situated than even Ames.

The integrity of Moscow agent meeting sites was one of the CIA's most closely held secrets. If the Russians knew in advance where Moscow case officers were going to make a meeting with an agent or indirect communications like a dead drop, every one of its agents was vulnerable to compromise. The worst-case scenario was the new mole had betrayed all the sites to the KGB, meaning Moscow station couldn't meet agents, period.

To give an idea of how sensitive the Moscow sites were, for a time neither the files nor the 3×5-card summaries were held at

Moscow station. When a case officer was due to make a dead drop or brush pass (an innocent-looking physical handoff of information), they'd cable to the USSR Branch back at Langley requesting it select a site. The Langley officer managing the case would check the available sites, among other things, making sure the one selected hadn't been used for another agent or somehow compromised. The latest satellite photography was also checked to make sure nothing precluded using the site. For instance, recent construction or a new police post nearby. If the site was suitable, Langley would cable its description to Moscow. In short, the CIA did everything possible to conceal its agent meeting sites from the KGB.

So it was no wonder, then, that Max's comments about a CIA double agent handing over copies of the 3×5 cards caused white-knuckle panic, especially considering how few people would have been in a position to do so. If his intelligence was accurate, they were near conclusive proof that at one time the Fourth Man had served on the USSR Branch. This tidbit of course helped to considerably narrow down the suspect list. Coupled with Max's claim that the double agent sat in on senior staff meetings, the profile for the Fourth Man was now in much sharper focus.

Even after the Caracas lead, Max still had his detractors. The scale of his new allegations didn't help things. Either in South America or at later debriefings, Max was challenged that in East Africa he'd said there were only two double agents in American intelligence, one in the FBI and the other in the CIA. Max bristled, saying that, no, all along he'd said there were three, two in the CIA and one in the FBI. This was never resolved to anyone's satisfaction, but nonetheless, Max's claims about a new, senior double agent in the CIA had to be taken seriously.

If Max was right and the Russians indeed had penetrated American intelligence at the level he alleged, it would be an utter catastrophe, likely to have done more damage than any spy in American history. As one Russian intelligence general later described the Fourth Man, he was the best agent the KGB's ever run. It's saying a lot, considering the KGB is the best intelligence service in modern times.

With Max setting off all sorts of new alarms, and the mounting inconsistencies related to what secrets Howard and Ames had and hadn't betrayed, the spy catchers in the trenches were convinced the CIA's seventh floor could no longer sit on its hands.

SEVEN

cir·cum·stan·tial ev·i·dence /ˌsɜr kəmˈstæn ʃəl ˈɛv ɪ dəns/ *n.*
An inference made from partial or contradictory facts.

Langley; May 1994

THE OFFICIAL HUNT for the Fourth Man quietly got under way in May 1994 when the head of CIA operations Ted Price tasked the number two in CIA counterintelligence, Paul Redmond, with conducting what Price called "a post-Ames cleanup investigation."

As the story floated down to the spy catchers picked to conduct the investigation, Price didn't tell Redmond he'd concluded there was another Russian double agent burrowed somewhere in the CIA. It's not something anyone would want to advertise around the CIA, an organization so grievously wounded and demoralized thanks to Ames. But since Ames had just admitted in court to wiping out CIA Russian operations on June 13, 1985, the only prudent thing to do was cross every *t* and dot every *i*. Price and Redmond never told the investigators how large a part Max's allegations played in their decision.

Redmond was the obvious pick to head Price's investigation. At Langley, he'd overseen Moscow operations, headed counter-intelligence in the Soviet division, was number two in the Soviet division, and then moved over to number two in counterintelli-gence, where he oversaw the mole hunt that ended with the arrest of Ames. This much time on a single portfolio was rare at the CIA.

Since Price wouldn't talk, there's no way for me to know what motivated him to open the Fourth Man investigation. Redmond said it was he rather than Price who ordered the investigation. "Within days" after Ames's arrest, he told me, he was certain the Russians had another penetration of the CIA, someone who either previously had access to Soviet/Russian operations, or possibly still did. Either way, neither Price nor Redmond needed to be reminded just how badly the CIA had botched Ames and Howard. Stories about what a loser Ames had been were now legion. The same went for Howard, who also was a drunk, not to mention a onetime cokehead and thief who also should never have made it through the CIA's background vetting. All of it left CIA management to wonder how deep the KGB had gotten into its pockets.

After Ames, the CIA was unsure how to put its house back in order and stop losing agents to the KGB. It started by mandat-ing more frequent and tougher polygraphs, offering better alcohol counseling, and taking a closer look at suspicious foreign contacts. But at the same time, it knew all this wouldn't be enough, because that regimen had pretty much been in place even as Ames was spilling his guts to the KGB (he passed two polygraphs). There also was the problem of how deeply the CIA could intrude into the personal lives of CIA employees. It's not like every time one of them inherited money from a maiden aunt the CIA had the resources to investigate the ultimate origins of the money. Falling for Ames's alibi about a rich Colombian wife, then, wasn't all that egregious a lapse. God help anyone trying to follow a money trail in Colombia, especially in the eighties when it was the cocaine capital of the world. The CIA had to find other ways to tighten up its security.

A raze-it-to-the-ground mole hunt definitely wasn't in the cards. James Jesus Angleton, who headed CIA counterintelligence from 1954 to 1975, had tried just that and failed miserably. Angleton became obsessed with the idea that the CIA was infiltrated by Russians. He not only never caught a Russian spy, with all of his thrashing around and wrecking careers, he caused the CIA to crawl so deeply into its shell that it all but stopped spying on the Soviet Union. Officers who understood the country and spoke fluent Russian unjustifiably fell under suspicion and were sidelined, all too often replaced by people who'd never in their lives met a Russian. Thanks to his witch hunt, Angleton turned away legitimate would-be Soviet defectors on the baseless suspicion they might be Trojan horses dispatched by the KGB to sow confusion. He also dismissed defectors who'd managed to make it to the United States, accusing them of being KGB plants. One, Yuri Ivanovich Nosenko, a Second Chief Directorate officer, was famously imprisoned in solitary confinement for almost four years.

In all fairness to Angleton, his paranoia wasn't entirely of his own invention. Thanks to the Army's breaking of Soviet codes, he knew that in the thirties and forties Stalin's intelligence services benefited from more than three hundred American spies, many well-placed and productive. Among the secrets they stole were American and British nuclear bomb designs. They also planted an agent in Roosevelt's White House. The Soviets also possessed more than a dozen spies in the OSS, the CIA's predecessor. In the absence of evidence to the contrary, Angleton had to assume Russian intelligence was doing just as well as the Cold War progressed.

The breaking of Soviet codes was one of the great triumphs in espionage history. But after NKVD double agents informed their handlers about it, the Soviet Union went about tightening up its encryption, making sure its codes were never broken again. Overnight, Soviet mole hunting went from hard to nearly impossible. Telephone taps and intercepts were of no help because the KGB knew better than anyone about the dangers of eavesdropping. As a matter of routine, Ames's handlers never called him at home or the office. They never sent him letters, either. Instead, they relied on old-fashioned spy tradecraft like dead drops and chalk marks on walls. After an initial set of face-to-face meetings in Washington, the KGB moved meeting with Ames outside the United States, in places where the CIA's and FBI's surveillance coverage was nonexistent or spotty. The KGB also knew that, rather than make direct wire money transfers to American accounts, it was safer to deposit money into banks out of reach of American banking oversight, like a nominee account in Switzerland or Panama. Or even better, pay them in cash. When possible, it didn't compensate a spy at all. Russian intelligence officers also never discussed an agent in spaces that could possibly be bugged. There were some occasions when even the Washington rezidentura wasn't informed of the identities of particularly sensitive spies to eliminate the risk of a defector from the rezidentura betraying them. In short, with the Soviets tightening up their codes and tradecraft, mole hunting was largely reduced to KGB agents like Max providing leads.

But since the Maxes of the world didn't come along often, the CIA was left only with the option of drastically limiting the distribution of sensitive Russian secrets, both to make it harder for would-be moles to get information and easier to identify the source of any leak. The first step was to reduce the number of people read into such information. Considering more than two hundred CIA officers had been given access to the names of the Russian agents lost between 1985 and 1986, it was clearly too many and completely unnecessary. Straphangers like Ames who made no real contribution to running agents were cut out of sensitive cases. Next to be thrown off the bus were clerical staff and executive assistants. Now that Russian operations were truly run on the basis of need-to-know, even the executive assistants in the director of operations' front office weren't privy to the identities of the CIA's most sensitive agents.

The process of tightening up Russian secrets was implemented at about the same pace as the dimensions of the '85–'86 Russian losses started to sink in. With the possibility the enemy was inside the tent, the head of Soviet operations, Burton Gerber, and his head of counterintelligence, Paul Redmond, in January 1986 sat down his Soviet team and told them, "Do anything you need to keep our guys alive." Accordingly, Russian internal and counterintelligence cases were moved into what they called "the back room"—a small, windowless, nondescript, never-unlocked room in Langley's Original Headquarters Building. The division's two most trusted officers, Sandy Grimes and Diana Worthen, were put in charge. They reported directly to Gerber and Redmond. Tritely enough, the new unit was called "Special Projects." Its existence was so secret, not even the people in the adjoining office knew what it was working on. Those in the Soviet division back then remember the back room's door as always shut and silent as the grave, the only sign of life the cigarette smoke drifting out.

As the back room added people, it would eventually move to a double-vaulted, alarmed, soundproof enclosure on the ground floor of the New Headquarters Building. It was always staffed by the most trusted officers. All veterans, they were almost invariably quiet, retiring women, all above suspicion. None of them drove Jaguars or paid for expensive houses in cash. A strange, gnomic tribe, their names—Jeanne Vertefeuille, Worthen, Sue Eckstein, Myrna Fitzgerald, and Grimes—were familiar to some in the Soviet division, but everywhere else in the CIA they were invisible. Only they, and at most two or three of their bosses, knew anything about the cases they were working on. It was perhaps the most exclusive club in the world.

Nevertheless, it's not as if things were a complete free-for-all before this point. These new measures, designed to limit distribution of Russian operations, joined others that had already been in place before the '85-'86 losses. For instance, "command channels"—standard CIA communications protocols—were tightened up by moving all sensitive agents into what are called "RH channels"—restricted handling. In order to read RH cables, an officer needed to be put on a "bigot list," which was as short as six officers and rarely more than twenty. The more sensitive RH cables weren't distributed through registries and secretaries, but rather at a window outside a special communications site at headquarters where authorized recipients would drop by to collect daily RH hard copy cables. Also, names in Russian RH cables weren't automatically indexed in databases, as names mentioned in CIA cables normally are, but rather manually entered in a special database that only a half-dozen analysts had access to. This is the database Bearden had wanted to get rid of in 1992.

There were a slew of other measures the CIA implemented to make sure as few people as possible had access to classified cables. Although these measures ultimately helped narrow down the identity of the Fourth Man, the CIA has asked me not to detail them. Presumably these measures are still in place, but it's just a guess on my part.

Russian operations were even more tightened up when it was decided to bypass electronic communication altogether, and instead have case officers fly back to Langley after meetings with the more important Russian agents and deliver their reports face-to-face with their bosses. Tape recordings from agent meetings would be transcribed onto standalone computers, or even written down by hand. Things got even stranger when Langley started—a lot like the Mafia—to keep two sets of books: one cooked and the other legitimate. The ruse started out as an attempt by Bearden and Redmond to smoke out a double agent at Langley. The way it worked was, an overseas CIA station generated what was called a "probe" or "eyewash" cable, falsely reporting the recruitment of a Russian official. The hope was that the mole in Soviet operations at Langley would see the cable, then run out the door to rat the official out to his KGB handler. If the framed Russian was precipitously recalled to Moscow, it would confirm the CIA had a mole problem and hopefully leave a bread crumb trail to the mole's front door. Although none of these traps caught a mole, they never lost their luster. In fact, over the years, eyewash became a cottage industry in Russian operations.

Needless to say, a shambolic system like this caused all sorts of confusion up and down the ranks. One assistant in the Directorate of Operations' front office told me all sorts of eyewash RH traffic passed across her desk every morning, but she had no way to know what was real and what wasn't. It was a complete mystery to her how her boss, the deputy director of operations, kept track of it all. She also had no idea how the CIA reconciled the fraudulent recordkeeping with laws governing federal records. A case officer who ran Russian operations for many years told me that by the early aughts it came to the point where Russia Group composed only eyewash RH traffic, with genuine write-ups from Russian agents typed up exclusively in hard copy and distributed by hand. He said it got even crazier when Russian operations stopped putting down anything on paper, with sensitive reporting instead locked up in officers' heads and, the way I understand it, lost forever when they retired. (Incidentally, I'd never heard of any of this when I was employed by the CIA, and it strikes me as not the most efficient way to conduct counterintelligence investigations, as I imagine it does to most.)

Max's reporting about the Fourth Man and the other double agents in American intelligence he exposed were treated according to these new protocols. When he was first met in East Africa, Max had been assigned a standard cryptonym and an agent file number, a so-called 201. Accounts of the meetings with him and his intelligence reporting were cabled back to Langley in command channels, with proper names indexed. But when he came around to talking about the two double agents, his case officers in East Africa started flying to London to send double-encrypted cables back to Langley from standalone, hard-case GRiD laptops: custom-built, air-gapped, and steel-encased computers that don't give off electromagnetic emissions called "tempest" that can be picked up from a distance. Soon enough, Max's reporting was taken out of communications channels altogether. Along with it, his cryptonym was substituted for a nickname, Maximillian, then simply Max. Officers who knew about the initial meeting in East Africa were misled into believing Max had broken off contact with the CIA. With fewer than a dozen at the FBI and CIA now read into his case, Max was turned into a phantom agent.

From then on, after a meeting with Max, a case officer would fly back to Langley with a taped recording of the meeting. A translator then would type up a transcript, a single hard copy of which would be put in Max's 201 file. When Max was met at Greenbrier, some of the debriefing notes were scribbled on napkins and then thrown in files at Langley. None of it was incorporated into databases or otherwise distributed around Langley.

Every other CIA Russian source with knowledge about the Fourth Man was removed from view by the same draconian regimen—cryptonyms dropped for nicknames, their reporting limited to a handful of people, and nothing logged in digital databases.

Moving sensitive information off computers onto hard copy and 3×5 cards was entirely predictable after Ames's arrest. But it was never expected to unearth the Fourth Man—if for no other reason than, already on the inside, she or he knew where the traps were and how to avoid them, and in the bargain could take advantage of all the chaos.

No surprise, jerry-rigged siloing and secrecy proved enormously inefficient. Looking for a mole was no longer a matter of sitting at a computer and searching for clues but rather knowing where to look for the evidence that mattered. It was now akin to picking through a crashed airplane's debris field searching for bomb fragments. At the same time, though, with the number of CIA officers with access to Russian secrets whittled down from more than two hundred to about a dozen, the Fourth Man must have considered that the noose was starting to feel a bit uncomfortable.

While Price's Fourth Man investigation wasn't going to make up for the Howard and Ames debacles, it was a start. Price, a compact, graying red-haired man with prep school sheen, was a credentialed spymaster. After graduating from Yale and a five-year stint in the Marines, Price joined the CIA as a case officer. He worked his way up the ranks the old-fashioned way, recruiting and running agents in the field. He spoke fluent Mandarin and served mostly in East Asia, including in China. Before taking over the CIA's Directorate of Operations, Price ran counterintelligence, a good remedial course for getting up to speed on Russian intelligence. Although by reputation he didn't hold a candle to someone like Redmond when it came to the KGB, he made up for it as a good reader with a talent for absorbing names and detail. But what Price had going for him when it came to counterintelligence was an ability to keep his cards close to the vest. Some wondered if it didn't have something to do with his having passed through Yale's Skull and Bones. Whether or not he was a member of that secret society, Price didn't need to be told that the only way to run an airtight counterintelligence investigation is to rigorously limit the number of people read into it. If only one spy catcher could do the job, all the better.

A cynic might interpret Price's Fourth Man investigation as a predictable cover-your-ass exercise. Or with Ames locked up in jail for life, a case of closing the barn door after the horse got out. But Price knew better. Max's claims about more Russian double agents couldn't be ignored, along with various other leads from the past decade. There were also the compromises of Russian agents and technical operations that didn't nicely fit either Howard or Ames, like Tolkachev. While Price and Redmond knew it would have been politically convenient to pin all the losses on Howard and Ames and leave it at that, it would be to ignore the evidence.

They weren't alone in their suspicions. The lead FBI agent in the Ames investigation, Les Wiser, told me that after the Ames damage was tallied up and accounted for, there was no doubt in his mind there had been or still was another Russian spy in the CIA. Dell Spry, the FBI agent who cuffed Ames next to his Jaguar, told me his squad operated on the assumption the Russians had another source in CIA Russian operations. A case officer who sat in on the Ames inquest—a "damage assessment," as the CIA calls them—agreed. Having meticulously picked through the secrets Ames confessed to betraying and the ones he hadn't, he said there absolutely had to have been another Russian penetration of the CIA. "With all the unexplained losses there just couldn't be another explanation," he told me. However, he was wide open to the possibility there could have been not only a Fourth Man but maybe a fifth, or who knows how many, other than the Russians. Milt Bearden would come around to believing there was a Fourth Man, which led him to write the op-ed piece about him in the *Los Angeles Times*. He believes the mole died sometime in the eighties, though. And so it went with most I talked to in the CIA and FBI who knew anything about Russian intelligence and had objectively weighed the evidence, telling me the Russians had been or were still running another spy other than Ames in CIA Russian operations. They wouldn't speculate as to his identity, but all the same they had no doubt about his existence. It's only natural this consensus would have informed Price's decision to order a post-Ames cleanup investigation.

One thing Price and Redmond also had to consider was just how badly a new spy hunt would go over in the post-Ames CIA. With the ratcheting up of security, the CIA was up to its eyeballs in personnel problems, worse than any in its entire history. One thing driving it was CIA polygraph operators raising their pass-fail baselines. Never far from an operator's calculations was that Ames had passed two polygraph exams while spying for the KGB. These new baselines meant the slightest blip on a chart and an operator would launch into aggressive interrogation. Which in turn would almost inevitably lead to an "inconclusive" exam result. I was told by someone in Price's office who kept track of the numbers in those days that more than four hundred officers were under a cloud of suspicion after an inconclusive polygraph or some other security problem. While no one believed all four hundred were Russian spies, caution dictated they be sent off to "holding pens," as my source called them.

Adding to Price's headaches were the endemic ills that afflict contemporary American society, and in particular the dangerous mix of hyperinflated egos and money problems. Both are well-traveled paths to treason. Although Ames attempted to sugarcoat his treachery with a contorted logic not worth repeating here, he ultimately was in it for money. Howard's immediate motivation was revenge, but the KGB also paid him well. The same went for Hanssen. The reality was that government salaries couldn't keep up with the cost of living, and in particular Washington, DC, area real estate prices. With the temptation for any CIA employee in financial straits to turn to Russian intelligence for quick relief, Price had to consider that if there was one bad apple like Ames, why not two. Or, again, who knew how many—other than Russian intelligence.

Price also had to contend with the reality that on White House orders, a collar of FBI agents was about to rain down on the CIA, the Howard and Ames debacles coming home to roost in a very ugly way. As soon as the FBI got inside the tent, it made no bones about how far it would go to clean up the CIA. An FBI agent, Ed Curran, was slated to take over CIA counterespionage, a section of the CIA charged with hunting down spies in its own ranks. It was a perch that would offer the FBI a death grip around the CIA's throat. With an FBI loyalty question mark hanging over an officer's head, there was no going overseas or getting promoted.

Curran was as straitlaced an FBI agent as they come. Like a cop, he saw the world in black and white, at variance with the CIA's world of gray. Unless you could show Curran solid evidence of a crime, he didn't have the time of day for it. Opening an investigation into Ames based on his cash deposits after meeting Soviets made perfect sense to him, but he couldn't have cared less about Tolkachev's blurred photography or that his family got to stay in their apartment after his arrest. Curran's coming on board was going to complicate things for Langley's spy catchers and, with his ability to put a career on ice, put Langley itself even more on edge.

An FBI agent would even be assigned to Russia Group, where he was given access to the CIA's most sensitive Russian cases, a first in the history of the CIA. It alarmed the Cold War old guard if for no other reason than the FBI didn't adhere to the same high standards of compartmentation. At the CIA, typically fewer than a dozen people were read into a sensitive case; now, with the FBI in the mix, intelligence from CIA Russian agents was distributed to hundreds of FBI field offices. When Hanssen was arrested in 2001, the idiocy of this decision was obvious.

To add to CIA jitters, with the FBI inside Langley, now anything that vaguely smacked of a crime on the part of a CIA officer was almost certain to generate a criminal referral to the Department of Justice. If you were caught arriving an hour late for work but claimed to have worked a full day, off went a letter to Justice offering you up for prosecution. (Okay, that might be a bit of an exaggeration, but still it was cause enough for many to bail on the CIA and look for a job where the boss doesn't spend his day looking for ways to put you in jail.) But as things would turn out, it was worse than Price could have ever imagined.

The rumor, accurate or not, quickly went around that the FBI would be riding into Langley with a hit list drawn up according to hunches and gut dislikes, and above all, an institutional distrust of the CIA. It meant that a transgression on the part of a CIA officer as minor as a foreign girlfriend or an ostentatious car would be cause enough to put them under an FBI microscope. It wouldn't necessarily lead to a Justice referral, but could definitely put the brakes on a career. A colleague I'd worked with told me that the FBI went after him for no other reason than he'd pissed it off years before. He didn't, in the first place, have much of a career left, but the FBI definitely snuffed out what was left of it. The witch-hunting weather turned all the heavier because the FBI kept its own counsel. With many investigations, it never notified CIA management. I was stationed in Langley at this time, and although I knew absolutely nothing about the Fourth Man investigation, the FBI witch hunting and general CIA angst were impossible to miss.

The level of distrust was so corrosive that Price felt compelled to cut out almost everyone around him from the Fourth Man investigation. His assistant knew nothing about the hunt. Price even excluded his deputy, John MacGaffin, who'd been the chief of the division handling Russia when Max told Corbin about Caracas. Having been at the Greenbrier conference, MacGaffin would have been in a position to offer Price context for Max's shoot-from-the-hip intelligence about double agents. MacGaffin's replacement, Jack Devine, got the same treatment. According to one of his aides, Devine regularly complained about how Price kept him in the dark about sensitive counterintelligence cases. Along with it, a rumor went around that Devine himself fell under FBI suspicion. As the story went, FBI agents showed up at Devine's office out of the blue one morning to aggressively interview him about his ties to Russian intelligence. Devine told me the story wasn't true. But the fact that the rumor started in the first place tells you how toxic things were at the CIA. The paranoia was rampant: Paul Redmond told me that one day Price invited him outside the CIA headquarters building to ask him if he thought the FBI might have bugged the CIA's seventh-floor executive suites. They never came up with an answer, but it further illustrates the environment that isolated Price and Redmond and deprived them of wise counsel they so badly needed.

The tight hold on the Fourth Man investigation never eased up in the least. At any one time, fewer than a dozen people were read into it. A chief of staff to one CIA director told me he wasn't allowed anywhere near Russian counterintelligence investigations. Although sitting at the CIA director's elbow when the Fourth Man hunt was still under full steam, he was told nothing about it. When I asked him why, he replied it was because the people in counterintelligence are "assholes." He added that things got worse than I could imagine, including the FBI ending its long-standing practice of informing CIA directors about secret counterintelligence court warrants on CIA officers. Frankly, the more I learned about the Fourth Man investigation, the more convinced I was it couldn't have occurred under worse circumstances.

A senior CIA official once told Bearden that case officers are of questionable utility because "all you guys do is take in each other's laundry"—that is, they're too busy rooting out traitors in their own ranks to get around to answering the important questions about the world. Like what would possess Boris Yeltsin to bring a hard-core ex-KGB agent into the fold and then appoint him his successor.

The CIA official wasn't entirely wrong, but what he missed, as Bearden did, is the inalterable reality that you can't possibly answer the important questions until you've cleaned your house of traitors. There's no way around it. If, for instance, a Yeltsin insider were to have approached the CIA to offer a firsthand explanation as to why Yeltsin had picked Putin, the Fourth Man (if he truly existed) would have quickly outed him to his Russian masters. Then the CIA would be right back to having no sources.

For Ted Price and Paul Redmond, Putin's budding political career was the least of their concerns in May 1994. Instead, what was on their minds was who would head the Ames cleanup investigation. It wasn't an easy choice. With the way the CIA was staffed, it pretty much came down to an either-or decision: someone from outside Russian operations and counterintelligence (someone like me, who knew next to nothing about either), or someone who knew what they were doing.

This may come across as a bit cattish, but I'll say it anyhow. The CIA's a place where intelligence—in the sense of expertise and intellectual depth—is the enemy of ambition. Spend a career trying to master a place like Russia or the KGB, and said career is likely to fizzle. The same goes for spy catchers. Spend twenty years tracking the KGB, and you end up pigeonholed and ignored as someone intellectually unequipped to see the big picture. As my former colleague on the Ames Damage Assessment Team put it to me, CIA management looks at its spy catchers as "too paranoid and in love with detail" to be entirely trusted.

There's no metric for it, but my experience is that most case officers, whether they want to or not, are forced to occupy the jack-of-all-trades, know-nothing end of the spectrum. Early on, they figure out expertise is a dead end to be avoided like the plague. As it is, they barely have the time to properly tend to their careers, punch the right tickets, and "hone their management skills" without trying to master a place like Russia or the KGB. As one of my colleagues once put it to me, "Who's got the time to pick the fly shit out of the pepper?" It's the same across the geographic board. Early on in my career, I intended to become an accomplished Arabist and fluent Arabic speaker, but along the way bureaucratic and career realities got in the way and I ended up well short of both.

Depending on which side of the equation you're standing on, the benefits that come with officers on the make are indisputable. As seas turn choppy, the ambitious can be depended on to not rock the boat. Should the Fourth Man hunt somehow uncover another Ames, they'd have enough sense to shield the bosses from blame and pin it on some poor schmuck down the line. Or, if doable, bury the whole thing altogether. The downside, of course, is someone safely dim and ambitious would stand little chance of unmasking the Fourth Man.

A counterintelligence veteran, on the other hand, would know how to go about the investigation efficiently and expeditiously, know exactly where to dig for the gems and skeletons. They'd know off the top of their head everything the CIA knows about Russian intelligence, and in particular how the KGB runs American double agents and dangles. They'd also know exactly where and how their bosses failed in the past, and could even put names to the failures— who made what mistakes with Ames, Howard, and now with the Fourth Man. But inevitably, people attached to unfiltered reality and facts tend to break a lot of china, given the opportunity.

To an outsider, Price and Redmond's choice should have been

no choice at all—pick someone who knows what they're doing. But that would be to overlook the reality that bureaucracies in their senescence and under attack lean toward survival rather than the truth. It's why the CIA dragged its feet with Howard and Ames. But Price and Redmond, having seen enough of the evidence to have their suspicions, decided not to take the easy way out and went with expertise. It was a courageous decision.

Even as Price ordered the investigation, he had to have understood the chances of success were next to nil, and in the bargain he'd run the risk of roiling the waters for no good reason at all. Unlike with Ames, Howard, and Hanssen, there was nothing like a smoking gun of the sort the FBI normally needs to make a case. Worse, the CIA's institutional ingrained resistance to admitting there might be another Ames also must have been particularly daunting. With the seventh floor and the Department of Justice certain to set an evidentiary bar at a level all but impossible to clear, Price and Redmond risked not only failing to nail the Fourth Man but also being dismissed as conspiracy theorists. It never pays to rub the nose of the powers that be in an unpalatable truth you can't back up with incontrovertible evidence.

All the same, it's not hard to see where the CIA as an institution was coming from. The exposure of a new Russian double agent at the top of the CIA would have hit with the force of a hundred-megaton nuke; who knows, it may have even been the final nail in the CIA's coffin. The *Washington Post* and the *New York Times* would have cheerfully feasted on its carcass. Congress would have had a field day, too, lopping heads right and left, just as it did after Ames's arrest. Then there would have been inevitable calls for the Pentagon to take over foreign intelligence.

Though Price and Redmond couldn't have relished the idea of undertaking a new hunt for another Russian double agent in the CIA, they did what they had to do. At the same time, needing to keep a lid on it, they had to carefully pick the right person to head the team.

EIGHT

call·ing / ˈkɔ lɪŋ / *n.* The feeling of being compelled toward a certain profession or path in life.

Langley; May 1994

LAINE BANNERMAN WAS at her desk wondering about where her career was going when she got a call from Paul Redmond asking her to come up and see him in his office.

As soon as she walked into Redmond's office, his body language signaled irritation, like he'd been asked to deliver a piece of unwelcome news he'd have preferred not to.

"I want you to do a post-Ames investigation," Redmond said.

Bannerman was surprised she was being offered an important assignment like this. It would mean running Special Investigations, the same unit that had unearthed Ames.

"What does Hall think about it?" she asked.

John Hall was the head of counterintelligence, Redmond's boss. As Redmond knew, Hall was the reason Bannerman was walking Langley's halls looking for a new position. Hall hadn't bothered to explain why, but he'd summarily forced her out of counterintelligence.

"I'll take care of Hall," Redmond said.

Bannerman waited for Redmond to explain how it was he came by a veto over the boss. But he didn't, and she didn't ask.

"Any conditions?" Redmond asked.

Bannerman knew she'd have to think fast; an opportunity like this wasn't going to come around a second time.

"Two," she said. "I want Diana Worthen and Maryann Hough."

They were two of the best spy catchers Bannerman knew of. She thought it was a long shot that Redmond would be able to finagle both their reassignments, but why not try.

Redmond looked at her skeptically. "You and Diana won't last two days before you kill each other."

"I'll make it work."

Redmond left it with asking Bannerman to write a memo to Price agreeing to take over the Special Investigations Unit (SIU) and conduct his "cleanup" investigation. Redmond was to be cc'd on the routing slip but not on the memo.

Bannerman smiled to herself. In asking for the memo to be addressed to Price rather than Redmond, she recognized the tried-and-true bureaucratic gambit of never putting your name on any piece of paper even vaguely controversial. Redmond evidently wanted it made a matter of record that the investigation was Price's rather than his. If for some reason it crashed and burned, it was all on Price.

During the course of the investigation, she would never see or hear from Hall, apparently the chief of CIA counterintelligence in name only.

Bannerman would often wonder why she'd been selected for the job, considering Hall had just let her go. Her best guess was that Price had asked for her by name. When Price headed counterintelligence in the early nineties, she'd worked directly with him on a couple of cases and he knew her to be unbiddable, with a real flair for counterintelligence. They'd crossed swords more than once, but Price let it go because he valued pushback from subordinates, especially when they could muster the facts and make a good argument. Counterintelligence is all about coming up with a coherent, fact-driven narrative, which is exactly what Bannerman had mastered. Price also understood that Bannerman knew the KGB backward and forward. Redmond told me he picked Bannerman because "she was as tough as nails and knew her stuff."

Although Bannerman would never describe herself in these terms, she was intelligence blue blood. Her father, Robert Bannerman, was one of the CIA's founders. In addition, a close relative was a senior counterintelligence officer in MI5 (roughly Britain's FBI), and a brother headed security at the Department of State. She grew up in Northern Virginia in Langley's shadow, where her father's CIA colleagues were her adult social milieu and rule number one was to never discuss work outside the office. She remembers Angleton coming over to the house for dinner when she was a child. He was the strangest man she'd ever met in her life. Reminding her of a werewolf, he terrified her. "If I'd been a dog, I would have bit him," she says.

Bannerman attended McLean High School with Ames, where they were both in drama. While Bannerman never minded that she didn't have the makings of a thespian and was more than pleased with the minor, lineless parts they gave her, she got an early look at Ames as a narcissist who insisted on occupying the proscenium. Even back then intuition told her his deep insecurities would cause him or somebody trouble. Both Bannerman and Ames worked summers at the CIA at the same time.

After high school, she studied Russian and Italian at William & Mary. Her Italian got good enough for her to read Dante in the original, while her Russian was good but never fluent. Still, it was Russia that became her true passion in life. The complexity of the place, its culture, and its people were of a lifelong fascination. As was the KGB. It helped a lot that she easily connected with Russians and would take genuine enjoyment in debriefing defectors. She likely would have made a magnificent case officer if it weren't for the fact she didn't have the time of day for the schmoozing and glad-handing that go hand in hand with the job.

In 1966, after graduating from William & Mary, inasmuch as these things are ever foreordained, Bannerman joined the Agency. Like Ames, she was a legacy hire. Without telling her, Bannerman's father lined up a job for her as an analyst in the Directorate of Intelligence; he didn't want her working in the grubby world of operations. But preferring to be where the action is, she arranged a transfer to the Soviet division (without telling her father). She was made an IA—an intelligence analyst. A lot like forensic accountants, IAs keep track of the minutiae of administering agents, tending to anything from cross-checking an agent's reporting to making sure there are no signs an agent has fallen under control of the local counterintelligence service. IAs are mostly assigned to Langley, but also overseas at larger stations. Bannerman quickly gravitated to Soviet and counterintelligence operations and would spend the rest of her career bouncing between the two.

Even before she was hired, Bannerman knew working for the CIA wouldn't be all roses and sunflowers. From her father, she already knew the CIA attracts a peculiar congregation, where institutionalized distrust and strictly compartmented lives are the rule. But when she moved over to KGB counterintelligence, she was inducted into a cabalistic world of forbidden knowledge. It was an existence so cloistered that there was no fraternizing with anyone from other parts of the CIA, and definitely not outside Langley. Called "the shit parties," Thursday night happy hours in the Soviet division were painfully dull affairs, with absolutely no gossiping about work and usually ending after a single glass of wine. The Ames and Howard aberrations were stains that would never come out, but the survivors still lived according to the iron law of "need-to-know." And as things would turn out, even when someone needed to know, they were still kept in the dark.

The need-to-know divider ran right up the center of the Soviet division. Bill Piekney, the deputy division chief who replaced Bearden in 1986, told me that in spite of his supervisory position, he'd been completely excluded from sensitive Soviet counterintelligence and internal cases. The only people read into them were the division chief, Burton Gerber; Gerber's third in command, Steve Weber; the division's head of counterintelligence, Paul Redmond; and their go-to field case officer, Dick Corbin. They'd all but slam the door in his face when discussing Russian cases. Piekney had served his career in East Asia, which was enough for them to not trust him.

"I couldn't wait to leave," Piekney told me. "When I was

offered another job I was out the door and never looked back."
As he'd find out later, he'd briefly been on the suspect list that
included Ames, but since he'd been overseas during most of the
compromises, he wasn't on it for long.

The keep-your-mouth-shut ethic even went all the way to the
top. When it came time to dish out punishment during the Ames
fallout, according to John MacGaffin neither he nor Price considered defending themselves by telling CIA director James Woolsey
it had been their agent Max who broke the Ames case. Rather
than make a point of it, they silently and stoically accepted being
shown the door.

It's difficult to explain to an outsider how suffocating and
invidious CIA culture has always been. Even for me, who never
worked in Soviet operations or counterintelligence, I found its
cult of secrecy excessive and all too often absurd. I'd regularly go
see a colleague about something, and before I got within reading
distance they'd instinctively flip over the papers on their desk.
The rudeness of it probably never occurred to them because they
were mindlessly submitting to their sworn duty. Even today, when
I no longer possess a single secret anyone would care about, I still
can't throw away a piece of paper without first checking to make
sure there's not something compromising written on it. Take
this paranoid ethic and multiply it by a hundred and you start to
understand why life in Soviet operations was as dark and narrow
as a coffin.

Secrecy like this leads to a knowledge-equals-power syndrome, and in the CIA of a kind easily and as a matter of course
abused. The CIA officer who knows a juicy secret and has the ear
of the CIA director knows he sits on an unassailable perch—if

for no other reason than no director has the time to corroborate the facts and has to take the word of those close to him. When Soviet and Russian recordkeeping was taken off paper altogether, it became all the easier to bend the system for personal advantage. It's why Bearden got to call the shots on Russia. Knowing exactly how it worked, Bannerman knew no matter what she and SIU dug up, it would be someone else providing the interpretation up the chain of command. In other words, if her bosses weren't happy with SIU's conclusions, they would brush them aside and the seventh floor would be none the wiser.

Another thing Bannerman walked into with open eyes is that as a woman, and especially a counterintelligence analyst, she'd always be looking through the wrong side of the glass ceiling. When she joined the CIA in 1966, it was very much an upstairs, downstairs divide—with women in the servants' quarters. In the seventies, the CIA did start to hire more women as case officers, but it wasn't until the late nineties that the Directorate of Operations started to see women enter the senior ranks. For Bannerman it came too late, her pedigree and expertise counting for little. On the other hand, her male contemporaries, many the issue of entitled, monied New England and expensive Ivy League educations, sat securely in their saddles, whether competent or not.

With a keen understanding of the CIA's bureaucracy and power structure, Bannerman knew when she agreed to lead Price's investigation she'd be at a distinct disadvantage. She wasn't sure where Redmond stood on the whole thing, but if he wasn't fully behind it, it could mean trouble. Owning the counterintelligence portfolio, he wasn't a man to cross. Yet at the end of the day, it didn't much matter to Bannerman because she was a CIA lifer, in the sense that Russian counterintelligence was her calling. As she liked to say, there's nothing like a bona fide mole hunt to stir the blood. She couldn't imagine going to work anywhere else, no matter what it paid.

While no one was going to tell Bannerman why she was picked to conduct the Fourth Man investigation, she knew exactly why she'd asked Redmond for Maryann Hough and Diana Worthen. Both were from Bannerman's mold, their calling Soviet/Russian counterintelligence. It helped a lot that neither had an ambitious bone in their bodies. In fact, their preference was never to be promoted into senior management because it would only have taken them away from the work they loved. But what mattered for Bannerman was they were just plain good at their jobs. If there was anyone with a chance of finding a post-Ames mole, it was them.

Langley's treacherous confines were a long way from Diana Worthen's picturesque heartland upbringing in a small town near St. Louis, Missouri. The downsides that ail modern American society felt far off; no one in the family ever even divorced. She lived in the same house with both parents until she went to the University of New Mexico, where she graduated with a degree in education. When she first interviewed for the CIA, she was so nervous she insisted the recruiter keep open the door to the motel room where they were meeting. She was hired as a secretary. Her mother put up a fuss about her going to work in DC, and especially for the CIA. Resigned, her father drove her all the way to DC to start work. When she was assigned to Vienna, Austria, her talents were quickly recognized, and she was turned into an analyst tasked with keeping track of Soviet intelligence operatives.

Spending her days sorting through names and pictures of them, she acquired a talent for spotting Soviet espionage tradecraft. She later worked in Moscow, Seoul, and then Mexico City while Ames was there.

Like Bannerman, Worthen was a dyed-in-the-wool introvert. She never married or for that matter ever drank. She would only socialize with other CIA officers, and she never talked about work. Even as the '85–'86 losses mounted, she never whispered a word about it other than to those read into the cases. And also like Bannerman, she was an unrepentant workaholic. On her rare days completely off, she'd go to the occasional cookout or craft fairs with CIA colleagues. All in all she was a perfect fit for Soviet operations.

Worthen brought to SIU's table a deep institutional knowledge of Soviet/Russian operations. Not only did she set up the back room in 1986, she at one time or another oversaw every important Russian case, making her a walking encyclopedia of CIA espionage on Russia. She was familiar with the names of every KGB officer the CIA knew about, and she could easily pick them out from their pictures and various aliases, as well as recite from memory their operational histories. She also personally knew every case officer who'd ever served in Moscow during her time.

Maryann Hough was born in Worcester, Massachusetts; her father worked as a truck driver and her mother was a factory worker. Graduating from Anna Maria College with a political science degree, she was directly recruited into the CIA and quickly assigned to Japan, then Mexico City. She soon married a CIA code clerk and spent the next twenty-five years on overseas assignment in places like Liberia and Bulgaria. Opposite her tight-lipped colleagues Bannerman and Worthen, Hough was a cheerful grade A extrovert, a prankster with a wicked sense of humor, and a connector with a Rolodex that wouldn't stop. When, for instance, SIU needed something from a personnel file or to find out about the travel of a particular officer, she'd be the one to do it. It helped SIU a lot that Hough had been originally hired by the CIA as a case officer and attended the CIA's basic operations course at the Farm. When called upon, she could do all the necessary schmoozing and case officering. Having gone through the denied area operations course, which was designed to operate in Moscow, she could also talk tradecraft with the best. She could also do odd jobs like check with the Office of Security to find out when someone logged in or out of Langley. She was always ready with a good joke to cut the tension.

Among the three, Hough was the only one to marry. Family always coming first, when her husband was assigned to Sofia, Bulgaria, she accompanied him as a dependent, abandoning her career as a case officer. From then on, she worked in counterintelligence analysis. She and her husband raised two children.

When Hough would have parties, which she often did, though limited to CIA colleagues, she had to put Bannerman at a separate table with the other introverted spy catchers. The "old farts' table," she called it. Despite their cloistered environs, Bannerman, Hough, and Worthen became close friends, regularly going out to lunch or dinner to unwind, though being of the Soviet division mold they never discussed work outside Langley's walls.

From my perspective as a former case officer, all three women were invulnerable to recruitment. None carrying debt, they were without expensive tastes or addictions, and their lives were meticulously measured. They didn't see psychiatrists or go to self-help groups. Their pleasures were simple: Hough was a competitive tennis player, always at one area tournament or another, and Bannerman rode horses to take her mind off work. Even if the Fourth Man had tipped off his Russian handlers to their identities, they would never have figured out how to approach them, let alone find a hook into their lives. When Price and Redmond chose them for the Fourth Man investigation, they would have known all of this.

The last member to join Bannerman's team was an FBI analyst named Jim Milburn. As I keep hearing, he's considered the FBI's best on Russian intelligence and counterintelligence. Like Worthen, he'd been part of the Ames hunt. And not unlike her, as an analyst rather than a special agent, the FBI tended to look at Milburn as a second-class citizen. He made up for it with intelligence, mastery of detail, and longevity on the Russian account, but just as important, an extraordinary ability to keep his mouth shut.

All four approached the Fourth Man investigation determined to stick with the evidence in the files. Any preconceived notions were deliberately put out of their heads. Having been part of the Ames hunt, Worthen knew early in the game that Ames couldn't have been responsible for all the mid-eighties compromises, but she was more than willing to take a fresh look at the evidence and assign the compromises to him if that's where the facts took her. As Price asked, they'd assemble the facts and give him their objective take.

The CIA and FBI were lucky to have people happy to spend their lives sorting through counterintelligence minutiae, perfectly content to patiently wait for the day the right Russian defector showed up and broke open a mole hunt. Poring through thousands and thousands of cables from the field, trying to figure out if small and seemingly unrelated inconsistencies amount to anything, isn't everyone's cup of tea. But for those passionately immersed in the work, it can be a thrill. And they weren't afraid to speak their minds. If Price and Redmond wanted pains in the ass who knew their stuff and would call a spade a spade, these three women and Milburn would be right at the top of anyone's list.

Bannerman went into the investigation knowing the odds that they'd find a new CIA double agent were slim. The head of the Ames investigation, Jeanne Vertefeuille, told Bannerman as she took over the new mole-hunting team, "There's nothing there. But have at it." But worse than finding nothing, Bannerman knew that if her team in fact were to unearth a new Russian mole, they wouldn't be hailed as heroes. They couldn't even be sure anyone would listen to them at all.

NINE

ma·trix / ˈmeɪ trɪks/ *n.* A pattern of facts that tells a story.

Langley; June 1994

THE FOURTH MAN investigation was conducted according to Redmond and Price's instructions: as far under the radar as these things can be. There were none of the bureaucratic trappings and grinding ordinances that come with official task forces—no memos portentously announcing its creation, no vacant job postings, and certainly not a word to anyone outside their small group about its mission. The investigation was administratively carried out under the name of an already existing counterintelligence entity, SIU, which technically fell under John Hall's Counterintelligence Center. But with Price and Redmond having kept Hall out of the investigation for reasons unknown to Bannerman, no one other than these two bosses knew the full scope and intent of the investigation. For brevity's sake, I'll refer to Bannerman, Hough, Worthen, and Milburn as SIU.

SIU occupied a small, windowless, vaulted room on the fourth floor of the CIA's New Headquarters Building. It had the feel of a large utility closet. It was served by a single reinforced metal door secured with a spin-dial combination lock. A bell by the door was intended for visitors, but it never sounded because there never were any. With only desk lights ever turned on, the place had an eerie, conspiratorial feeling. From the corridor outside, there was absolutely no hint of what went on inside. When friends would ask Bannerman what she was working on, she said she was cleaning up some old cases and sending unneeded files to archives. She of course didn't whisper a word that there could be a Russian penetration of the CIA's senior ranks. Bannerman knew as well as anyone how to downplay whatever it was she was working on.

SIU started by collecting every relevant Russian file it needed from the Central Eurasia (CE) Division, which handled Russia, and the Counterintelligence Center (CIC). At night, the files were locked up in four-drawer safes. In order to maintain the investigation's complete integrity, SIU worked off a closed computer network, a LAN. If the Fourth Man was still employed by the CIA and had the sort of access he was thought to have, the last thing SIU needed was for him or her to hack into their computers. Which is exactly what Hanssen would do to his FBI boss.

SIU's principal resource was the Soviet/Russia division's counterintelligence database. It allowed them, for instance, to instantly pull up the dates and circumstances of all Russian agents arrested and details like what defectors had to say about Russian double agents in the CIA. SIU's collective memory proved an important complement to the database, and all the more so Milburn, who had stored in his head the unexplained, unique FBI compromises to the Russians. Most important were the bigot lists, which keep track of which CIA officers have access to which sensitive cases. These lists allowed SIU to quickly eliminate as suspects those who had no or tangential access to Russian operations.

Unlike most units in the Directorate of Operations at Langley, SIU was unable to generate cable traffic. That meant it couldn't do things like query foreign liaison services or overseas CIA stations. If, for instance, it needed to know more about a KGB officer who'd served in London, it could only search what was already in CIA files. As for checking leads with Russian agents, no doubt it would have been extremely helpful, but Ames outed all the ones they would have asked. SIU also couldn't interview CIA employees. The moment SIU started sitting people down and asking them questions about unexplained compromises to the KGB, the CIA rumor mill would have shifted into high gear, with everyone correctly assuming another mole hunt was afoot. SIU also had no law enforcement authorities, meaning it couldn't depose witnesses or subpoena documents. Nor could it search things like credit reports or FBI and police databases. Anything specific it needed from the FBI had to go through Milburn, a laborious and time-consuming process to be tapped only sparingly.

In limiting the investigation to a scrubbing of the files and archives—and confining it to four of the most tight-lipped spy catchers in the government—Redmond and Price's plan worked like an expensive Swiss watch. Not even the Ames Damage Assessment Team, which ran concurrently with SIU's investigation and dealt with much of the same material, knew about SIU's Fourth Man investigation. SIU's investigation was even kept from the CIA's directors. As I was to find out, it's one reason so few of my ex-colleagues who'd worked in Russian operations knew nothing about it.

At this point, none of these limits Price and Redmond put on SIU mattered because what they'd asked for was a preliminary investigation, a simple search through the files looking for the odd, stray inconsistencies in Soviet/Russian compromises in the eighties and nineties, ones that didn't completely fit Ames's or Howard's betrayals. These more than likely would add up to nothing more than a series of unrelated compromises. As I understand it, that's the outcome Price and Redmond expected.

But if SIU were to make something of the anomalies, it was understood that their work would be followed by a proper, full-fledged investigation, one involving formal interviews, a review of security files, checks for unexplained foreign travel of officers, background checks, et cetera. The National Security Agency also would be queried to check for telephone intercepts and metadata. If all this pointed to a new mole, the FBI would be called in to conduct a criminal espionage investigation, just as it had with Ames.

In short, with the limited tools it was given, SIU knew it would never be in a position to assemble an indictment-ready case of espionage. Whatever it came up with would be a matter of inference and conjecture. SIU knew just how hard it is to catch a spy. No matter what the FBI and the CIA claim about their brilliant analytical work on Ames, it was hard evidence of espionage found in Ames's house and trash that allowed the FBI to make an airtight case against him. Reportedly, Hanssen was identified as a Russian spy thanks to a Russian double agent smuggling out of Russia a trash bag with Hanssen's fingerprints on it and a recording of him calling his handler. (It bears mentioning that multiple well-placed sources told me the published accounts of how Hanssen was caught are inaccurate, though none would go on the record or tell me what actually happened.) While obviously SIU would have preferred to have that evidence of the quality that reportedly nailed Hanssen, it would have to make do with the files. Not that this in the least discouraged them; they'd been through it many times before and as always rose to the challenge.

The currency spy catchers deal in are called anomalies. Anomalies run the entire gamut from the obvious to the frustratingly ambiguous. An agent arrested, tried, and jailed is an obvious clue there's a problem. But an agent who inexplicably stops showing up for meetings might be one or it might not. Either way, it's marked down as an anomaly. An agent's loss of access to secrets is another one. It might be thanks to some routine or nothing-to-sweat bureaucratic decision, or it could mean the agent's been unmasked, but either way it goes in the anomalies column. It's even considered an anomaly when an agent's reporting starts to look too good to be true, another potential red flag that he's been discovered and turned into a conduit for disinformation. An even more ambiguous anomaly is when the local counterintelligence service inexplicably alters its surveillance array and shines a spotlight on a particular CIA case officer. It's hard to know whether it's a coincidence or the local service is the beneficiary of some tip-off. Anomalies, in other words, amount to a grab bag of discrepancies, doubts, and suspicions. Looked at individually they mean little, but analyzed in context and over time, the hope is they begin to resolve into a pattern.

Technical operations, things like bugs and intercepts, are plagued with the same ambiguities, which may or may not add up to something. One day the National Security Agency is reading an adversary's top secret diplomatic cable traffic, the next day the codes are changed and now unreadable. The NSA has to wonder whether it's thanks to a double agent's betraying its code-breaking or something as benign as a routine upgrade of encryption software. The same concern holds for when a counterintelligence service inexplicably digs a hidden mic out of the wall. It could be thanks to a routine sweep, or maybe a double agent betrayed it.

In a mole hunt, the anomalies are then curated and ranked into what spy catchers call a matrix. Sometimes referred to as a "deep chronology," the hope is that over a long-enough time span, the anomalies will start to make sense chronologically and tell a coherent story. When overlaid by means and opportunity—which officers had what access to which secrets and at what time—it ideally will lead the spy catchers to a traitor's door.

In order to understand the limits of matrices, it helps to know that one wouldn't have worked with Howard. The damage he did as a new employee was limited because his access was limited. Dozens of others had access to the same secrets he did. For instance, to one degree or another, in total about a hundred officers were aware of Tolkachev's existence. Not to mention all the people at the Pentagon who'd read Tolkachev's reporting and could make an educated guess as to the origins of it. It means that without Yurchenko's outing him, it would have taken years of Howard's spying for a matrix to finally pick up his trail.

A matrix is a rigorously empirical exercise. It never excludes evidence, no matter how seemingly inconsequential, irrelevant, or secondhand. Nor does it exclude anyone as a suspect, including the CIA director himself. Intuition plays no part in drawing up a profile. Drunks and philanderers may be tempting targets, but it doesn't mean they're traitors. Going after such low-hanging fruit leads to too many false positives, as well as causing an investigation to over-look a traitor who might to all appearances be of long, impeccable standing. At the same time, spy catchers fully recognize a matrix isn't take-it-to-court evidence. It's at most a faint and broken bread-crumb trail that may or may not lead the spy catchers to a name.

Bannerman and the others didn't invent matrices and pro-files, but rather learned their subtle arts from one of their bosses, a storied officer by the name of Dave Blee. A Harvard Law School graduate, he was an alumnus of the OSS, the CIA's forerunner. After serving many years overseas, he headed the Near East and Soviet divisions before taking over counterintelligence. Like any field operative, what he brought to counterintelligence was street smarts, having been burned by his share of fabricators, dangles, and agent operations souring for no apparent reason. And know-ing just how vulnerable computers are, he used a typewriter. I'd imagine he would have been the type never to go near a cell phone.

According to Blee's rule-of-thumb basics, here's how matrices and profiles are composed:

1. Define your problem, in the sense that you need to deter-mine whether the unexplained compromises point to a human, technical, or tradecraft problem. If human—a double agent in your organization—move to step two.

2. Draw the widest circle possible of suspects to include everyone who's had direct or indirect access to compro-mised assets. Even if it's in the hundreds, every single name is put on the suspect list. Again, no one's excluded due to rank or reputation.

3. Every anomaly is noted and none excluded—from compromised agents to compromised mics and every other unexplained oddity. As Blee never stopped reminding his understudies: "Never prejudge. Collect all the evidence first, and only then judge." (By the way, this isn't the FBI's normal approach. Like a good prosecutor determined to present a coherent, compelling narrative, it downplays or discards evidence that doesn't fit the case it's trying to make.)

4. All leads are followed to the very end, never discarded because there's not a quick or obvious explanation for them. The reason they're not discarded, as Blee told his spy catchers, is because you never know when at some point in the future they'll make sense.

5. Don't throw the baby out with the bathwater. Just because a KGB defector or agent has exaggerated or even made up something, it doesn't mean everything he's had to say should be dismissed as a lie. Max, as I wrote, held back information and even lied because he didn't like one of his CIA handlers in East Africa. Then later Corbin coaxed a lead out of him that put Ames in jail.

6. Rank sources and leads according to reliability and access. An agent who has a record of inflicting consistent, demonstrable damage to an adversary should be trusted more than an agent who's been providing so-so intelligence. The KGB came to trust Ames only because he'd proved himself by wiping out CIA Soviet operations.

7. Draw up a thorough, complete, and annotated chronology noting all the anomalies and why some are ranked higher than others. For instance, the anomalous travel of a KGB

counterintelligence operative (Line KR) is of more weight than the travel of an ordinary KGB operative, because Line KR officers are the ones who normally handle double agents in foreign intelligence services. The same goes for unusual foreign travel of suspect CIA officers, and especially ones who work in Soviet operations. Had the CIA early on been in a position to correlate Ames's travels to Caracas and Bogotá with the travel of a KGB counterintelligence officer to the same cities at the same time, it's possible he would have been caught a lot earlier.

8. Draw up a profile of the traitor based on means and opportunity. It's no surprise that a motor pool driver won't find his name high on the list of suspects. But every officer who's had access to all the compromised cases automatically finds himself on the list, and a short one at that. Again, with the evidence allowed to take investigators where it will, absolutely no one's excluded as a suspect, including the investigators themselves. In the middle of the Fourth Man hunt, everyone in SIU would be polygraphed. During the Ames hunt, more than once Paul Redmond told his analysts his name should not be eliminated as the Russian penetration responsible for the '85–'86 losses.

9. No one outside the core investigators is allowed to edit either the matrix or the profile.

The coda to a matrix is to take a "black hat–white hat" team approach. In plain English: a brutal fact check of the conclusions drawn from a matrix, ensuring that neither paranoia nor too strong an attachment to a particular set of facts has skewed it.

When these standards are strictly adhered to, the hope is the matrix will point to a single individual whose access will account for all the unexplained compromises. Then the real investigation begins—credit checks, background investigations, interviews, and eventually the FBI.

SIU started exactly where it should have, sorting through the secrets Howard and Ames were thought to have betrayed and the ones they hadn't. Although most of the spadework had been done during the Ames investigation, SIU deliberately took a fresh look at the evidence. One reason is they didn't need to be told the Ames investigators had been under implicit pressure to attribute to Ames as many compromises to the Russians as possible, even the ones that didn't quite fit. Their objective had been to get Ames locked up as fast as possible rather than get sidetracked.

Auditing Soviet (and later Russian) operations was a fairly straightforward exercise thanks to the Directorate of Operations keeping accurate records of who'd been read into which cases, and in particular the sensitive cases administered by bigot lists. Bigot lists record not only the date an officer's read into a sensitive case but also when they're read out. But even less sensitive cases are also closely audited. To order an agent file from archives, an officer needs to be on the "badge table," which records when a file was ordered and when it was returned. SIU made quick work of subtracting the bigot-list-administered cases Howard and Ames had been read into and presumably compromised to the KGB from the total number compromised to the KGB.

With the clear-cut compromises that could be laid at the doorstep of either Howard or Ames out of the way, the first set of anomalies that drew SIU's attention was the outing of three Russian intelligence officers in May 1985. Two had spied for the CIA and the third for Britain's MI6. What immediately struck SIU is that the timing of their outings was starkly inconsistent with Ames's confession. Both the FBI and CIA agreed that Ames didn't betray any active, bona fide Soviet agent until his June 13, 1985, meeting with his KGB go-between at Chadwicks.

There's always the possibility Ames lied about what he passed the KGB and when, or he could have passed their names to the KGB at an earlier meeting and forgot about it, but it was heavily discounted because the consensus of everyone who questioned Ames after his arrest was that this wasn't the case. Working through Ames's confession, SIU agreed he hadn't given up the names of the three Soviet intelligence officers until his June 13 meeting.

The timing of the KGB's arrests of agents will be a constant focus in SIU's investigation. In spite of what many assume, Russia is a legalistic society where there's invariably a lengthy, involved due process before someone is arrested and tried, or for that matter executed. For instance, when Stalin's successors decided to get rid of his security chief Beria, they went out of their way to make it appear that he'd been fairly tried and convicted according to Soviet law, although a summary execution would have been quicker and cleaner. The same legal niceties were accorded KGB officers suspected of espionage, evidence against them formally presented before a military prosecutor and a judge before they could be arrested. Thus, according to SIU's rough calculations, the KGB likely learned about the three Soviet intelligence officers long before May 1985—and probably as far back as 1984.

This anomaly is the reason SIU initially devoted its time to looking into the circumstances under which the three intelligence agents were outed. The most intriguing of the three was a KGB colonel turned MI6 double agent named Oleg Antonovich Gordievsky. MI6 recruited Gordievsky in 1974 in Copenhagen. By 1985, he'd been promoted to the rank of colonel, assigned to the London rezidentura, and was about to become chief there (though before he was due to assume the job, he fell under suspicion as a British spy). There wasn't a secret he didn't pass on to MI6, effectively closing down KGB spying on Britain. Gordievsky is widely thought to have been Britain's best penetration of the KGB ever. But then on May 16, 1985, with no warning, he was abruptly recalled to Moscow under the pretext of consultations, taken to a dacha outside Moscow, drugged, and accused of spying for MI6. However, since his interrogators were neither able to extract a confession from him nor did KGB counterintelligence have enough evidence to formally arrest him, he was allowed to return to his Moscow apartment to await his fate. Thanks to the KGB's spotty coverage on him, MI6 smuggled him out of Russia by car to Finland. He now lives in exile in Britain. According to a former colleague who interviewed him, Gordievsky is unsure who compromised him. And so is MI6.

While Gordievsky was never "declared" to the CIA—that is, it was never supplied his identity and position—MI6 did occasionally pass the CIA intelligence from him, enough for the CIA to guess Gordievsky was the source. Ames knew about Gordievsky and admitted to giving him up at the June 13 meeting. There's a very remote possibility Gordievsky is right that Ames gave him up at an earlier meeting, but again it would mean Ames lied or forgot about it. There was no one I talked to involved in the Ames investigation who gave this credence. If the FBI and CIA interrogators are right about Ames's extraordinary memory for operational detail and believe he gave a frank confession, someone else gave up Gordievsky. It's the version SIU accepted as most likely.

There are several other possibilities to explain Gordievsky's compromise. One is a Russian penetration of MI6 we don't know about. The same consideration holds for the Danish service, which was aware MI6 had been courting Gordievsky while assigned to Copenhagen and recruited him as an agent. Sandy Grimes now supports the Danish angle, but it's just a guess. Alternatively, Bearden blames MI6's mishandling of Gordievsky. In an effort to boost Gordievsky's KGB career, MI6 supplied him with sensitive policy background briefings. The briefings were so authoritative and well sourced, Bearden believes it led Gordievsky's London KGB colleagues to suspect the truth and alert Moscow. This version of Gordievsky's compromise has been peddled by former KGB officers.

Not in the business of speculation, SIU instead examined the facts it could establish. For instance, it made a list of who in the CIA for certain knew about Gordievsky. Like all sensitive cases, there were only a handful on his bigot list. In the Soviet division's front office, there was the chief Burton Gerber; his deputy Bearden, another front office executive; and lower down the chief of the USSR Branch, Paul Redmond; Ames; and an officer who headed SE/X/EU—a branch that handles Soviet cases in Europe. Considering the way things work at Langley, SIU also couldn't exclude the possibility that word about Gordievsky had gotten around thanks to gossip. Not all sensitive operations remain completely airtight. For instance, when Bill Lofgren, who would later succeed Gerber as Soviet/Russian division chief (after Bearden and MacGaffin), was assigned to Copenhagen as a case officer, he'd observed Gordievsky's MI6 recruiter first start to court him and suspected the relationship ended in a recruitment.

One intriguing detail that caught SIU's attention is that a First Chief Directorate counterintelligence officer by the name of Viktor Budanov was brought in to interrogate Gordievsky. He was known as one of the best spy catchers in the KGB: "The most dangerous man in the KGB," as a recent bestseller described him. What didn't nicely fit was that Budanov's specialty was American counterintelligence rather than British. It made SIU wonder if Budanov hadn't been brought in because he was the one running the American double agent in the CIA who'd first outed Gordievsky. There was no evidence to support this theory, but SIU put it on the back burner hoping it would eventually make sense.

SIU kept coming back to the KGB's cautious, legalistic, and methodical history of moving against spies. Even if Ames were to have improbably given up Gordievsky's name at an earlier contact with the Russians, there still simply wasn't enough time for Gordievsky's May 16 recall. Not to mention the KGB initially considered Ames a CIA provocation and treated everything he had to say about CIA spies in its ranks as disinformation. It's highly unlikely the KGB would have recalled a senior, well-respected officer like Gordievsky and harshly interrogated him based on an accusation from a suspicious walk-in who had absolutely no hard proof that Gordievsky was a British spy.

Jeanne Vertefeuille and Sandy Grimes wrote a book about the Ames investigation in which they shared SIU's doubts about Ames's responsibility for betraying Gordievsky. They write:

One could speculate that the real story of Gordievsky's downfall has not yet come out. . . . . Ames readily admits he gave up Gordievsky, but believes it took place in June, at the time of the big dump. . . . As far as the two of us are concerned, Gordievsky's compromise remains a mystery.

Les Wiser, the lead FBI agent in the Ames investigation, also doesn't believe Ames was the first to betray Gordievsky. The timing just doesn't work. Wiser didn't offer an alternative suspect, adding that as far as he knew, no one on the American side ever decided who first betrayed Gordievsky.

SIU had to consider the possibility that Gordievsky might even have made a mistake all of his own, like leaving a compromising piece of paper on his desk at work. Or he could have said something to his wife, and she turned him in. But without evidence and considering Gordievsky was a professional, it was dismissed. It's why Gordievsky's compromise was treated as such a noteworthy anomaly.

Incidentally, long after the SIU Fourth Man investigation, Ames's first handler, KGB colonel Victor Ivanovich Cherkashin, would claim in his memoir that a British Washington-based journalist first tipped him off to Gordievsky's spying for MI6. Cherkashin offered no details other than the time frame he flew back to Moscow to report it. It was an odd comment to make, more than likely a piece of disinformation.

Gordievsky's compromise on its own didn't mean much. It could easily be explained as an isolated incident, the KGB getting lucky. And on its own it didn't constitute proof of another Russian penetration of the CIA beyond Ames. But throw in the compromise of two other Russian agents in May 1985, and it became a pattern that couldn't be ignored. In counterintelligence, a pattern is often all you get.

On May 21, 1985, Sergei Ivanovich Bokhan, a GRU colonel assigned to Athens but spying for the CIA, received an ominous message from KGB headquarters in Moscow. It recommended he come home right away to take care of his son, who was having problems at school. Seeing through the ruse—he'd just talked to his son and knew it wasn't true—Bokhan defected to the United States. As with Gordievsky, Ames was certain he hadn't given up Bokhan's name until the June 13 meeting. Howard knew nothing about Bokhan. The bigot list for Bokhan was about as short as Gordievsky's, fewer than a dozen.

Like Gordievsky, Bokhan had been an outstanding agent, loyally serving the CIA. When he first approached a CIA case officer in Athens, the officer's Russian was so bad that he thought Bokhan was trying to recruit him rather than vice versa. Dick Corbin was brought in to straighten things out, quickly turning Bokhan into a fabulously productive agent. One time, snooping around the GRU office he found evidence that a young CIA officer had flown to Athens and sold the GRU a copy of a manual for the CIA's most advanced satellite surveillance system, the KH-11. Confronted with the evidence, the CIA officer confessed and went to jail.

In trying to identify who outed Bokhan, SIU faced the same

problem as it had with Gordievsky. In theory, bigot lists are a good idea, but in practice they're not foolproof. People gossip, documents are misdirected, and mistakes are made. One day, the Athens chief sat down his station and proceeded to inform them about Bokhan. Although they weren't on the Langley bigot list, both Lofgren and Redmond found out about Bokhan thanks to this slipup. As Lofgren today will tell you, with his knowing about both Gordievsky and Bokhan, he, too, should have been on the Fourth Man suspect list.

The third CIA agent to be inexplicably outed in May 1985 was Leonid Georgiyevich Poleshchuk, a KGB First Chief Directorate officer recruited in Lagos, Nigeria. That month, he was lured back to Moscow. Poleshchuk was arrested, tried, and executed. The case officer who handled him in Lagos told me there'd been no security hiccups in Lagos, which led him to believe someone at Langley must have passed his name to the KGB. As with Gordievsky and Bokhan, Ames admitted to giving him up at the June meeting but not at an earlier one. Howard knew nothing about him. Hanssen's spying for the KGB also doesn't fit the timeline.

What all three cases started to suggest to SIU is that the KGB likely had a source on the USSR Branch at Langley who gave them up months earlier than Ames's June 1985 meeting at Chadwicks. Or if not on the desk, a supervisor higher up the ranks whose name was on the bigot lists for all three agents. All told, that amounted to no more than two dozen officers in the Directorate of Operations. Someone like the Athens chief or Lofgren were eliminated as suspects because neither had access to the identities of all three agents. The anomalies kept pointing back to a Langley-based officer.

SIU then moved to the less obvious anomalies. These included unexplained compromises of two technical operations against Soviet embassies in South America in the 1984–85 time frame, and, as the CIA learned from Yurchenko, a sensitive counterintelligence document from the USSR Branch or a description of it that found its way to Moscow in 1984. Thanks to meticulous recordkeeping, SIU was certain Howard and Ames had never seen the document. Another memo the Russians got their hands on dealt with a long-dormant GRU agent named Nikolai Chernov. A technician, Chernov volunteered to the FBI in the sixties, but contact was broken off in 1972. Then, for no apparent reason, Chernov, long into retirement, was arrested in the early nineties. Howard knew nothing about him. Ames had known about Chernov, but had no memory of giving up the memo or his name to the KGB. With the Chernov case ancient history and a man as good as dead from an intelligence perspective, there would have been little point.

One significant detail about the Chernov memo was that the only copy had been squirreled away in Angleton's safe, then moved to the USSR Branch. If it wasn't Howard or Ames who'd ousted Chernov to the KGB, it had to be someone else who'd once served on the branch. Since Chernov was recruited by the FBI and a file on him existed there, it could have been a KGB agent in the FBI. But at this point, SIU, having nothing solid on Hanssen, put it on the matrix, where for the moment it bolstered the case that the post-Ames mole had sat in the USSR Branch (or Russia Group after it changed names).

There were other, earlier compromises that bothered SIU. While previous investigators dismissed them as unrelated coincidences,

SIU revisited them. One was the compromise of Boris Nikolayev-ich Yuzhin, a KGB officer assigned to San Francisco under cover as a correspondent for Russian news agency TASS, where he was also spying for the FBI and CIA. He returned to Moscow in 1982, but sometime between then and Yurchenko's defection on August 1, 1985, he was caught and tried for espionage. Yurchenko said he'd been caught thanks to a CIA-issued spy camera disguised as a lighter found in the San Francisco Soviet consulate offices. The KGB, according to Yurchenko, pieced together that the CIA had issued it to Yuzhin. But because Yurchenko was not entirely trusted, SIU put Yuzhin in the anomalies column.

Another odd compromise was that of a French penetration of the KGB by the name of Vladimir Ippolitovich Vetrov. Inside French intelligence he was called FAREWELL. FAREWELL was an extremely valuable agent, passing thousands of documents from the KGB's Science and Technology Directorate (Director-ate T) to the French. As for Gordievsky, the French didn't tell the CIA his name, but the CIA correctly guessed it. Back in Moscow, FAREWELL reportedly murdered a man, and while in prison, as Yurchenko told the story, he confessed to a fellow prisoner that he was a French spy. His hope was the prisoner, who was about to be released, would go to the French embassy, which then would help free him. But instead, he went to the KGB and ratted out FARE-WELL. FAREWELL was reportedly executed in 1983.

One afternoon, Worthen looked up from a stack of files on her desk, FAREWELL's on the top. "The KGB sure had a great streak of luck," she said. "In 1983, they somehow cottoned on to a spy in Tolkachev's institute, then they magically find a Tropel lighter in San Francisco, and FAREWELL makes an idiotic confession."

Bannerman nodded her head: "More luck than they'd ever had. Short of Ames, that is."

"As the old-timers used to say," Worthen said, "one compromise is a coincidence, two nothing much to worry about, but three in a row it's time to sound a five-alarm fire."

"Why didn't anyone else see it?" Hough asked.

"Because they weren't looking."

Now with the possibility there might have been a KGB double agent active in the early eighties who betrayed both FAREWELL and Yuzhin—as likely as not someone on the USSR Branch—Hough pulled out the branch staffing table for the pertinent years and jotted down their names on the matrix and profile.

Add up the unexplained compromises, from the French agent FAREWELL to the British agent Gordievsky, from the GRU officer Bokhan in Athens to the long-retired agent Chernov, and these unexplained compromises started to tell a story. They kept pointing an accusatory finger at someone on the USSR Branch, which oversaw the running of all Soviet agents. Everyone who served on the branch would have had access to their identities. What the compromises also had in common was they occurred before Ames's big dump on June 13, 1985, and couldn't have been Howard (or, as is clear now, Hanssen).

Although there was no concrete evidence to tie these compromises together, they constituted the best evidence that there was a problem in the Soviet division at Langley beyond Howard and Ames, and maybe it was still in place. Another thing becoming

increasingly clear to SIU was the emergence of 1982–84 as a pivotal time frame, very likely the one in which the Fourth Man may
have started to spy for the KGB. It would account for discrepancies in the Tolkachev compromise, supporting the hypothesis he'd
been outed at least a year before Howard's betrayal in late 1984. It
chimed with the compromise of the "angry KGB colonel" Vasilyev,
suggesting it had occurred earlier than Howard's outing him.

SIU's doubts about Howard's giving up Vasilyev kept circling
around the fact that because he wasn't administered by the USSR
Branch, Howard didn't have access to his file. It wasn't until Vasilyev was ready to transfer back to Moscow in mid-1985 that his
file was moved to the USSR Branch in preparation for running
him there. Which made the circumstances of Vasilyev's betrayal
better fit either someone on the USSR Branch, likely with across-
the-board access to Soviet files or, again, someone more senior
overseeing Soviet operations.

Another set of anomalies SIU examined was the mid-eighties
compromise of FBI listening devices installed in Soviet diplomatic
facilities in Washington, New York, and San Francisco. Their dis-
coveries by the KGB were initially ascribed to Ames, the hypothesis being he'd somehow found out about them from an FBI agent.
But working with Milburn, SIU determined it couldn't be true
and instead indicated there had to be some problem at the FBI.
It supported Max's allegation that the KGB was running a source
in the FBI. It wouldn't be until Hanssen's arrest in 2001 that both
Max and Milburn were proved right. What it meant for SIU in the
moment, though, was that the Ames investigation was starting to
look shakier and shakier. If it missed a mole in the FBI, what else
had it missed?

SIU then went about overlaying the anomalies with the patterns of Russian operatives assigned to the Washington, DC, KGB rezidentura. In particular, they focused on the movement around town of First Chief Directorate counterintelligence officers (Line KR), any one of whom would most likely have run the Fourth Man. Any odd pattern on their part, like a Line KR officer switching from driving to taking taxis, was of interest. Or something as seemingly innocuous as a Line KR operative starting to walk around a part of Washington he never had before, or even something like one taking up walking a dog. As any CIA case officer who's spent time on the street will tell you, there's nothing like the alibi of an incontinent dog to explain walks in the middle of the night.

One day, Milburn arrived with a chronology of KGB "starbursts" in the Washington, DC, area. A starburst occurs when a rezidentura pours all its people out into the streets in order to swarm and tie up FBI surveillance teams. With the FBI chasing decoys, an operative is freed up from surveillance to make a meeting with an agent or service a dead drop. For SIU, the takeaway was a heartening revelation: During many of the starbursts on Milburn's list, Ames was assigned to Rome or temporarily out of the country. (As it would be learned after Hanssen's 2001 arrest, the starbursts occurred when he wasn't in contact with Russian intelligence.) It was one of those a-ha moments for Bannerman, Worthen, Hough, and Milburn, everyone considering how nicely the KGB starbursts fit the narrative of a double agent other than Ames. At the same time, it was acknowledged the starbursts very well could have been a case of the KGB spoofing the FBI.

What was becoming increasingly apparent to SIU is that

while it had been convenient to deposit all the mid-eighties compromises on the doorsteps of Howard and Ames, it's not where a close, objective reexamination of the evidence was taking it. At this point, SIU couldn't completely rule out that the anomalies were unconnected mishaps, but with the reality taking shape, it was looking less and less likely. And what if they were all connected by a new mole in the CIA? Crazy as it might have sounded to some, it was beginning to look that way.

SIU's assembling of the matrix and profile never went other than smoothly. Much of it had to do with everyone knowing exactly what they were doing when it came to counterintelligence. Considering that between the four of them they'd spent something like a century working at it, they should have. What also helped was that all four in SIU were more and more convinced that Russian intelligence indeed had run—or was still running—another double agent in CIA Russian operations. Having taken part in the Ames hunt and gone through the evidence with a fine-tooth comb, both Worthen and Milburn were almost certain of it. It also helped that everyone in SIU assigned the evidence pretty much the same weight. For instance, they agreed Max's leads about the Fourth Man couldn't be taken at face value without some serious, well-sourced corroboration.

One reason Milburn worked so well with the team is because he never let FBI institutional biases get in the way of facts. Unlike FBI special agents trained and under instructions to help make a prosecutor's case with court-admissible evidence, he was comfortable working with the ambiguities of intelligence. While hearsay and rumor are worthless in a courtroom, Milburn knew how important they are for drawing up a matrix. Also, by dint of long experience, Milburn understood the CIA's byzantine recordkeeping practices and its other bureaucratic eccentricities. For instance, how (polar opposite the FBI) some of the CIA's best intelligence never makes it into easily searchable records.

Milburn's mind was open enough to be one of the first to suspect that the Russians were running a high-level penetration of the FBI. Not only had Max reported there was one, but any objective parsing of the anomalies convinced him that too many unique FBI operations had inexplicably gone bad to come to any other conclusion. This went against the ingrained FBI institutional bias that it wasn't possible Russian intelligence could turn an FBI agent. Every time Bannerman brought up the possibility the KGB had a source in the FBI, Ed Curran, visibly irritated, would say, "Moles are your problem, not ours." It was just as the CIA deluded itself into believing the same about itself before Ames. Milburn relayed SIU's suspicions about FBI problems back to his bosses in the Washington field office at Buzzard Point, but it would take seven years before enough hard evidence could be collected to arrest Hanssen. Years later, Milburn would tell his former SIU colleagues the matrix helped make the case against Hanssen.

Curran, now in charge of counterespionage at Langley, had other problems with SIU, seeing little sense in the approach it was taking to the investigation. One day he walked into the vault and took a close look at the matrix displayed on the easel, which tracked travel and movement of KGB counterintelligence officers around the Washington area. "What's that?" he asked. When

Bannerman explained, Curran's response was "Who cares?" Bannerman considered reminding him that soon after Ames's June 13, 1985, meeting, the Line KR chief made a quick, mysterious trip back to Moscow. No one at the time thought to connect it to the agents lost after his trip, but now, with twenty-twenty hindsight, the Line KR chief's trip turned out to be of extreme significance: He'd gone back to coordinate the running of Ames with Moscow Center. With each interaction, Curran let it be known he was less and less impressed by SIU, and when given the chance intended to hijack its investigation.

In general, though, despite the high stakes for their superiors, SIU's four spy catchers were mostly left alone to piece together the matrix and draw up the profile. Price never checked in, and neither did their boss John Hall. Redmond occasionally would pop into SIU's vault to make sure things were running smoothly, but he never asked for a progress report. If he noticed the two large easels with thick blocks of paper, the matrix and profile scribbled across them like a Jackson Pollock painting, he didn't say anything. Redmond wasn't a fan of matrices, believing they'd have never caught Ames. SIU did consider it odd Redmond never offered his thoughts about the Fourth Man, not even his opinion whether he existed or not. It was curious considering Redmond had helmed the Ames investigation. Surely, SIU thought, he must have come away from that investigation with some opinion about the possibility of a post-Ames mole. They often wondered if Redmond knew something about the Fourth Man he didn't feel he could share with SIU. Or maybe it was as simple as he didn't want his personal biases to taint their investigation.

For Bannerman, Hough, and Worthen, the Fourth Man investigation was the most rewarding thing they'd ever done in their careers. They got to put to use everything they'd learned over their professional lives. For the fans of John le Carré's classic spy novel *Tinker, Tailor, Soldier, Spy*, Bannerman and Worthen were like an amalgam of the Connie Sachs character, "granaries" of counterintelligence fact and history. Stored in Worthen's memory was a staggering number of names and details about the KGB and the CIA's Soviet operations. She could tell you which case officer ran which agent in which years. What Worthen didn't know, Bannerman could fill in. She could cite chapter and verse the histories of the various KGB directorates, and the rivalries and feuding between them. She could even cite obscure facts like the exact date the KGB's Third Directorate (military counterintelligence) started to poach on First Chief Directorate American operations in West Germany. On the rare occasions when Bannerman and Worthen couldn't remember something, they knew exactly where to find it in the files. As for Hough, she was a font of obscure details in her own right—for instance, where to dig up old paper travel records or retired personnel records from archives.

While Redmond had feared Bannerman and Worthen wouldn't get along, in fact, all three delighted in working with each other. As Bannerman would explain it, "We meshed perfectly. Diana knew all the KGB files inside and out, Maryann spent her days breezing around Langley assembling pieces of the puzzle not found in the files, and I spent fourteen-hour days at my desk sifting through it all."

They celebrated each other's breakthroughs, with high-fiving, eureka moments, and along the way a couple of impromptu jigs. For instance, when Milburn showed up at Langley with the starbursts chronology, it set them off excitedly talking late into the evening, all three agreeing how it was the closest they'd come to genuine forensic proof of a post-Ames mole. They eagerly began looking for a compromise that coincided with a starburst. When they decided there wasn't one, it was one more reminder that the Fourth Man was run by true professionals.

They had their moments of hilarity, too. When one of their friends was in the hospital dying of cancer, they brought her a mechanical duck, which quacked when someone entered the room. They named it Phil. Bannerman was convinced Phil could detect the presence of someone with "high energy." Be that as it may, when their friend passed, they brought Phil to the office, hiding it in a dark corner. Every time Curran popped in, Phil would start quacking furiously. It unnerved Curran, but the women held their poker faces, pretending they hadn't heard anything. As soon as Curran left, they'd break out into gales of laughter. All three would become lifelong friends, agreeing the Fourth Man hunt was the most exciting and happiest time of their lives. It says a lot, considering that early on they knew that if they were right about another Russian double agent, they knew they'd end up being treated like skunks at a wedding.

For many in the CIA, these women may have appeared to be humorless, green-shaded bookkeepers, but what got them out of bed in the morning was an unswerving passion to solve what was starting to look like the most damaging case of espionage in American history. In fact, it remains an obsession for them to this day, just as it would become for Milburn and others in the FBI.

When SIU moved from tallying up the anomalies to examining what Russian agents and defectors reported about double agents in the CIA, the evidence was no less ambiguous but nonetheless pointed in one direction. Like Max, none of the agents was able to identify the double agent by either name or position, but what they had to say supported the hypothesis that there indeed were more Russian double agents in American intelligence Soviet operations.

In the early nineties, the FBI in New York recruited a Line KR officer who the CIA and FBI referred to as Adolf. Like Max, he wasn't assigned a cryptonym, and everything related to him was kept off computers. Although Adolf was considered a so-so agent, he passed on rumors about two double agents in American intelligence, one in New York and the other in Washington. One in the CIA and the other in the FBI. At the time, Ames wasn't in Washington, and Hanssen as it turned out wasn't active. But that's the best his CIA and FBI interlocutors could get out of him. Nor could they induce Adolf to dig deeper with his colleagues. An engineer, he was bored by espionage. The one tantalizing piece of corroboration for Adolf's claims was that starbursts that didn't fit Ames (or Hanssen, as it would turn out) occurred during the time frame Adolf reported the Washington, DC, double agent was active.

But the little Adolf did have to say about a high-level penetration of the CIA fascinated SIU, in particular what he'd heard from a colleague in New York about a KGB Line KR communications specialist named Vladimir Tsymbal, who several times traveled to Washington in support of an agent operation run there. Adolf wasn't certain but suspected Tsymbal helped handle contacts with the CIA double agent. Whether it was a CIA agent or not, one assumption the FBI and CIA worked off was that Tsymbal operated burst radio transmissions, which would be used to communicate with a high-level agent. As Bearden wrote in his book, "When Tsymbal showed up somewhere, the CIA's first instincts were to start looking for a spy." But what's most telling about the Tsymbal story is that neither Ames nor Hanssen were issued covert communications by the KGB. Bearden rightly asked, "What agent operations in Washington were so important that they required Moscow's best covert communications tech?"

SIU reviewed the videotapes of Adolf's debriefing in New York. It was evident Adolf was an indifferent agent who cared little about whether or not he pleased his FBI and CIA handlers. On the other hand, his absence of salesmanship gave SIU some confidence he wasn't the type to embellish or tailor what he had to report. It didn't help matters that Adolf's debriefers had clearly given up on him. In one sequence, SIU could hear off camera, "Food and beer here!" The debriefers jump up, leaving Adolf alone on the couch, sputtering, "But I'm trying to tell you something."

Adolf's vague references to two double agents in American intelligence aside, what SIU kept coming back to was Max's allegations about the 3×5 cards summarizing the Moscow meeting sites. The fact that Max, and thus the KGB, even knew about the protocols for handling the cards was compelling evidence the KGB at one time had a source on the USSR Branch or someone in the Soviet division front office. Again, the KGB's detailed knowledge about the cards was something neither Ames nor Howard possessed.

Max's other allegation about the double agent attending Directorate of Operations division chiefs' meetings remained an important part of the matrix. At one point, Max reported the agent had provided either summaries or copies of the minutes to the Russians. But Max couldn't provide any details, like the date or the subject of the meetings. Nor, as usual, would Max reveal the name of his source. Was it because he thought the CIA would try to recruit him and risk his compromise? It's often the reason why agents won't fill in details on where they get their information. Nevertheless, after Max's Caracas grand slam, his allegations could only be taken very seriously. And this allegation was very serious: If true, it meant the whole function and purpose of the CIA was in jeopardy every moment the Fourth Man was active.

Putting aside Max's tip about the 3×5 card and the Fourth Man holding a senior position in the Directorate of Operations, the deeper SIU got into its investigation, the more the anomalies kept pointing to an officer who'd served in counterintelligence and did a stint on the USSR Branch. Taken as a whole, the anomalies now pointed to a dozen or so suspects. For an investigation perhaps never expected to succeed, getting that far along was a triumph, as well as an inherent danger. No one in SIU dared say their names out loud. It was much too early for that, not to mention they frankly didn't want to believe any one of them could be a traitor. Ames was bad enough. But like a compass that points to true north, it's where the evidence kept pointing.

TEN

wil·der·ness of mir·rors /ˈwɪl dər nɪs əv ˈmɪr ərz/ A term lifted from T. S. Eliot's "Gerontion" to describe an espionage case so complicated and riddled with lies and disinformation that it's impossible to get at the truth of it.

Moscow; September 1994

SIU WEREN'T THE only ones increasingly certain about the Fourth Man. In September, four months after they had begun their investigation, Diana Worthen was quietly pulled out of SIU for a different mission. Although it touched on the Fourth Man hunt, it was so sensitive not even SIU could be told about it.

After Corbin's meeting with Max in South America, the FBI was more convinced than ever about the existence of a post-Ames double agent in the CIA. As it did before the 1993 Greenbrier conference, it threatened to track Max down in Moscow if the CIA wouldn't. Considering the CIA still was better equipped to make a clandestine meeting there, it had no choice other than to come up with a plan of its own. And with Russian surveillance on the Moscow CIA station as relentless as ever, one thing the CIA was absolutely certain of was that it couldn't use a Moscow-based case officer to meet Max.

Langley came up with a plan, one as ambitious as it was dangerous. They decided to send two officers "black" to Moscow to find Max. By black, it means they'd travel on alias tourist passports and have no affiliation whatsoever with the American government. The two officers, made to look like a married couple meeting up on vacation, would be less likely to be noticed. On the other hand, traveling as tourists, they wouldn't have the protection of diplomatic immunity. If caught meeting Max, there'd be no innocent explanation for it, and they'd likely face years in a grim Russian prison. For some reason, they called the attempt to drop in on Max a "probe." The two case officers who volunteered for the mission were named Phil and Michele. In order to limit the Russians' reaction time, Phil would fly in from a Baltic state, so he wouldn't need a Russian visa. The Russians of course would receive the flight manifest in advance, but it was highly unlikely they'd have enough time to assemble a surveillance team. Michele flew in from Europe.

Fewer than a dozen officers at the CIA knew about the trip. Though Worthen was brought in to help organize it, she was given direct orders not to tell her SIU colleagues about it. Moscow station wasn't informed, no cables were sent anywhere concerning their travel, and there were no internal CIA travel orders. Their credit cards and driver's licenses were "backstopped"—that is, a cursory check would not have detected any irregularities and the credit cards had a history of purchases behind them. But the reality was the two were operating far beyond the pale, at the mercy of luck and gaps in Russian coverage. Their trip was one of the riskiest operations the CIA's ever run in Russia using its own staff officers; in the past CIA case officers always enjoyed the Get Out of Jail Free card known as diplomatic immunity. This time their freedom might be on the line.

I knew Phil from when I was in the Agency and called to ask him if he'd share the details. He was friendly, but cut me off, saying, "I'll never talk about that to anyone." I wanted to say, "Come on, Phil, it's been more than twenty-five years." But there was no mistaking that he intended to take the secrets of his Moscow trip to the grave. It left me to wonder how he and Michele had intended to make contact with Max, or for that matter what they had planned to say to him when they did. According to press reporting around this time, the FBI was openly offering KGB officers bounties to identify double agents in American intelligence. I suspect, then, that Michele and Phil were authorized to offer Max a large pot of money if he were to produce another Caracas-like gem as he had with Ames.

When Michele and Phil were en route to Moscow, the only help Worthen could offer was having NSA monitor patterns of Russian police and intelligence communications. Encrypted, they weren't readable, but she was looking for unusual radio spikes near the airports indicating some sort of out-of-the-ordinary surveillance team patterns. Such spikes would suggest the Russians had been tipped off to their arrival and were watching the airports.

As meticulously planned as the probe was, something went wrong. When Phil and Michele disembarked from their flights in Moscow, everything looked fine. There were no menacing security types at the end of the gangway. At immigrations, it took about the right time for them to clear. But outside baggage claim they couldn't miss it: men and women with earpieces talking into their lapels. They looked away when Phil and Michele happened to make eye contact, a bad sign. As the two passed through the airport, they couldn't miss the teams tailing them. It almost seemed as if the Russians wanted to be spotted. Michele and Phil had no choice other than to abort. Rather than going to look for Max, they headed directly to the hotel, stayed the night, and returned to the United States without incident. With few willing to talk about it, this is the best I've been able to piece together about the story.

There was no evidence for it, but there was strong suspicion at Langley that someone had tipped off the Russians to Michele and Phil's trip. There wasn't a better explanation for the blanket surveillance coverage at the airport, which led to the suspicion it likely was a double agent at Langley who tipped off the Russians. But now, with Phil and Michele safely back in the United States, what mattered was Max. If indeed someone at Langley knew about the trip, they almost certainly knew about Max, maybe even his true name. Which led to the inevitable question: Had Max been arrested?

As this grim road kept winding, this in turn led to another troubling question: Was Max a provocateur, a dangle? Or somewhere along the line had he been turned into one, wittingly or not? The purpose would have been to channel disinformation through him, which could have been done even without his knowing he'd been made. Max's tipping off the CIA to Ames's Caracas trip would strongly suggest it wasn't true. That aside, Max possessed many of the hallmarks of a dangle. He never named his sources. More than once he made it clear that he wouldn't tell the CIA everything he knew about the double agents at Langley and the FBI. He never provided classified documents or submitted to CIA direction. His comments about American double agents were more tantalizing than something you could act on. It was as if he were primed to bait some sort of trap. It also was extremely suspicious the way Max had showed up at Beria House as a notetaker, almost as if the Russians put him in the CIA's path. The same went for how Max was fortuitously included in the 1993 Russian intelligence liaison trip that ended up at Greenbrier. Be wary of the unbidden, Max's detractors said.

Aside from the chief in East Africa, another Max skeptic was David Rolph, the Moscow chief who attended the Greenbrier meeting. Among many things, Rolph has a hard time believing Max was able to get away from his fellow attendees and go fishing with Corbin without his Russian colleagues knowing. Rolph said that through the entire conference the Russians kept close track of each other, and he never once saw an occasion when one pulled away from the others to socialize alone with a CIA counterpart. He wonders, then, how it would have been possible for Max to steal away and meet Corbin without the other Russians noticing.

If indeed Max did get a brief moment with Corbin, the best explanation for it is that the head of the KGB delegation permitted it, or even instructed him to do so. If so, for those with a deeply conspiratorial view of Russian intelligence, it meant Max—again wittingly or unwittingly—had been ordered to flag Ames's Caracas trip to Corbin. The obvious problem with this version of events is you end up tumbling down Angleton's rabbit hole, where the KGB's behind every bush and calling every shot, and every Russian spy and defector is a plant to drive the CIA crazy. The Monster Plot, as it came to be called.

Bill Lofgren, the division chief overseeing Russia during the

Fourth Man hunt, said early on he'd been led to believe the Russians intentionally gave up Ames. As Lofgren tells the story, he had just been reassigned from overseas to Langley as deputy to John MacGaffin, then the division chief. Shortly afterward, MacGaffin pulled him aside and whispered that Ames had been unmasked as a Russian spy and would soon be arrested. Although MacGaffin didn't mention Max by name, he said it occurred at a conference with Russian intelligence. According to MacGaffin, a Russian attendee at a break walked up to a CIA attendee and handed him a note. When the CIA officer later opened it, it read: "It's Ames."

The way MacGaffin told the story, it distinctly sounded to Lofgren as if the Russians had indeed sacrificed Ames. Lofgren couldn't fathom what would motivate the Russians to give up an active agent. But it nonetheless tells us something when someone who knew Russian intelligence as well as Lofgren would consider the possibility Ames was sacrificed for a strategic objective. As Lofgren wonders to this day, for all the CIA knows, the Russians did it to protect a more valuable agent. The calculation being that when the CIA caught on to Ames, they'd stop looking any further at the '85–'86 losses. A pawn sacrifice to save a queen.

One thing the pawn-sacrifice gambit has going for it is that by the time of Greenbrier, Ames was all but worthless to the Russians, a throwaway, as the CIA and FBI call them. Even Ames was aware of his greatly diminished value to the Russians. With barely disguised desperation, he'd repeatedly begged Bearden, MacGaffin, and Lofgren to let him back into Russian operations. In coordination with the FBI, Lofgren offered Ames the position heading Russia Group, the idea being to allay any suspicion on Ames's part that he was under investigation.

Another possible motivation for the Russians outing Ames could have been to humiliate the CIA by subjecting it to an embarrassing public trial. First, with the spectacle of it, any Russian considering volunteering to the CIA would have second thoughts. Second, if the Russians indeed had another source in Russian operations, she or he had almost certainly caught wind of the fact that Ames was about to go down, as Redmond's SIU team already suspected by the time of the Greenbrier meeting. The Russians could have decided to preempt the inevitable and outed him themselves at a time of their choosing. Granted, if any of this is true, it would be a plot twist wild enough to turn le Carré green with envy and warm the cockles of Angleton's heart.

SIU had an alternative theory why the Fourth Man didn't betray Max to his handlers. In early 1992 and continuing through 1993, the Fourth Man seems to have put himself on ice, cutting off contact with the Russians. There were no unexplained compromises of Russian agents during this period and no unusual pattern activity at the DC rezidentura to suggest it was running an important agent. One explanation for this long a gap in contact was a case of prudent cold feet. With Russia coming apart at the seams and Russian intelligence under attack, the Fourth Man had every reason in the world to pull back. Hanssen did the same thing, breaking contact with the Russians in 1991 and not resuming it until 1999. While the Fourth Man almost certainly would have known about Max, he could have decided it was too risky to tip off his handlers. Or, there's this: The Fourth Man very well could have welcomed the Ames investigation and arrest because it took the heat off him.

None of this proves Ames was sacrificed to protect the Fourth Man. But for what it's worth, the KGB does have a history of sacrificing lesser agents for more important ones. For instance, in the fifties, the KGB sacrificed an active and productive source in Germany's foreign intelligence service in order to protect Heinz Felfe, the chief of that service's counterespionage. (It gave Felfe nearly a decade of breathing room, but eventually in 1961 he was arrested as a KGB spy.) But the question is whether the Russians would treat Ames the same way. While one former Russian intelligence officer I talked to found the theory very plausible (a chess player, he called it a "queen sacrifice"), another told me he highly doubted Ames had been deliberately outed by Moscow. He said no matter what tactical advantage it might serve, it would destroy the reputation of Russian intelligence if the story ever came out.

Then there's the question of whether they'd risk a staff officer like Max as bait, even if the end game was to protect a more valuable agent. There was a precedent for it, though. In 1988, a KGB agent with the Second Chief Directorate by the name of Aleksandr Vasilyevich Zhomov approached the CIA Moscow station chief Jack Downing on a Leningrad-bound night train and passed him a packet of classified KGB documents. Zhomov offered himself up as a spy in the Second. When Downing got to the American consulate in Leningrad and read the documents, he had no doubt they were genuine. The documents accurately described his activities during a previous posting to Moscow.

Although the CIA wouldn't learn Zhomov's name until a couple of years later, Langley treated him as a legitimate agent and encrypted him GTPROLOGUE. Eventually, the CIA would figure out the Second had run Zhomov into Downing as a dangle with the intention of leading the CIA down the garden path of believing its '85–'86 losses were caused by a problem other than an agent, like bugs in Moscow station. After Bearden retired, he met Zhomov in Moscow, where the Russian fessed up that the KGB had offered him up in order to divert attention from Ames.

In the KGB's eyes, the Zhomov operation must have looked like it was worth the risk, giving Ames a much longer shelf life. Which is one reason it might have been encouraged to try it again—anything to throw dust in the CIA's eyes. And the time was opportune. The Russians somehow knew all about the blood-letting going on at Langley, the post-Ames paranoia, and would have seen the advantage to opening the veins wider. In November 1994, Valentin Klimenko, a senior Russian counterintelligence officer, pulled aside Rolf Mowatt-Larssen, the CIA's acting chief of station in Moscow, to needle him about another Russian mole in the Agency beyond Ames. Mowatt-Larssen would have dismissed it as a ham-fisted provocation, but because Klimenko was in the possession of detailed and intimate knowledge of the current workings of the CIA's Russian operations, Mowatt-Larssen could only conclude someone in the CIA was at the very least talking out of school, if not serving as a genuine double agent. Then in 2005, Ames and Hanssen's KGB handler Victor Cherkashin alluded in his memoir to the KGB running another penetration of the CIA beyond Ames. Considering Cherkashin wasn't a defector and wrote his book in retirement in Russia, it's a fair assumption Russian intelligence vetted and approved it, and very likely even concocted the reference to its still-active, mysterious CIA double agent.

Lies illuminate as much as they conceal, but in the end it makes little sense why, if indeed the Russians had another double agent in the CIA, they would see the benefit of rubbing the CIA's nose in it. As far-fetched as it sounds, it's possible the new double agent was so secure in his position, Russia was confident the CIA and FBI could never catch him. Another consideration is that the Russians, knowing how much damage Angleton had done to the CIA, might have decided to run the risk of exposing the Fourth Man in hoping to kick off a new open-ended mole hunt. If all this sounds preposterously conspiratorial, you're right, but at the same time it's not beyond the Russians. That's the level of sophistication at which they play the game.

Which brings the story of the Fourth Man hunt to this very real consideration: There's no certain way to know whether or not the Russians didn't frame the Fourth Man from day one. It would take herculean effort, planning, and patience, not to mention genius. But the KGB certainly had done it before. It nicely framed Jeanne Vertefeuille, the lead Ames investigator. During an assignment in Africa, the KGB pitched her via a proxy. She turned it down and reported it. But in the middle of the Ames investigation, the Russians started wiring money into her account as if she'd accepted the pitch and was now a KGB agent. The evidence was compelling enough for the FBI to open an investigation into her code-named "Gray Mouse." The FBI eventually figured out she'd been framed, but in the meantime the Russians managed to deepen the distrust between the FBI and CIA, further slowing down the Ames hunt. With no one in the CIA above suspicion, especially post-Ames, framing a high-level American intelligence officer would be guaranteed to wreak havoc on the CIA. If I were the Russians, it's what I'd do. Apologies for the sodden spy cliché, but welcome to the wilderness of mirrors.

But that's not what SIU believed. There was too much specific evidence to believe the Russians fabricated the mole out of thin air. Among many things, there were the 3×5 cards summarizing the Moscow meeting sites. Someone clearly had informed the Russians about them, and it wasn't Howard, Ames, or Hanssen. Just as it's certain none of them outed the three Soviet agents in May 1985. The waters were still murky, but the trail wasn't lost. They also believe Max was the real thing.

With the failure of the probe, and all the dark complications its loss added into the mix, Worthen went back to SIU to continue the investigation. Since it seemed very unlikely Max would show up anytime soon, if ever, SIU was left to speculate how the KGB could possibly have gotten away with the Fourth Man for so long, with no spy or defector emerging to give up the game as they had with Howard and Ames and hundreds of other KGB moles caught over the years. There had to be some explanation.

ELEVEN

in·ner sanc·tum /ˈɪn ər ˈsæŋk təm/ *n*. A private, closed-off space, often intended to protect the secrets of those who trust no one on the outside.

Langley; October 1994

INDEED, WHAT NEVER stopped bothering SIU is how the Fourth Man had managed to remain so elusive for so long. Sort of like the Loch Ness Monster, evidence of his or her existence was always episodic and thin. No one could come up with a satisfying explanation why more KGB defectors and spies wouldn't have heard more about him. And if he was as high up in the CIA as Max said he was, how could the KGB keep him a secret for so long? These were questions that followed him into the darkest, most perplexing depths of KGB lore.

With the exceptions of Max and Adolf, Russians crossing the lines hadn't heard the faintest echo of the Fourth Man. Yurchenko had nothing to say about him; neither did any of the dozens of Russian intelligence officers who'd served in the New York and Washington rezidenturas and then defected. At least one of them should have picked up something—anything—when they were back in Moscow. But not a word. It was as if a phantom Russian intelligence agency other than the KGB and GRU had recruited and run the Fourth Man. Or maybe some invisible KGB clique that truly knew how to keep a secret. One Soviet defector might have provided an answer.

In 1989, at the age of thirty-four, a Russian named Sergei Papushin resigned from the KGB and went into the oil business. On a business trip to New York, he got into a drunken scuffle and was arrested. The NYPD called the FBI, who sent agents to interview him. Refusing to cooperate, the next day Papushin ran to the KGB rezidentura to report the FBI approach, only to have the KGB security officer tell him not to sweat it. Discouraged and at his wit's end, Papushin revisited the FBI offer and defected. Papushin was debriefed by both the FBI and CIA and later by MI6 because, when assigned to Moscow for the Second Chief Directorate, he was in the section that spied on the British embassy.

Landing a source with any knowledge of the KGB's Second Chief Directorate, even one no longer employed, was a big deal. Anyone who worked in Soviet operations in those days knew the Second was a different animal. Known to be staffed by hard-boiled, provincial, xenophobic operatives, they looked at the West as corrupt, corrupting, and ultimately doomed. They were perfectly happy living in cramped cold-water apartments, driving around crappy Soviet cars, and serving as the Soviet Empire's trusted storm troopers. They sometimes traveled abroad on short trips, usually to ride shotgun on traveling Soviet delegations. But it wasn't enough to file off the jagged Soviet edge. Nor did it undermine their sincerely held belief that the United States was the Soviet Union's mortal enemy and needed to be fought tooth and nail. In other words, getting your hand on one was akin to catching a blue lobster.

On the other hand, defectors from First Chief Directorate were a dime a dozen, coming over all the time. One reason was they were the KGB's pampered and untrustworthy elite. Spending careers abroad, many fell for the allure of shopping malls, shiny Mercedes, and restaurants with more on the menu than borscht, pelmeni, and cheap vodka. First Chief Directorate officers may have learned the difference between a salad and a dessert fork, but the downside was they were susceptible to waking up one morning, reassessing life's prospects, and coming to the momentous decision to drop by the nearest American embassy and defect to the CIA. Russian military intelligence (the GRU), where many operatives typically spent their careers abroad, suffered the same vulnerabilities. Naturally, the KGB was less inclined to trust operatives from the First with its most sensitive secrets.

By the end of the eighties, the CIA knew the names of only four Second Chief Directorate officers. It's a noteworthy lapse, considering the Second was a persistent and real threat to Western governments thanks to an Olympic-class record of recruiting diplomats and spies assigned to Moscow and other postings around the Soviet Union. The Second Chief Directorate was just as successful with Western businessmen, enlisting them to smuggle in embargoed technology and rob the West blind of advanced technology. Not to mention Putin reportedly got his start on rotation to the Second Chief Directorate in Leningrad.

One thing the CIA made no mistake about was that the Second Chief Directorate had a better track record of observing the discipline of espionage than the First.

"The fact is Ames wasn't run by the KGB's A-team," Bannerman told me. "It made sloppy meeting arrangements on the fly, which went unobserved by the FBI thanks to sheer luck."

She was referring to the KGB cutout (i.e., an intermediary), a Soviet diplomat, not showing up for a meeting, forcing Ames to make an uninvited visit to the Soviet embassy. The KGB's writing him notes that clearly were couched instructions—even noting what it had paid him to date—was another case of sloppiness. Equally risky, the Washington rezidentura Line KR chief, a man well known to the FBI, came to a meeting at Chadwicks. These are all practices the Second Chief Directorate would never have countenanced. Then there's the case of Max. The Second would never have allowed any of its officers who knew about double agents to fraternize one-on-one with a CIA case officer, as Max had in East Africa and later at Greenbrier. Finally, it's unlikely the Second would have been so quick to arrest the agents outed by Ames, putting him in an extremely exposed position. The Second would have had the good sense to quietly ease them out of their sensitive jobs, or at least waited longer to arrest them.

The Second was so little known and so feared that some in the CIA came to believe that in the eighties it was given free rein to recruit and run agents outside the Soviet Union without having to tell the First anything about them. It was thought that Second Chief Directorate operatives bypassed KGB rezidenturas, meeting their agents when they happened to be on short official trips outside the Soviet Union. Carrying diplomatic passports, the Second operatives didn't run the risk of arrest were they to be caught meeting an agent. The express purpose of cutting out the First was to reduce the risk that a defector or spy from rezidentura could out the agent.

There was some hope Papushin might clear this up. But as it turned out, he was an incorrigible drunk, worse than Ames. His CIA cryptonym, GTDECANTER, tells you all you need to know about what Langley thought of him (the digraph GT denotes the Soviet Union). Mike Sulick, a Russian-speaking case officer who would rise to become the CIA's director of operations, took Papushin on a three-city tour of the United States. Papushin barely drew a sober breath the entire trip. In one bar, Sulick had to rescue him from an imminent brawl when Papushin overheard someone criticize America's role in the Vietnam War and squared up on him. Another time, Papushin dropped a twenty-dollar bill in a panhandler's cup, assuming since he was wearing an army surplus jacket he must be a vet and deserved more respect. In short, anything Papushin said had to be taken with a grain of salt.

The one thing in Papushin's favor is that he was the one who first identified GTPROLOGUE as Aleksandr Zhomov. If it hadn't been for Papushin recognizing Zhomov in a photograph, it would have taken the CIA years longer to figure out Zhomov was a dangle run into the CIA to throw it off its mole hunting. Also in his favor, British intelligence found Papushin's information about Second Chief Directorate operations against MI6 in Moscow to be credible.

Then in August 1990, Papushin out of the blue made the sensational claim that when he was still employed by the KGB, he'd heard a rumor the Second Chief Directorate had recruited a CIA officer in Moscow, presumably a case officer. A claim like this would normally have rung all sorts of bells, but because it came so long after his defection it barely registered. Most thought Papushin was either suffering from delirium tremens or lying to make himself relevant again to the CIA and FBI. It was all the easier to dismiss the notion of the Second recruiting a CIA officer because at this point, few at the CIA and FBI accepted the possibility the Second was running agents outside the Soviet Union.

If anyone doubted Papushin's drinking was as bad as claimed, those doubts were put to rest when he was found dead in February 1991 under his bed next to an empty bottle of bourbon. At the time, he was living in a CIA apartment in Maryland. Papushin's death of course did nothing to lend credence to his allegations about a CIA double agent.

But in reexamining the Papushin case, there were a couple of things that caught SIU's attention. One is that the KGB, totally out of character, had desperately tried to get Papushin to return home soon after his 1989 defection. It even allowed his KGB father, Viktor Papushin, to travel to the United States to talk sense into him. The younger Papushin unpersuaded, his father returned to Moscow only to find his career in ruins. SIU had to ask why the KGB would go to this extreme to get back a low-ranking defector who supposedly couldn't do all that much damage. Was the KGB anxious Papushin might know something about a double agent in the CIA and needed to get him out of the clutches of the Americans before, in a moment of clarity, he might remember a crucial detail?

SIU took a close look at what exactly Papushin had to say about the CIA double agent. One thing that caught its attention was that Papushin had said he *assumed* the CIA officer had been posted to Moscow; he didn't say he knew it for a fact. For all Papushin knew, as he'd made clear, the Second had recruited the CIA officer when he happened to be passing through Moscow on temporary assignment, or even outside the Soviet Union. In SIU's eyes, hedging his allegation in this fashion made Papushin's claim somewhat more credible. This, combined with Papushin not having a record of making things up, led SIU to give his claim of a Second Chief Directorate double agent in the CIA more credence than others before. Although Papushin's allegation about the Second recruiting a CIA officer was wafer-thin, it stayed on the matrix—with an asterisk in bold that it didn't constitute anything close to proof. As their mentor David Blee had taught, a lead (no matter how far-fetched) stays on the matrix.

This would only become significant later, but SIU found it extremely odd that against usual practice, Papushin's lead about a mole in the CIA hadn't been incorporated into the Soviet division's counterintelligence database. The way the system was expressly designed to work, even if Papushin's claim was dubious, it nonetheless should have been logged into the database. SIU had no way to know whether this was an oversight or done on purpose.

And as if the Papushin case didn't have enough loose ends, there was yet another. Not long after Papushin's death, Ames dropped by the back room, the off-limits vaulted area set up after the '85–'86 losses for the administration of internal, counterintelligence-related Soviet operations, and casually mentioned he'd visited Papushin the night before he was found dead. Ames didn't say why, other than he'd tagged along with Papushin's normal handler, Rod Carlson. It struck the back room as odd that Carlson would have invited him, because Ames was no longer in Soviet operations and had no business meeting a defector. One hypothesis SIU considered was Ames had asked Carlson to let him meet Papushin to make absolutely sure Papushin didn't know anything that could point a finger at him.

Or alternatively, Ames's KGB handler might have tasked him with determining if Papushin knew anything about the Fourth Man. However, since SIU had no way to check with Ames in prison, it was just a hypothesis.

So much about the strange case of Papushin remains unresolved to this day, but for SIU—and those who would take up the case after that group—it opened the door a crack to the possibility the Fourth Man was recruited by and reported to the Second Chief Directorate. It was one possible explanation why First Chief Directorate agents and defectors would only hear the vaguest rumors about him, and how it was he could remain a phantom Russian agent for so long.

As far as I know, there's been no official determination whether the Second Chief Directorate (or its successor, the FSB) operated independently in Washington. Mike Rochford, the FBI agent credited with collaring Hanssen, wrote me that Yurchenko told his CIA and FBI debriefers he was aware the Second ran agents outside the USSR independently of the First. But as I heard from other CIA and FBI counterintelligence officers, there's no confirmed consensus on this; there's simply not enough evidence to support it one way or another. But there is an old case suggesting it did at one time. In 1957, Vladislav Kovshuk, the head of the Second Chief Directorate section responsible for the American embassy in Moscow during the fifties and early sixties, made a ten-month trip to the United States. Although he traveled in alias and appeared to operate independently from the Washington rezidentura, he was sometimes accorded assistance from it in the way of countersurveillance. One hypothesis is that Kovshuk had been sent to Washington to activate a CIA double agent his section had recruited in Moscow. The Washington rezidentura very likely would have wanted the Second to establish a track record for the agent before agreeing to take over his running. In the end, with no double agent arrested, no one's exactly sure what was so important that Kovshuk dropped his Moscow duties to go work in Washington—or if the Second continued to operate in Washington after he left.

A former MI6 officer told me his service at one point looked into the possibility that some of the KGB's most sensitive cases abroad were run by the Second Chief Directorate. He believed it worked that way because the KGB's most trustworthy operatives were in the Second and consequently trusted with its most important cases. MI6 also heard that the officers supervising those cases, the ones who knew all the details about them, never left Moscow in order to preclude their defecting. The former MI6 officer wrote me, "It apparently was an explicit part of the deal with them— the best casework in return for a foreign travel ban." Instead of the Lubyanka-confined officers making face-to-face meetings, as MI6 heard it, the Second Chief Directorate took the precaution of using special couriers to meet the agents, often Second operatives traveling with trade delegations. Or sometimes Aeroflot crews.

Someone else who often wondered how active the Second Chief Directorate had been in the United States was a former colleague who once headed CIA Russian operations. He couldn't cite for me any known examples of the Second running agents in Washington, but he did offer me that the Second did indeed have the advantage of possessing a limited number of completely trusted officers it could employ for handling an agent like the Fourth Man, either internally or outside the Soviet Union. As he put it, the Second was "pre-wired" to handle high-level cases. It was one reason, he added, that the Second Chief Directorate always had more clout than the First.

He cautioned me, though, that it would be a mistake to draw an arbitrary line between the First and Second Chief Directorates. They weren't always competitors, and as a matter of practice their most trusted officers coordinated on important cases. In some cases, First Chief Directorate officers trusted by the Second were sent abroad to handle particularly valuable agents recruited by the Second. To protect their cover, they were embedded deep in Russian embassies, usually in menial jobs like a driver or a cook. It made phantom case officers like these almost impossible to spot, let alone unearth the phantom agents they were sent to run.

A former FSB officer—the successor to the Second Chief Directorate—told me the Second's preference was always to use its own officers when making meetings with agents outside the Soviet Union. Most often, the Second operatives embedded in official delegations where they'd have more than enough opportunities to break away and meet their agents. The meetings were never coordinated with the local rezidentura, and certainly not the Soviet embassy, due to lack of trusting the First.

The former FSB officer went on to say that Second operations run abroad were overseen by an ultra-secret section inside Lubyanka, the Second Chief Directorate's Baroque Revival headquarters in central Moscow. (Before the 1917 October Revolution, it was occupied by the All-Russia Insurance Company.) The section was simply called "Intelligence." Its office was in the old part of the building that hadn't been refurbished since the twenties. There were no pictures or maps on its somber walls, the carpets a dull green. There was no evidence of safes or filing cabinets. None of its offices had signs on them, only numbers. In fact, in order to find the Intelligence Section's offices, you needed to know where to look. There also was no way to directly call any of its officers, who didn't appear on staffing tables or in any KGB directories.

The Intelligence Section, he explained, didn't handle agents according to the normal KGB practice. The former FSB officer confirmed to me that Lubyanka Second operatives overseeing sensitive agent cases weren't allowed to travel outside the Soviet Union, not even with official Soviet delegations. He also said they arranged for Second "legal travelers" to make contacts with agents. These go-betweens weren't trusted enough to be told the names or positions of the agents, and instead were only told where to pick up or put down a dead drop or make a brief meeting. Incidentally, the former FSB officer told me that this regimen held through the most chaotic days of the Yeltsin presidency and still exists today, with Intelligence Section officers still forbidden from traveling abroad.

He continued that Intelligence Section files also were not handled in a normal fashion. Rather than appending an agent's true name to a file, they used pseudonyms. Telephone numbers and any other possible identifiers were coded. Source descriptions for intelligence reporting produced by an Intelligence Section agent were obfuscated. For instance, while the source of a report might be an agent, the report would attribute it to an intercept. Finally, the Intelligence Section was generally disinclined to act on the information it acquired. If, for instance, it were to catch a British spy somewhere in the Soviet government, it would allow the spy to remain in place rather than risk losing the agent who'd outed him.

When I started poking around Moscow, quixotically searching for a retiree from the Second Chief Directorate to corroborate information about the Intelligence Section, I was met by stony silence. As I was told over and over again, the Russians even today look at the eighties as yesterday, with retired Second officers under the same strictures as during the worst of the Cold War. It didn't matter to them that I saw it as a good news story for Russia, proof of Russian intelligence at its best. The one Second Chief Directorate defector I did manage to find stopped answering me as soon as I asked him about the Intelligence Section.

This leaves me with the observation that nothing about the Second Chief Directorate should be taken as scripture and that the mechanics of the Second's running agents abroad and successes pretty much remain unascertainable. But it's easy to see why the hypothesis the Second ran the Fourth Man was so tantalizing for SIU. The team turned over every stone to see if there was any support for it. It certainly would explain how the KGB and the Fourth Man could have gotten away with it. It's a possibility the FBI has also increasingly entertained over the years. With the Second—and perhaps the mysterious Intelligence Section—in the mix, SIU was looking at a level of tradecraft that could make a spy more or less impossible to catch.

TWELVE

in·tu·i·tion /ˌɪn tuˈɪʃ ən/ *n*. A gut feeling.

Langley; October 1994

SIU COULDN'T SWEEP any of it under the rug—that Max might be a dangle, that the Fourth Man could have been framed, that they were up against an intelligence service within an intelligence service. But they had to find a way through, to make sense of it all. With the Venn diagram intersection between the unexplained Russian losses and those read into them winnowed down to fewer than a dozen, it was time to zero in on a unique profile for the Fourth Man.

The problem now was SIU was about to ruffle some feathers—and they knew it. All the suspects had been or were senior officers who'd climbed a hill of broken glass to get to where they were. Fancying themselves as quasi-royalty, they wouldn't take well to anyone questioning their loyalty. On top of it, as soon as any one of them was put under a microscope, the others could be counted on to close ranks and return fire. I got a taste of how it worked in my reporting.

When I started asking questions about the short list of Fourth Man suspects, half of my heretofore forthcoming sources clammed up. They stopped answering my emails and calls. When I called Gerber—the Soviet division chief when Ames volunteered to the KGB in 1985—to tell him I possessed the short list of suspects, he was furious. "No one should ever have given you that."

If SIU had ended up with a list of less ambitious, less entitled suspects—of the type you could put on ice until the investigation was finished—things would have been a lot simpler. But the longevity of the Fourth Man's treason almost certainly meant he was a senior officer (as Max had alleged), one not lightly accused of treason.

On top of it, there was still a smoldering civil war in the CIA and FBI about Russia's ability to deceive its enemies. To one degree or another, everyone lived unhappily in Angleton's shadow and his fever fantasy about the KGB's Monster Plot, where every Russian defector or spy who showed up at American intelligence's door was an avatar of an elaborate disinformation conspiracy. Debates about fake Russian defectors were nearly theological, which meant suspicions swirling around Max and the Fourth Man were like pouring kerosene on an already blazing fire.

The paranoia and distrust went so deep that Price and Redmond both ended up on the suspect list. Had they been told, it wouldn't have surprised them much. They'd been read into the unexplained compromises and knew they should have been on the list. Worthen and Bannerman were on it, too. They tried to laugh it off, treating it almost as a badge of honor confirming their status as insiders. But deep down, it worsened the already poisonous atmosphere they were forced to work in. After all, if you're suspected of being a traitor, it couldn't be otherwise. It was another thing that would come to taint the findings of the Fourth Man investigation.

As much as SIU did its best to ignore intuition and personal animosity, it couldn't avoid them entirely. On top of the Fourth Man suspect list sat Milt Bearden. With his winding down Russian operations in the early nineties, he'd done more damage to intelligence collection on Russia than anyone else other than Howard and Ames. It didn't help that he had a foreign wife (French) or that he'd served in Africa—that happy hunting ground for spy recruiters. It was all the worse because Bearden didn't even pretend to conform to the Russian division's strict protocols of compartmentation, and in fact went out of his way to ridicule them. When he accused the spy catchers of "circling the wagons to protect their rice bowls," they took the insult in the worst light—that he didn't give a damn what slipped out the door and ended up in Moscow. To remind everyone a new broom sweeps clean, Bearden kept a swagger stick in his office that he'd slap on the desk to remind people who was in charge.

The hostility toward Bearden got so bad that at one point Sue Eckstein, a backroom denizen, printed her thoughts on him and handed out copies for everyone in the division to scotch tape above their desks. "Arrogance without substance breeds disaster," it read. No one said it to Bearden's face, but everyone knew he was the target of their wrath. The way those in the trenches of Russian operations looked at it, Russian intelligence couldn't have done better than Bearden.

During his assignment to the Soviet division in the mid-eighties, Bearden knew exactly how much the rank and file distrusted him, or for that matter how much the CIA's leadership distrusted each other. One day, he and the head of counterintelligence, Gus Hathaway, were called up to see Bill Casey, Reagan's CIA director. The '85–'86 losses of Russian agents were very much on everyone's mind, and Casey wanted to know where the investigation stood. When the conversation turned to suspects, Casey mumbled, "Am I on the list?" Bearden couldn't resist: "You're right at the top of it." Casey of course knew Bearden was joking, but it shows how relentlessly Angleton's ghost stalked the CIA, or how it was possible a senior officer like Bearden could be suspected of being a Russian mole.

Bearden was well aware he was on the short list of suspects for the '85–'86 losses, the ones Ames would largely be held responsible for. As he tells the story, one day the head of counterintelligence, Gus Hathaway, pulled aside Burton Gerber, the chief of the Soviet division and Bearden's boss, and asked him, "How far can we trust Bearden?" Hathaway cautioned they couldn't be too careful when it came to outsiders to Soviet operations, someone who hadn't been properly vetted and forged in the crucible. He reminded Gerber that Bearden, having served in East Asia and Africa, was inherently suspect. Gerber said he was wrong about Bearden, that he could be trusted as well as anyone. Reassured or not, Hathaway asked Gerber not to say a word to Bearden about the conversation. Gerber did anyway. Incensed, Bearden told Gerber to let Hathaway know that if he made another insinuation about Bearden's loyalties, he'd drag Hathaway to Langley's roof and throw him off.

But Bearden was far from the only suspect. When John Mac-Gaffin took over from Bearden in 1992, they flew to Moscow together so Bearden could introduce MacGaffin to the Russians.

As soon as the plane lifted off from Dulles, Bearden asked if Mac-Gaffin knew why he'd been given the division. MacGaffin had no idea. Bearden said it was because MacGaffin was the only senior officer who wasn't in a position to have given up the agents lost in 1985 and 1986. As MacGaffin told me, Bearden was only half kidding.

Despite overseeing the Ames hunt, Paul Redmond also was on the list. A man in a class of his own when it came to Russian intelligence, he'd been the obvious choice to supervise the Fourth Man investigation. After Ames's arrest, he was now a strutting rock star of counterintelligence. At one point MacGaffin, then Price's number two, made a life-size Redmond cardboard cutout and put it in the corner of his office to celebrate Redmond's new-found status. It was just good-natured ribbing, but nonetheless it gives you an idea about the plinth Redmond occupied at the CIA.

Like any good spy hunter, Redmond kept an open mind when it came to counterintelligence. Had the occasion come up, he would have been the first to tell SIU that it needed to take a close look at him, just as he had told colleagues in the middle of the Ames hunt not to exclude him as a suspect. Redmond also had a reputation for knowing Russia and its intelligence services as well as anyone at the CIA. One day, Redmond's status as a master spy catcher would spread via the small screen when ABC ran a scripted series based on the Ames hunt, with Redmond portrayed as a good man on a dark night.

Central casting couldn't have done better depicting a spymaster than Redmond. A short man, he favored bow ties, plaid shirts, and rolled-up shirtsleeves. He sported a paunch, suggesting he'd spent a life poring over files rather than at the gym. He owned a shabby genteel townhouse on Capitol Hill and drove an exhaust-belching beater with a bumper sticker that read: "This car is not abandoned." People who passed his car in the executive parking lot noticed the driver's side seat belt was always hanging out the door. It all telegraphed he wasn't just another plodding, minivan-driving federal bureaucrat relegated to Northern Virginia's dull suburbs. Along with it, he let anyone and everyone know he'd attended Harvard. To fill out the persona, Redmond worked hard at a reputation for aloofness turning into in-your-face arrogance at the drop of a hat. When he'd catch his colleagues idly chatting about something like an upcoming NFL game, he'd cut the conversation short with something like "Who with a brain would give a fuck?" Some thought his sour disposition was thanks to his career plateauing, stuck overly long in a series of mid-level jobs at Langley. It wasn't until after Ames's arrest that things would finally take off for Redmond.

He wasn't without a sense of humor, though. In 1989, when Redmond was number two in the Soviet division, he visited an East European station that was under particularly heavy surveillance. On the day of his arrival, the station chief drove him around town, pointing out all the cars following them around. As the chief pulled up in front of his residence that evening, he told Redmond a pedestrian would soon be rounding the corner with a bag over his shoulder. The chief explained it contained a concealed camera with which to get a picture of the chief's guest, Redmond. Redmond got a glimmer in his eye, and said, "Watch this." As soon as the man with a shoulder bag came within hearing distance, Redmond started talking loudly in Russian. The following days, the chief was blanketed with surveillance trying to identify the mysterious Russian. One morning the chief came out of his house to find all four tires on his car were flat. The people who tailed him, as the chief told me, apparently didn't appreciate Redmond's little joke.

A veritable who's who of Langley's Russian operations was on the suspect list. Gerber was on there because he'd served as chief of station in Moscow, and then chief of the Soviet division when the '85–'86 losses occurred. He'd been in a position to give up Gordievsky and the other two Russian intelligence officers betrayed in May 1985. He also would have been in a position to betray Tolkachev before anyone else. Not to mention he had his quirky side, which the KGB would have tried to exploit. In Moscow, he forbade station officers from dancing, deeming it lascivious behavior. Then, back at Langley, he banned men in his division from wearing pink shirts. (A Soviet division officer assured me Gerber had been joking about the pink shirts.)

Hathaway, the head of counterintelligence before Price and a former chief in Moscow who first ran Tolkachev, also had his name on the list. His access to Russian internal cases and marriage to a German wife—some accused her of having a family in East Germany—was cause enough. His plodding, almost indifferent approach to the mole hunt did nothing to ease up SIU's suspicions about him: It had almost seemed as if he was uninterested into getting to the bottom of the '85–'86 losses.

SIU gave the same consideration to the CIA's directors. But most weren't briefed in detail about Russian operations. No director, for instance, would have known anything about how the USSR Branch handled the 3×5 cards. Nor certainly would they ever have been in a position to make copies of them. Anyhow, their terms of service didn't fit the timeline of the Fourth Man's spying for the Russians.

SIU also put Ted Price on the list, as well as his predecessor in counterintelligence and former Moscow chief Jim Olson. They'd both been read into many of the compromised Russian cases. Olson was Soviet chief of operations in 1985 when Ames betrayed most of the Soviet agents. But their tenures in those positions didn't match many of the other unexplained compromises. (Of course, there was always the possibility the Russians were running more than one mole in the CIA's senior ranks, but even with SIU's darkest suspicions, it wasn't something they'd consider without good evidence for it. It left them to narrowly focus on settling on one suspect.)

SIU tried its best to avoid intuition and stick with the facts of the matrix and profile, knowing how deceiving character eccentricities and winning personalities can be. For instance, all four had liked Howard, and before he defected they thought he would have been the last one to betray his country. They knew Ames was a loser, but that alone didn't mean he was a spy. So nothing related to intuition was added to the matrix or profile. But SIU did keep what it called a "gab book"—a running list of potential vulnerabilities and character flaws they saw in their list of suspects. It would have helped if they could have cross-checked any details that mattered with security files, but they didn't have that authority.

Despite their tireless professionalism, all three women in SIU couldn't get around the fact that, to put it mildly, they weren't always impressed by their CIA bosses. One good reason is they'd had front-row seats to how their bosses had dropped the ball with Howard and Ames. The way Ames was handled particularly irked Worthen. She'd worked with him in Mexico City and recognized him for the alcoholic and terminally lazy officer he was. At the time, she knew it was an act of utter idiocy appointing him head of Soviet counterintelligence. But no one asked her. She'd flagged Ames's spending to Jeanne Vertefeuille in 1989, but because Vertefeuille had her own mole candidate instead of Ames, Worthen was ignored. It was all the more frustrating when, even as Ames moved up the mole suspect list, Bearden arranged a promotion for him. To add insult to injury, he tasked Ames with writing the worldwide cable effectively closing down spying on the KGB. To this day, Worthen is convinced the bosses failed spectacularly by not ordering a serious mole hunt in the eighties. The way she sees it, it was thanks to them that he got away with treason for nine years.

Bannerman, Worthen, and Hough were convinced the problem with their bosses boiled down to unbridled ambition and unfettered egos, alpha male case officers climbing their way up the greasy pole. They also knew the feeling was mutual, case officers looking down at them as unnecessary speed bumps to their careers. Not until Redmond's team finally caught Ames was counterintelligence considered a stepping-stone to the top. Also, a lot of the animosity had to do with a classic "field versus headquarters" syndrome—stereotyped, overly cautious nail-biters at Langley stopping the big ballers from bringing home the bacon. One chief of station who served in Eastern Europe told me he considered spy catchers "frauds" who would never stop lecturing him about surveillance even though they'd never been subject to it themselves.

Bannerman definitely had her grievances with management. When Hall let her go from counterintelligence, he hadn't bothered to explain his reasoning, let alone help her find a new position. Her best guess was it had something to do with her writing what she'd thought was a fair but mildly critical counterintelligence study of a European station years before when Hall was chief there. When Hall became her boss as head of counterintelligence, he apparently decided now was the time to act on his bleeding grudge. Not that Bannerman was much surprised. CIA station chiefs never appreciate hearing they're running sloppy operations, and especially from Langley carpetbaggers.

But it was Bearden she truly mistrusted, largely thanks to what she saw as the damage he'd done to her beloved Soviet division. When Bearden took over, she headed a small counterintelligence unit within it called Production Review Branch, or PRB for short. Contrary to its innocuous name, PRB was an indispensable part of Soviet counterintelligence because it kept the Soviet/Russia counterintelligence database. The CIA has asked me not to describe what was in this database or how it was composed, but what I can say is that it was the jewel in the crown of CIA KGB counterintelligence, irreplaceable and indispensable to the Fourth Man hunt. In short, much of the CIA's Russian counterintelligence program rested on the shoulders of Bannerman and her PRB analysts.

When the Soviet Union collapsed in 1991, the Soviet/Russia counterintelligence database initially stayed in the new Russian division. But with the political winds shifting, Bearden made noises about destroying it, reasoning that with Russia now an ally, the database was no longer needed. He apparently didn't care that it would be all but impossible to reconstruct. "Why not at least send them to archives?" Bannerman asked. As Bannerman put it: "It was clear to anyone who wasn't blind and deaf the Russians knew exactly what they were doing. They set a trap for us, and we fell for it hook, line, and sinker."

The CIA got a peek into how dismissively Russian intelligence viewed Bearden and the CIA thanks to a Russian agent providing a transcript of a meeting in Moscow between Russian intelligence officers and their CIA counterparts. As usual, nothing came of the meeting other than the perfunctory vodka toasts and empty promises of eternal friendship. But when the Americans left the room, the transcript went on to quote the Russian participants who spent the next ten minutes laughing about the naivete of Bearden and the CIA, who they saw as having no idea how Russia worked. The gist of it was: *Do these arrogant bastards really think they beat us and we're some colony meant to kiss their ass in thanks?* Of course, this tail end of the transcript was seen only by a few and not disseminated within the division.

Normally Bannerman would have kept quiet, but when the matter of the Soviet/Russia counterintelligence database came to a head, she'd had enough. At a staff meeting where Bearden said it was time to destroy it, she made it known in no uncertain terms it would be an act of sheer folly. Even if there were a change of mind down the road, she pleaded, there'd simply be no reassembling it.

She looked around the room hoping for some support, but was met with embarrassed silence. Redmond didn't say a word, even though he knew as well as Bannerman how important the database was, and he had a history of standing up to Bearden. One colleague whom she'd closely worked with for years only looked down at his shoes. Bannerman lost. When the meeting ended, she immediately ran to Jim Olson, the new head of counterintelligence, and asked him to house the Soviet/Russia counterintelligence database in his Counterintelligence Center. He agreed, which is why Bannerman followed the database there and ended up working for Olson.

Bannerman didn't like Redmond either, but in particular she didn't appreciate his hoarding of secrets. She knew that on occasion he even cut out the bosses, including Bearden. When he pulled the same thing on her, she couldn't understand why he didn't see she couldn't do her job without all the facts. She also didn't like Redmond's habit of running what she called "back pocket" agents. Like Max and Adolf, nothing related to them went in cable traffic. But the real problem was that Redmond didn't even write up memos, or even make notes from what he learned from these agents. For all she knew, Redmond had come on some gold mine that would completely change her take on a case she was working on. Along with it, Redmond couldn't be bothered to explain his thinking. To her, his approach to counterintelligence was more like one of King Arthur's errant knights on a quest than a civil servant charged with keeping a record of his activities.

The one time Bannerman worked directly with Redmond was when he asked her to evaluate a Second Chief Directorate volunteer. The case remains so sensitive that the CIA has asked me not to use his cryptonym or of course mention his name. I'll simply call him Alex. When Alex was first met in 1990, Redmond was still deputy chief of the Soviet division working for Bearden. Under normal procedures, Alex should have been at least initially met by a case officer where the first meetings took place, Berlin. But as with Redmond's other back-pocket cases, he took personal charge of Alex, dispatching Langley case officers under his direct orders to meet him in Berlin. There could have been all sorts of reasons for it—such as the Ames hunt—but what bothered Bannerman is that none of the take from Alex was ever logged into the Soviet/Russia division's counterintelligence database or even shared at all with the analysts who followed the Second Chief Directorate. The lapse was all the more befuddling since at this point the CIA still knew next to nothing about the Second. Who knows what Alex had to say about the Intelligence Section and the agents it ran outside the Soviet Union.

With Bannerman, Redmond was cagey about Alex from the start, showing her only Alex's production file, which held only the substantive parts of his debriefings. Redmond didn't give her Alex's name, position, or any other identifying details. He also didn't tell her things like Alex's motivation for volunteering to the CIA, whether for money, revenge, or ideology—all crucial in determining an agent's bona fides and the reliability of his reporting.

Another thing that bothered Bannerman about Alex was that his production file consisted of only notes and handwritten memos rather than the cables and memos that normally make up a 201 file. Accordingly, Bannerman was unsure what to make of Alex. On the face of it he seemed legitimate, but without knowing more about him she couldn't be absolutely sure he wasn't a KGB dangle.

All Bannerman could tell Redmond was that Alex's reporting tracked with that of other agents. It was good enough for Redmond, who walked out of her office grumbling a parting thanks. As she watched him disappear around a corner, Bannerman had to wonder how many other Alexes Redmond was running she didn't know about. It made her wonder if he wasn't running his own private mole hunt. She wasn't the only one to suspect that.

When Moscow chief of station David Rolph was invited to attend the first Alex debriefing in Berlin, he was just as baffled about him as was Bannerman, unable to make up his mind whether or not Alex was a bona fide KGB volunteer or a dangle. He told me it was one of the oddest volunteers he's ever run across.

Without explanation, Rolph was summoned from Moscow to Berlin, his only instructions being to make his way there by a circuitous route so the KGB couldn't track his travel. When he got to Berlin, he was directed to a hotel where a meeting was to be held with what was described as a new, unvetted Russian volunteer. Attending the meeting with him was Mike Sulick. Jeanne Vertefeuille was also there to help with the questioning. Rolph was never introduced to Alex by name.

While Sulick debriefed Alex, Vertefeuille listened into their meeting remotely from another room. She would periodically relay written questions to the debriefing room as they occurred to her. To Rolph, the questions made little sense. The same went for Alex's answers. The best he could determine was Vertefeuille's questioning had something to do with the '85–'86 compromised Russia agents. Alex wasn't particularly helpful, from what Rolph took away from the meeting. Alex also provided nothing about Russia or anything of general interest concerning the Second Chief Directorate. Rolph walked out of the meeting feeling like he'd only been invited as some sort of window dressing.

What astonished Rolph was that he'd never seen a cable or even heard about Alex until he got to the Berlin meeting. Even then, he was uncertain about the chain of acquisition, how Alex had been first met, how Langley communicated with him, or whether Alex was paid or not. He'd worked on Soviet Bloc cases for many years, but had never heard of a chief of station kept in the dark about the origins and circumstances of a case run from the country he was supposed to be in charge of. The next time he was back at Langley he asked around about Alex, but no one seemed to know anything.

On the other hand, Sandy Grimes, who helped manage Alex from headquarters, told me it wasn't all that strange the details were kept from Rolph, because at the time the CIA didn't know whether the KGB had somehow bugged Moscow station and was reading CIA cable traffic.

And unlike Grimes, neither Bannerman nor Rolph were fully read into what turned out to be the Ames hunt. If it looked to them like Redmond was up to something, perhaps it's because he was, and for good reason. Adding to the mistrust, counterintelligence analysts are convinced they need to have the full picture to do their jobs and resent getting cut out of anything. Redmond's stovepiping and the arrogance that comes with restricting access to information could only have muddied the waters all the more.

In any event, none of this—whether Bearden's kneecapping of Soviet operations, Redmond's back-pocket agents, Hall's firing of Bannerman, or whatever other inexplicable actions the SIU spy catchers witnessed over the years—makes a case for treason. But it does speak to SIU's determination to overcome their personal biases and conduct a rigorous, systematic hunt, regardless of how well they knew the suspects. Just because someone disliked pink shirts, slapped their desk with a swagger stick, or was obsessively secretive didn't make them a spy. Only in sticking with the facts as they knew them could they hope to come up with a profile that pointed to a single officer, someone with the means and opportunity to account for the unexplained compromises. For all SIU knew, the Fourth Man could be their favorite officer in the Directorate of Operations.

THIRTEEN

fact /fækt/ *n.* Something held to be self-evidently true.

Langley; November 1994

LAINE BANNERMAN LEARNED early in her career that counterintelligence isn't a fairy tale. Cinderella doesn't always make it to the ball, Beauty doesn't always fall for the Beast, and complex mole hunts plagued with thin and contradictory leads rarely get tied up with a pink bow. Minus a lazy mole like Ames leaving proof of treason in his trash and on his computer, the evidence is too often ambiguous, conflicting, and sometimes just wrong. It takes priestly nuance to make anything of the details. It's the world Angleton tried to navigate, and it eventually drove him over the edge. But it never stopped Bannerman from plowing on, letting facts take her where they would. What she counted on was that if SIU presented a thorough case, the bosses would see things the way she and SIU did, then pick up the ball and run with it—pursue a full-fledged mole hunt with all the resources and the legal authorities of the FBI backing it up.

One November morning in 1994, it all clicked for Bannerman.

Without saying a word, she walked over to SIU's two easels, one with the matrix and the other with the profile. She took one step back and turned to face Worthen and Hough, who were sitting at their desks. "Are you seeing what I'm seeing?" she asked.

Bannerman ticked off the anomalies, from the most important to the least. Max's leads still stood at the top, and in particular what he'd had to say about the 3×5 cards and the double agent's attending Directorate of Operations staff meetings. She then came to the compromises of Gordievsky, the MI6 recruit in Denmark; Bokhan, the GRU agent in Athens; and Poleshchuk, the KGB agent handled in Lagos, Nigeria. You couldn't get around the reality all three had been compromised almost a month before Ames's big dump in June 1985. From there, she ran through the compromised technical operations, plus Vasilyev, the GRU colonel in Budapest; and Chernov, the GRU officer arrested after lying dormant for so long. Those losses also couldn't be assigned to Ames or Howard, nor to the yet-to-be-identified Russian mole in the FBI—the one who would turn out to be Hanssen. Finally, there were the compromises of Tolkachev, the TASS correspondent in San Francisco, and FAREWELL, the French agent and murderer who supposedly confessed to espionage to a fellow prisoner.

Bannerman then went through the Fourth Man's profile. She or he likely had served on the Langley USSR Branch from 1984, which is the best explanation of how various classified documents mentioned by Yurchenko and a sensitive counterintelligence document from the USSR Branch made its way to Moscow. Also, anyone sitting in that position would have known the identities of Gordievsky, Bokhan, and Poleshchuk. The technical operations compromised in South America were all administered from

the USSR Branch. Max's 3×5 cards could only have been compromised by someone on the USSR Branch. The same went for
Vasilyev, whose file was transferred to the USSR Branch before he
returned to Moscow on reassignment in 1985. In short, it all kept
coming back to the USSR Branch.

Then, after the collapse of the Soviet Union, the compromises
were from Langley's Russia Group, either someone still working
there or higher up. The compromise of the probe to track down
Max in Moscow, led by Phil and Michele, was another blinking
red light. It was extremely tightly held, even in SIU only Worthen
knowing about it thanks to her having been pulled in to help run
it. But otherwise, knowledge of it was confined to a handful of
senior officers, along with the officers who flew to Moscow to conduct it.

Then there were Max and Adolf. Their descriptions of the
Fourth Man were too vague to close in on an identity, but on
the other hand they weren't contradictory—someone in the CIA
serving at Langley. The unexplained Washington starbursts and
the travel of the courier, Tsymbal, both supported that assumption. Papushin's claim about a Second Chief Directorate mole was
included in the profile, but again only as a possible explanation
for why the CIA hadn't heard more about the Fourth Man. What
it all added up to was a senior officer who'd served continuously
at Langley since the mid-eighties, had done a stint on the USSR
Branch and counterintelligence, and likely as not still active.

Bannerman hadn't really needed to go through the evidence
because everyone in the room already knew it cold. Neither
Worthen nor Hough said anything, and only nodded.

"There's an old CI rule Blee used to teach us," Bannerman told me. "When you keep turning over stones and see the same thing, it's not an accident."

Bannerman also didn't need to remind them that over the last seven months they'd whittled down the list of suspects. SIU's biases and visceral dislike aside, they had stuck with the facts and crossed off Milt Bearden's name, the bottom line being that during the critical time span covering the main compromises, he was either in Khartoum or Islamabad, then later Berlin—all places where he had no access to the compromised internal Russian cases. He also knew nothing about Phil and Michele's trip to Moscow. The evidence was also categorical that the Fourth Man had to have been assigned continuously to Langley from the mid-eighties on, which Bearden wasn't. There were dozens in the division who met this last criterion, but definitely not Bearden.

There also were too many anomalies that occurred outside Burton Gerber's time in the Soviet division to leave him on the list. Gus Hathaway's access to the post-Ames compromises didn't match the unexplained compromises. Nor did that of a number of other potential suspects who'd served in the USSR Branch and Soviet counterintelligence. By going through the bigot lists and badge table, others were eliminated. The sifting was also helped thanks to some suspects serving overseas when key compromises occurred.

At the end of it, the conclusion now rudely staring them in the face was so shocking that no one dared say out loud the name of the man who stood alone on the suspect list as by far the most plausible candidate.

What they also didn't need to be told was if the matrix and profile were right, this man was in a position high enough to betray every important secret the CIA possessed to Russian intelligence. No CIA source or undercover operative anywhere in the world would be unknown to the Russians. If SIU was right, it amounted to a monstrous breach of national security, unlike anything in American history.

At this point, one thing the three women couldn't exclude is that they'd somehow been led astray by the evidence. Part of it could have been that Max fabricated or embellished information, or, as remote a possibility as it seemed, it was an elaborate Russian intelligence disinformation campaign designed to frame one of the CIA's best. Either way, it was now definitely time to run it up the flagpole and have someone check their work.

Those attending Bannerman's briefing, along with Hough and Worthen, were the head of the Central Eurasia Division, Bill Lofgren; Paul Redmond; the FBI agent in charge of counterespionage, Ed Curran; and Ruth Olson from CIA security. Milburn was at his office at the FBI. Bannerman made sure SIU's vaulted door was closed and locked so no one would interrupt them.

Bannerman stood at the two easels and proceeded to go through the matrix point by point, starting with the 3×5 cards.

Redmond immediately objected. He said Max's reporting about the 3×5 cards shouldn't be on the matrix at all, and he wanted it taken off. Max, he said, was untrustworthy.

Redmond then objected to the "angry KGB colonel" Vasilyev as soon as Bannerman mentioned his name. "He was given up by Howard," Redmond objected. Bannerman let this go, too.

No one said anything when Bannerman went through Michele and Phil's Moscow trip.

As soon as Bannerman raised Papushin's allegation that a CIA double agent had volunteered to the Second Chief Directorate, Redmond wanted that taken off, too. Papushin, he said, had been completely discredited, and nothing he had to say was of relevance. Bannerman considered replying that per rule #9 of matrices no one outside the process should be allowed to edit the matrix, and especially delete leads. But she decided it would be best to keep moving along.

Bannerman looked at Curran. His face was expressionless. It had always been a long shot, but she'd hoped that Curran would come around to seeing the logic of the matrix, or at least at this point ask some questions demonstrating some degree of interest. But he never said a word. Her hope that the FBI would pick up the ball was quickly vanishing.

But it didn't matter; Bannerman had never backed down from a fight, and she certainly wouldn't now. She had run her investigation by the numbers and was completely confident in the matrix that came out of it.

When Bannerman came to Gordievsky and the two other compromised Soviet intelligence agents, Redmond could no longer hide his irritation. He said she was wrong: Ames had betrayed all three, period. Bannerman calmly refuted him, saying the timing simply couldn't work. She pointed out that everyone agreed Ames didn't pass their names until the June 13, 1985, meeting at Chadwicks, but these three were rolled up in May. The only plausible alternative is that someone assigned to or supervising the USSR Branch had betrayed them. Redmond snorted.

When Bannerman came to the documents from the USSR Branch, how copies of them or their summaries found their way to Moscow in 1984, Redmond looked visibly shaken. He growled, "Yurchenko said it was Howard who had compromised them."

Bannerman challenged that, too, replying that Yurchenko may have said that, but the bigot list showed Howard never had had access to them. Moreover, the documents were compromised after he was fired, not to mention he never had the opportunity to steal and pass documents to the KGB. Redmond refused to concede the point, saying Howard had somehow gotten his hands on them.

Bannerman considered bringing up a sensitive counterintelligence study held on the USSR Branch that the Russians also got their hands on (in addition to the ones Yurchenko mentioned), how the document was compromised long after Howard defected. Not to mention Ames never had access to it. But by now it was clear Redmond was growing weary of the matrix's nuanced details, and she let it drop. It was time for her coup de grâce.

As soon as Bannerman came to Max's claim the Fourth Man was a senior officer in the Directorate of Operations, Redmond leaped up, his chair skidding backward. His face was flushed and contorted in anger. He stormed to the vault door, threw it open, and was gone. It was one of those moments when you could hear the proverbial pin drop.

No one in the room said anything, but if they'd been paying attention, they understood the profile alone fit Redmond, an officer who'd been continuously assigned to Langley for the past ten years, from 1984 to 1994, and who had access to all the unexplained compromises of CIA Russian agents and technical assets during those years. Bannerman, Worthen, and Hough looked at each other. They didn't say a word, but all three were thinking the same thing: *There's our mole.*

Lofgren finally broke the silence: "Well, I guess this meeting's over."

Redmond says he does not recall any of this. Meanwhile, an FBI agent more than twenty years later would ask Bannerman, "Wouldn't the reaction of an innocent man be to order SIU to keep digging, even broaden the investigation? After all, that's exactly what Redmond's job was."

FOURTEEN

blind /blaɪnd/ *adj.* Unable to see.

Langley; June 1995

I WAS AT my desk at Langley one morning when the front office secretary called. She said the boss needed to see me right away.

Lofgren had recently taken over the Central Eurasia Division (Russia, the ex-Soviet republics, and Eastern Europe) from John MacGaffin when MacGaffin moved up to the seventh floor as associate deputy director for operations. I was in charge of South Group, which oversaw CIA operations in Central Asia and the Caucasus. I got the job because I'd served in Central Asia.

By now, what I knew about Lofgren was that he didn't suffer fools, conspiracy theories, or for that matter any bullshit at all. Like me, he'd spent a long career on the world's ragged political edge. He'd fled Beirut one step ahead of assassins, then an unrelated terrorist group targeted him during a posting to Manila. He'd been pitched by the KGB in New Delhi. I'm not sure if any of this had anything to do with it, but Lofgren took his authority seriously and felt obligated to exercise it. Coupled with a notoriously bad temper, it was a combustible mix.

I'll never forget one morning when I showed him an interview the CIA director had just given to the *New York Times Magazine*. It was bad enough the writer took a chicken-shit swipe at the CIA, but when Lofgren came to the part where the director said something about military officers standing head and shoulders above the CIA's, he growled that a general never blames his troops for losing the battle. He stormed back to his office and slammed the door so hard the walls up and down the front office enfilade shuddered. He proceeded to pound out a cable to all his field stations and bases to the effect of: *The director is an ambitious ass and pay no attention to what he said about you.* As it turned out, the director respected—or feared—Lofgren too much to fire him.

That morning, without bothering to ask me to sit down, Lofgren said there'd be three people coming to work for me, at least for a while. Considering South Group was an understaffed backwater, I didn't see why not. And in those days, CIA operations divisions were run along the lines of medieval fiefdoms, where the lord of the castle got to call all the shots. Which meant I wasn't about to say no.

I was about to leave when he stopped me. "There's one other thing. All three'll be working on a special project for me. I can't tell you what it is, so don't bother asking."

That's flat-out nuts, I thought as I walked out of Lofgren's office. In all my time in the Central Intelligence Agency, I'd never heard—never once—about a supervisor not knowing what his subordinates were working on. Maybe I was just naive, but then again the times were decidedly strange. There'd been the murder of my boss in 1993 in the Soviet Republic of Georgia, and then the Ames arrest in 1994. But more than anything, I'd been in the CIA too long to be surprised by anything. Serving back at Langley for who could say how long after years abroad, I started to wonder what I was doing drifting into middle age in a rudderless, stultifying intelligence bureaucracy. Espionage had lost its mystique, for me at least. Counterterrorism had definitely come into its own; it's all I did when assigned to places like Beirut. But to my tastes, it didn't hold a candle to the KGB versus CIA stuff. Part of it, I think, had to do with the simple fact that Moscow pointed nukes at us and the terrorists didn't. But more had to do with the Graham Greene cloak-and-dagger intrigue of it all, the Great Game played out in the foggy alleys of Berlin and Vienna. Not that I'd ever been a varsity player in it; I missed the Cold War.

The three graying women who showed up for work in Lofgren's division one June morning were in their fifties, prim, dressed in conservative pantsuits and comfortable flats. I'd seen enough of their type to know the only thing in their lives was the CIA. When still on good terms with them, Bearden called them his Rosie the Riveters, those fiercely industrious and single-minded women of World War II fame. Only one of them in the end would come to work for me, while the others Lofgren placed in other parts of his division. The one who did, Laine Bannerman, I assigned to a floating position until a country desk opened up for her.

Bannerman quietly went about her job as efficiently and thoroughly as I'd expected. One morning I tried to lighten things up. "So what are you in for?" I said. She answered me with an illegible smile. I read it to mean she was resigned to being rusticated to my little backwater. We didn't have much to talk about, but we got along just fine. I'm sure inasmuch as she trusted me it was because, per Lofgren's instructions, I never brought up the "special project." I know trust is a hard thing to win with an endemically suspicious crew like Bannerman's, but I'm pretty sure whatever trust I earned is the reason that twenty-five years later I was allowed a peek into their world, and I'm now able to tell this whole story.

After a couple of months, I wondered why I never caught Bannerman working on Lofgren's project. What I did notice was Bannerman and her two compatriots would meet up in the bullpen just outside my office, then go outside the building to talk. One time I caught them on a bench in the middle of some sort of pow-wow. They stopped talking as I passed. I could have been reading too much into it, but it looked like they were holding a hush-hush, special project staff meeting. But that wasn't the end of it.

The gloomy, windowless vaulted area with drab cream walls South Group inhabited was served by a single reinforced steel door. The first person to work in the morning opened the spin-dial combination, recorded the time and date of opening on a sheet of paper, and jotted down their initials. They then called security to say they'd just opened the door, reading aloud their badge number to verify they were who they claimed to be. It was the same shtick at the end of the day when the last person out closed up for the night.

It wasn't something I normally checked, but one day I decided to examine the spin-dial lock log. Looking over the last month, I could see Bannerman had been in on weekends. One thing I knew for sure was she wasn't working on my group's stuff on her days off. Nothing we were doing could justify that amount of time. I decided it had to be something to do with Lofgren's project.

Then one day I caught Bannerman putting away in her safe a GRiD laptop like the ones case officers in the field used to cable in reporting from sensitive agents. I'd worked off a GRiD in Central Asia and knew they were standard in "denied areas"—places like Moscow or Beijing where the secret police take an acute interest in what the CIA's up to—but I'd never seen one used inside headquarters. Was someone afraid the Russians or Chinese had installed intercept equipment inside Langley?

I had no way to connect the next incident to Lofgren's project other than a hunch. But a couple of weeks after I caught Bannerman with her GRiD, I came into work early one day to find a colleague's office across the hall yellow-taped, an FBI crime scene. *This is a goddamned federal building*, I thought. I had no idea what to make of it. Other than it was another bright shining WTF in my otherwise uneventful and placid existence as a mid-level bureaucrat marking time at Langley. Apparently, while I was away overseas, someone had switched out the rule book.

I didn't know much about my colleague under FBI scrutiny other than that he'd served in Moscow before getting reassigned back to Langley, where he, like me, was doing his penance waiting for his next overseas assignment. (Any CIA case officer worth their salt wants to work overseas running agents.) I checked around to see if anyone knew what was going on, but no one had a clue. Nor did anyone know where they'd taken him. All they could tell me was that FBI agents were still in his office going through it with rubber gloves and crime-scene cameras.

I never would see my unfortunate colleague again, and heard nothing about him until many years later when I was told he'd gotten into a legal beef with the CIA. As I remember it, it didn't have anything to do with Russia, but the FBI investigation couldn't have helped his cause. And as I'd soon find out, he was only the tip of the iceberg.

Unlike Price and Redmond, I had no idea why FBI agents were swarming the building, but obviously it had something to do with Ames. The White House, for one, wanted answers to how the CIA had so badly screwed up with him. It, too, could only have been struck by the picture of Ames cuffed next to his Jaguar. (By the way, I'd hazard a guess it was the FBI who made sure that iconic moment was splashed across the press in pursuit of its age-old rivalry with the CIA, which goes back to 1947 when the CIA was founded over J. Edgar Hoover's strong dissent.) Everyone knew the CIA needed a good housecleaning, and the FBI was the one to do it. Nothing like a legal whip to put the fear of God into a bureaucracy.

It's no surprise the FBI arrived at Langley with its all too pre-dictable institutional biases. It was a lot like the Second Chief Directorate's distrust of the First. In the eyes of the FBI, CIA case officers drank too much, had too many foreign girlfriends, and put on cosmopolitan airs, among all their other moral failings, real and imagined. In one notorious incident, the chief of station in Kabul swapped wives with a French academic, profoundly offending the Afghans and just about everyone else. But at the bottom of it, the FBI thought it should be the organization collecting foreign intel-ligence. Or at least that's the case J. Edgar Hoover tried to make.

Nothing was ever made official, but we kept hearing about dozens of officers put on ice. By some accounts—and I was sure they had to be wildly exaggerated—the number was in the hun-dreds. Hallway chatter had it they'd been tripped up in polygraphs thanks to one indiscretion or another, like shoplifting or keeping a Russian chorus girl on the side. But there seemed to be more to it, some sort of Augean cleaning of the stables.

What we didn't need to be told is that anyone under even routine FBI investigation was screwed. These poor bastards now had an indelible scarlet letter etched deep in the middle of their foreheads, and little doubt for the rest of their spy lives. They were sent off to the CIA's version of a gulag, a soul-crushing office park near Tysons Corner, the "holding pens" I mentioned earlier. Their security clearances pulled, they were doomed to spend their days reading newspapers, doing crossword puzzles, and ordering out for pizza. No one dared call them, even to say hi. Or, for that matter, even ask after them. I wasn't around in Angleton's time, but I suspect it must have been about the same.

Trust me: For a spook, getting cut off from all secrets and purpose amounts to a miserable purgatory unimaginable for someone who has never worked in intelligence. It must also seem odd to an outsider that no one in those days even attempted to seek an explanation for their banishment. But the fear was that in showing any curiosity, you'd be on the next shuttle bus to the Tysons Corner gulag—on a one-way trip.

Although my job had nothing to do with Russian counterintelligence, like my colleagues I could only conclude that given Ames's arrest and the FBI's invasion of Langley, all this spooky stuff going on around me had something to do with a new Russian mole hunt. What else were we to think after Ames? I'd never been the victim of a mole hunt (that I know of), but I can tell you there's nothing like an old-fashioned CIA witch ducking to fan the flames of a tribe already gripped by blinding paranoia. So hell if I was going to stick my nose into it.

What I absolutely didn't know until now—and definitely wouldn't have wanted to—is that Bannerman and company were at least indirectly responsible for the holding pens and the yellow taping of my colleague's office. Nor would I ever have suspected that Bannerman was in the middle of a battle royal with someone I considered a CIA legend or that she was at the dead center of the most secretive mole hunt in history. Nor that her hunt was now hidden from CIA counterintelligence and the FBI as well. It was more off the books than even Redmond's private mole hunt, whatever that was. In fact, it was completely unsanctioned, other than by Lofgren.

After Bannerman's briefing-turned-confrontation in November, things quickly got ugly. As Bannerman now believes, at the start of Price's investigation Redmond initially hadn't seen her and SIU as a threat. But as soon as he understood that the matrix and the profile pointed at him—and they weren't going to back down—Bannerman and her colleagues believed he panicked. He very well might have worried Curran might take the matrix and profile seriously, and maybe even put Redmond under an aggressive FBI investigation. After all, that's how it was supposed to work with this kind of investigation. As they saw it, there could be no other explanation for the reprisals taken against them. Whether Redmond was truly guilty of spying for the Russians, worried he was a victim of Russian framing, or merely concerned the whole thing might tarnish his reputation, he launched what looked to them like a scorched-earth counteroffensive.

The first sign came when Milburn was yanked out from under Bannerman's authority, depriving SIU of all FBI input into its investigation—information like the dates of starbursts, what new FBI sources had to say about Russian double agents in the CIA, and the catalogue of unique FBI compromises that couldn't be attributed to Howard or Ames. As Bannerman would bitterly complain, "Had Milburn stayed we would have caught the Fourth Man." (What she wouldn't know until years later is that in pulling out Milburn, the unmasking of Hanssen was delayed by nearly seven years.) While none of the FBI side of the investigation was vital for nailing the Fourth Man, it did help substantiate evidence the CIA already possessed that there were Russian double agents in American intelligence.

Seeing the writing on the wall, Milburn did what he could. He couldn't do anything about Redmond, no matter what his suspicions were. Even if he suspected Redmond, he didn't have the clout at the FBI to force an investigation. So he preserved what he could of the investigation. He ripped the sheets outlining the matrix and profile off the easels, rolled them up, and drove them right to the FBI Washington field office at Buzzard Point.

It was a savvy move. One Monday morning shortly before Christmas 1994 Bannerman came into the office to find out that over the weekend Curran's people had let themselves into SIU's office and seized all of its paper files. (She never found out if it had been FBI agents or Curran's CIA subordinates who'd done the job.) There was no way to know for sure, but she could only assume Redmond was behind the raid. Who else could have been?

According to Redmond, it was in fact the FBI. He told me what occurred was that as soon as the FBI heard about the Fourth Man investigation, it came "roaring in" and hijacked it. There was nothing he could do about it since it was now a criminal matter.

Since Bannerman stood her ground with the FBI, refusing to allow it to more widely expose the CIA's sensitive Russian agents within the FBI, he was forced to replace her with Mary Sommer, a CIA analyst. (I was never able to reach Ed Curran to get his take or obtain a comment from the FBI. But I was assured by many CIA senior officers that the FBI never had the authority to take over an internal CIA investigation.)

Either way, Bannerman now understood SIU's investigation had been sidelined. And little doubt it was soon to be completely out of business. But that wasn't all that bothered her. As she feared, with the Fourth Man investigation snatched out of SIU's hands and put directly into those of Redmond and Curran, the FBI was given unfettered access to SIU's sensitive files, and most importantly Max's. Whereas previously no more than about two dozen at the CIA and FBI were aware of his existence and allegations about double agents, now hundreds of FBI agents and field offices across the country working in counterintelligence were read into Max's intelligence. If the suspected FBI traitor didn't know about Max already, as Bannerman feared, he certainly would now—and soon after, his Russian handlers. She turned out to be right.

Bannerman had spent a long career doing everything possible to limit knowledge of agents to the fewest people possible. It was expressly done to protect them from the likes of another Ames. The system wasn't perfect, but it had worked as intended. Now in one fell swoop it was all unraveled; it was heart-wrenching for her. There was nothing she could do about it other than appeal to a higher authority in hopes of getting someone to take one more look at SIU's investigation. If she failed to get it reopened, she knew she'd pay for it in spades, but that wasn't going to stop her.

At the November briefing, Bannerman had shot off her ammunition, and the target was unmarked. No one asked explicitly if the profile described Redmond, no one asked for a follow-up briefing, no one for that matter had any questions at all for her. It was extraordinary; an official, expert-led investigation had all but called a senior officer a Russian mole to his face, and seemingly no one but him flinched.

Bannerman's only choice now was to take it up the line to Price, the man who'd ordered the investigation. There was one little problem, though: Redmond and Curran insisted Cindy Webb, a Redmond protégée, attend the briefing. A Directorate of Intelligence analyst, Webb had come over to counterintelligence as part of the CIA's grand strategy of putting analysts and operators in the same room, hoping the "synergy" would produce better intelligence. Never mind that Webb had no background in counterintelligence nor in running agents. It didn't bode well for Bannerman.

At the briefing with Price in early January 1995, Webb started off. However, Price quickly interrupted her: "I want to hear it from Laine."

As soon as Bannerman dove into the gritty details of the matrix and the profile, Price understood that more time would be needed and stopped the briefing. He asked Bannerman to come back the next morning at six. He added that Bannerman should come alone. Webb couldn't hide her outrage at the snub and stormed out of the office without saying a word.

Bannerman showed up the next day, five minutes before six. For the next three hours, she walked Price through the matrix and the profile. He was familiar with all the agents, including

Max, and the compromises not explained by Howard and Ames. He asked a lot of questions, but made no comments. He seemed to quickly catch how rigorous SIU's investigation had been, how it had nothing to do with intuition or precooked conclusions. He also understood that it didn't prove the guilt or innocence of anyone. Redmond's name was never mentioned, but it was clear that Price understood he alone fit the profile SIU had constructed. Bannerman's briefing went on for three hours. It's unheard of for a director of operations to spend that much time on a single topic. Price only stopped it when his secretary stuck her head in the door to let him know his nine o'clock staff meeting was about to begin.

As Bannerman walked out of the office, she knew that unless Price stepped in to protect her, she didn't have a shadow of a doubt Redmond would come after her with a hatchet. She wasn't scared, just fatalistic.

FIFTEEN

re·venge /rɪˈvɛndʒ/ *n.* Striking back at someone in response
to a real or imagined injury.

Langley; January–June 1995

THE THREE WOMEN were convinced that Redmond, had it
been within his authority, would have summarily fired them.

Bannerman, for one, learned at an early age about the treach-
eries of CIA power politics. Her father's career came to an abrupt,
early end when the wife of CIA director Richard Helms asked
him to spy on her husband because she believed he was having an
affair. She expected Bannerman's father to have Helms's security
detail supply her with proof of it. Bannerman's father said no, but
the whole thing somehow got back to Helms. As these things so
often go, Helms took care of the problem by getting rid of Bannerman's father.

Instead, it appeared to them that Redmond had launched a
war of attrition against the three women. It looked like one of his
first moves was to enlist Curran and the FBI to his side. Curran,
already skeptical about Bannerman and SIU, wasn't a hard sell.

The first step Curran took was to order FBI polygraphs of Bannerman, Worthen, and Hough. They were single-issue polygraphs: *Are you a KGB spy?* The polygraphs were described to them as routine, but all three knew better.

Any doubts about how serious things had become vanished when Curran ran across Bannerman in the hall shortly before the polygraph. He barked at her: "If it turns out you're the mole, I'll kill you." It was clear he'd meant it metaphorically, but it's not the kind of threat you want to hear come out of an FBI agent's mouth.

All three passed their polygraphs, and lucky for them, because if they hadn't, they could have been charged with perjury. This small victory aside, they now knew that the shoe was on the other foot. They were the pursued rather than the pursuers.

It wasn't as if Redmond made any bones about his dislike of them. He'd come across them in the hallway and sneer, under his breath but loud enough for them to hear, "Fucking bitches." Not that he was circumspect about it. At an office party for Corbin's retirement, Redmond walked past Worthen, again calling her a "fucking bitch" loud enough for those around them to hear. Worthen was flabbergasted. "Say that again," she said, "and you'll hear about it from the seventh floor." Knowing it was a hollow threat, Redmond just smiled and made the rounds of the party. Granted, this type of behavior was in keeping with Redmond's gruff personality. Yet Worthen interpreted it as Redmond in effect telling her and everyone in earshot he was untouchable.

All three were pried out of counterintelligence in stages, they could only assume at Redmond's behest. It had started with the FBI seizing SIU's files, leaving them with nothing to do other than review whatever evidence and analysis was in their computers. They sat in the SIU vault for months doing nothing. Then one morning, with no warning, Curran sat down at the counterespionage daily staff meeting and announced there would be "a change of management" at SIU. He didn't even look over at Bannerman. Cindy Webb would be overseeing it, he said, and a new SIU head would be appointed. Bannerman, Worthen, and Hough were moved to a bullpen with about fifty analysts in rows of cubicles. They were seated at the very end of it, the farthest reach from the front office suite. Their new duties were to review old files that had nothing to do with Russia or the KGB. Stultifying make-work, they couldn't miss the message: They were done in counterintelligence.

Bannerman also had to wonder how long before it would be before Redmond would sic the Office of Security on her, as he had on Ames. She had nothing to hide, but it would mean an intrusive background investigation and another polygraph examination, this time from the CIA rather than the FBI. If Redmond were to mislead the polygrapher—lie that Bannerman was definitely guilty but polygraphic proof was needed—it very easily could have gone very badly, with the slightest blip on the chart registered as a deception. Then chances were good she might spend what was left of her career in a Tysons Corner holding pen.

Redmond's attack, however, came from a different direction.

In May 1995, a secretary in Price's office appeared one morning at Bannerman's cubicle with a sealed manila envelope. She left it with Bannerman without saying a word. When Bannerman opened it, she found a half-dozen memos written by Redmond to Price accusing Bannerman and Worthen of withholding evidence from the FBI related to the Fourth Man investigation.

Redmond recommended that Price immediately conduct an investigation. Looking at the dates of the memos, Bannerman noted that Redmond had written them shortly after the November 1994 confrontation, and as framed they represented a potential felony—obstruction of justice. Bannerman didn't need to be told that had Price chosen to, he could have referred the matter to the Department of Justice for prosecution.

As Bannerman read through the memos, she now finally understood why Curran and Cindy Webb had stopped returning her phone calls and gave her only an ice-cold nod in the hallways. Although they hadn't been the recipients of Redmond's memos, they almost certainly had heard about Redmond's accusations. Curran later described his feelings toward Bannerman: "[She was] very protective of the CIA. She thought she was in charge and would decide what the FBI got. We had to resolve that right away. We immediately had conflicts. She's trying to protect the agency's jewels, and we're trying to investigate."

With a potential criminal charge like this hanging over Bannerman's head, Curran didn't have the authority to sit down Bannerman and get her side of the story. If the charge was taken seriously, someone else in the FBI would have to investigate it. The only thing Curran could do was give her wide berth, which is exactly what he did.

Bannerman suspected that Redmond had misled Curran into believing Max's reporting had been deliberately withheld from him. It's complicated, but the way Max's reporting was processed was that after a meeting with Max, the case officer would travel back to Washington, then turn over a tape recording from the meeting to a translator to transcribe onto hard copy. The transcript was then sent to Lofgren, the chief of the division overseeing Russia (CE), who then would approve sending it to counterintelligence and the FBI. Needless to say, this process took time. If Lofgren were on a trip, even longer. Unless someone had walked Curran through the process, it's easy to see how he easily could have been misled into believing Bannerman was guilty as Redmond charged.

Fortunately, Price had chosen not to forward Redmond's referral to Justice. She now had the only copy of Redmond's memos, which she shredded. Bannerman had no doubt what a close call it was: If Justice had gotten its hands on it, who knows whether or not it would have pursued a federal indictment. With the CIA in such bad odor with federal law enforcement, it wasn't beyond the realm of possibility. An internal investigation would capsize her career, but with this one, her freedom could have been in the balance.

Now, Bannerman could only fear what would come next. A few evenings, after leaving work, she was all but sure she'd caught surveillance, a pair of cars hanging back at relatively low speed to keep pace with her. She knew the Counterintelligence Center ran surveillance teams inside American borders, usually to follow CIA employees under investigation. But since the cars weren't right on her, then dropped off, she couldn't be sure her fear of Redmond hadn't driven her into a state of paranoia. In any case, there was no way she could bring this up with CIA security, which would dismiss it out of hand. Hough, too, was sure she had surveillance, but decided there was nothing she could do about it, either.

Things went beyond strange when one evening Bannerman came home to find her two large dogs unusually agitated. Her first thought was that there'd been a robbery attempt while she was at work. She put it out of her mind until the next day when an FBI agent phoned her to ask if he could come over and ask her a few questions about the boss of Russia Group. She said fine, but when the FBI agent asked her to keep her dogs under control when he got there, she had to ask herself how the FBI even knew about her dogs. Had the FBI paid a visit to her house when she wasn't there? It's another thing she couldn't bring herself to seriously believe, but it fleetingly crossed her mind that the FBI might have attempted a black bag job, only the dogs encouraged them to change their minds.

Things went from bad to hopeless when Price, abruptly and without ceremony, retired in May 1995. When any deputy director of operations retires, he normally makes the rounds around the building saying goodbye, offering what a pleasure it had been to serve together and promises to keep in touch. But Price was there one day, gone the next. He'd never called Bannerman for a follow-up on her January one-on-one briefing. It was a wasted thought, but she had to wonder if Redmond hadn't somehow been instrumental in forcing Price out. There was zero evidence for it, she knew, but with everything that had happened over the past eight months, it would cross anyone's mind.

Now, with Price gone, she knew the three of them were cut adrift with no patron. She was almost certain it wouldn't be long before the Office of Security was knocking at her door. They'd have no clue about the bad blood between her and Redmond—it was too sensitive to ever read them into the SIU investigation—and there'd be no point in trying to explain. Fear isn't the word to describe what Bannerman felt, but something closer to utter powerlessness, at the mercy of an opaque system.

One morning Worthen was standing at her cubicle. "Let's see if we can't get jobs in CE," she said without any prelude. Lofgren, she reminded Bannerman, had thought Redmond's reaction was telling of something when he went into meltdown at the November 1994 briefing. Lofgren may not have completely grasped the implications of the matrix, but his witness to Redmond's bizarre reaction would at least earn them a hearing. Bannerman didn't think twice. "No hurt in trying."

Worthen showed up at Lofgren's office the next morning at six thirty. She closed the door and sat down on the sofa facing his desk. As soon as she said the three of them needed jobs, explaining that they were all but certain Redmond was after them, he didn't think twice. He picked up his phone to call his division's personnel office.

It was the first good news they'd had in a long time. Worthen, Hough, and Bannerman met up at Bannerman's house that night for a glass of wine to celebrate. They knew Redmond didn't have the clout or courage to try to get through Lofgren to get to them. For now, they were safe. As importantly, they had the breathing room to pick back up the investigation.

SIXTEEN

coun·ter·at·tack /ˈkaʊn tər əˌtæk / n. Responding to one act
of aggression with another.

Langley; June 1995

WITH THE UNLICENSED SIU Fourth Man investigation now
embedded deep in Lofgren's division—and operating right under
my clueless nose—the only thing to do was get back to work. The
three women may have been driven from the field of battle, but it
didn't mean they didn't know how to fight a guerrilla campaign.
They started by reconstructing the matrix from memory. More
importantly, they now had access to Russia Group's files, where
they came across more than a few gems.

More than anything, though, they still hoped Max or another
Russian spy would come along to provide a key piece of evidence
either against Redmond—or, if not him, the real Fourth Man.
They did not buy the possibility Redmond had been framed by
the Russians, because they didn't think the Russians were that
good. Their problem was that the evidence against Redmond was

still far from airtight. It would have to get materially better than what they presented in November 1994.

In the meantime, they started to compose on a GRiD what they called the "in-case memo." It amounted to a summary of all the evidence they had against Redmond, plus what they were now assembling. The name was a reference to the possibility that a piece of evidence—tomorrow, next year, in a decade—might come across the transom that would make their case. For security, they kept only one copy of it, saved on a GRiD stored in Bannerman's safe. Since only she knew the combination, the Office of Security would have had to open it with a blowtorch to get their hands on the memo.

One central part of the in-case memo was a record of how they believed Redmond had attempted to undermine SIU's investigation. For instance, every time SIU would send the matrix up to Redmond's office for review, someone there would edit out references to the 3×5 cards and the double agent attending division chief meetings. Each time it happened, SIU would put both references back on the matrix. But off they would come again. The only explanation they ever got was at the November confrontation when Redmond claimed Max was unreliable.

This is not what SIU believed. Throughout the investigation, they remained convinced that although the CIA couldn't control him, Max was a bona fide agent who volunteered to the CIA of his own free will. The Caracas lead trumped all suspicions about him. SIU didn't entirely dismiss the possibility the KGB had sacrificed Ames to divert attention from the Fourth Man—that Max was some sort of unwitting vehicle for this—but without any evidence, it barely made it to the matrix as a footnote. And SIU couldn't exclude the possibility that Redmond knew something about Max they didn't; for instance, maybe he'd found out Max had fallen under Russian control. But if that were true, there was no earthly explanation why SIU hadn't been informed about it. In either event, according to the rigorous rules by which SIU conducted its investigation, no evidence is ever discarded, no matter what someone's suspicions are about it, and an outsider to a mole hunt should never be allowed to edit a matrix.

Someone in Redmond's office also had regularly removed references to Papushin from the matrix, along with the possibility the Second Chief Directorate was running agents in the United States. No explanation was offered for this, either. Curious, Bannerman went back to the archives to see if there might be something to explain it. There'd been the strange case of Alex, the Second Chief Directorate volunteer whom Redmond ran as one of his back-pocket agents. Why, the SIU-in-exile had to ask, was the Second Chief Directorate such a touchy subject for him?

Whatever Redmond's motivation for assuming personal control of the Alex case, the three women saw it as part of a pattern of running off-the-books Soviet counterintelligence operations. In 1986, someone claiming to be a Second Chief Directorate operative dropped an envelope in a case officer's mailbox in Bonn, West Germany. Not knowing his name, the CIA referred to the anonymous letter writer as Mr. X. The first letter was followed by five more. The gist of the mysterious KGB volunteer's message was to blame a CIA communications breach for the '85–'86 losses of Soviet agents. Eventually, the letter writer would falsely accuse a CIA case officer named Chuck Leven of being a double agent.

Normally with an approach like this, an officer in field would manage the case. But when it was thought Mr. X might surface, Redmond himself flew to Germany to make the meeting. For some reason, he took a taxi halfway across the country to get to Bonn. As it turned out, Mr. X never showed, and it was eventually determined that he was a dangle intended to throw Langley off the Ames scent. All the same, the question at Langley was what had gone through Redmond's mind to make him believe he had to be the one to talk to Mr. X rather than a Bonn-based case officer. It was all the stranger because, for the levelheaded at Langley, Mr. X looked like a clumsy KGB provocation. (When an agent refuses to provide hard, verifiable intelligence and won't meet face-to-face, they almost invariably are.)

Fitting the same pattern of treating the Second Chief Directorate differently from the rest of the KGB, Bannerman pieced together that when Redmond headed the USSR Branch and later counterintelligence in the Soviet division, he as a matter of course turned away Second Chief Directorate walk-ins, not even giving them a hearing. One of the defectors turned to the French and would become an extremely valuable source. Another just disappeared. On top of that, it was suspicious that mention of these cases had never made it into the Soviet/Russia counterintelligence database (as Alex didn't). Bannerman didn't know if it was Redmond's doing, but she suspected it was. She had to ask herself why he so consistently either rejected volunteers from the Second or made sure what they had to report was funneled through him and kept out of counterintelligence databases. He didn't do this with the Third Directorate or any other directorate, so why the Second?

Just as intriguingly, she recalled that Redmond had refused to

incorporate the Mitrokhin Archive—documents smuggled out by
a KGB archivist—into counterintelligence databases. After he was
turned away by Bearden, Mitrokhin defected to MI6 in Riga and
brought with him six trunks of notes copied from KGB records.
The notes turned out to be a gold mine, leading to the identifica-
tion of numerous KGB agents and operations around the world.
In spite of the obvious use for counterintelligence analysts, Redmond refused to allow Mitrokhin's notes from being entered into
any database. When asked why, Redmond said it was because MI6
asked that they not be. As Bannerman later learned, however, one
person at MI6 disputed this. It was a shot in the dark, but Bannerman wondered if Redmond was worried that Mitrokhin might
have identified KGB couriers—"agents of the route"—traveling to
the United States to service Second Chief Directorate–recruited
agents.

Another odd case involving Redmond occurred after the 1989
Velvet Revolution in Czechoslovakia. One day, the head of the
Czech intelligence service called his CIA contact to ask why the
CIA had arranged to meet Karl Koecher, a former Czech intelligence officer, in Germany. He asked why the CIA hadn't simply
asked him to arrange a meeting with Koecher in Prague. Embarrassed, the CIA officer said he knew nothing about it but would
check with Langley.

Koecher had immigrated to the United States in 1965 posing
as a dissident. In 1973, the CIA hired him as a linguist, of course
having no idea he'd worked for Czech intelligence—and still did.
In the course of his CIA employment, Koecher betrayed numerous CIA operations to the KGB via the Czechs, including a Soviet
diplomat spying for the CIA, Aleksandr Dmitrievich Ogorodnik,

who inside the CIA was known as TRIGON. Koecher was eventually arrested by the FBI for spying, then traded with the Russians on Berlin's famous Bridge of Spies in 1986 for Natan Sharansky, among others. He returned to Czechoslovakia a minor celebrity.

Perplexed why Langley would have met with a notorious spy, the CIA officer wrote a cable back to Langley asking if anyone had met Koecher in Germany. Rather than writing back, Redmond called the officer on a secure line and told him that yes, one of his people had met Koecher, but he couldn't put in writing what the meeting had been about. He would explain when the officer was next back at Langley. When he did run into Redmond on his first trip back, all Redmond would say was that the Koecher meeting was part of a mole hunt.

Another thing they included in the in-case memo was the number of times Redmond had driven out to Dulles International Airport in Northern Virginia to meet case officers returning from meeting Russian agents. He'd done so with Adolf, the Line KR officer who reported the mysterious travel of Tsymbal and the existence of two double agents in American intelligence. After transferring from New York to Moscow, Adolf was met there by Mike Sulick, the station chief. Because Adolf was a sensitive source, Sulick would fly back to Washington to relay his Adolf reports. Although Adolf was a Russian case rather than counterintelligence's, Redmond would drive out to Dulles and intercept Sulick gate side, then grill him on the drive back to Langley.

On another occasion, Redmond drove out to Dulles to meet an officer from Athens who'd just gotten a dump of documents from a Russian intelligence agent met there. Redmond never said, and no one ever asked him, why he thought it necessary to take the trouble to drive out to Dulles. It struck people as particularly odd because it's an almost unheard of practice for a senior officer. Moreover, there was nothing the agent had reported in Athens of any counterintelligence interest. Bannerman's suspicions now in high gear, she had to wonder if it was because Redmond had been assigned to Athens in the eighties around the time Bokhan was met there. Was he worried the Russian had something to say about Redmond's tour there? As Bannerman knew, suspicions counted for little and it wasn't worth giving much thought.

Bannerman also discovered Redmond had a history of short-circuiting the CIA's recordkeeping system, never checking out files or conducting traces in his own name. Although he was on the "badge table" and could check out any file he wanted, he always instructed a subordinate do it. Whatever his justification was, it's highly unorthodox, if not unheard of, for someone in counterintelligence as it undermines the principle behind bigot lists and other recordkeeping procedures. Even if he thought he was above grunt work like ordering up files himself, it was inexcusable, because he knew mole hunts depend on complete and accurate recordkeeping. Bannerman asked herself, *Why would he do it unless he has something to hide?*

However, it bears mentioning that throughout this period of apparently suspicious behavior, Redmond *was* hiding something: the Ames hunt. Though Bannerman and her colleagues believed counterintelligence could only be done by following strict, tried-and-true protocols, it's not unreasonable to consider Redmond decided to cut more than a few corners to preserve the integrity of the Ames hunt. What looked from the outside like underhanded and self-serving acts might after all have been the result of spending so many years hunting double agents that he ended up trusting no one other than himself. Still, the Ames hunt was part of what troubled SIU, and in particular the dumbfounding oversights committed by the Ames investigators, ones Redmond ignored. Most importantly, he should have thrown a red flag on Gordievsky and the other two Soviets compromised in May 1985, acknowledging the timing of their compromises wasn't consistent with Ames's statement that he hadn't betrayed them until June 13, 1985. *How could the leader of the investigation,* SIU wondered, *have missed a bright shining clue like this?* (While he helped set up SIU's Fourth Man investigation, which investigated loose ends like these, to this day he stubbornly remains convinced Ames gave up those agents, despite believing there may have been a Fourth Man.)

Similarly, Redmond never raised a doubt with Bannerman's SIU about the compromises of FBI telephone taps and bugs that neither Howard nor Ames knew about. Bannerman also had a problem with Redmond's approach to the Ames hunt, especially the way he relied on intuition rather than evidence. During the Ames hunt, he, Jeanne Vertefeuille, Jim Olson, and the others voted on their favorite suspect, basically turning the investigation into an unpopularity contest. No one for a moment stopped to consider that a tactic like this would be guaranteed to overlook compromises Ames couldn't have been responsible for, or the possibility there'd been two double agents in CIA Soviet operations. Redmond definitely should have known better, Bannerman was convinced, but for some reason he let it go. Just as he hadn't objected to Bearden ordering the destruction of the Soviet/Russia division's counterintelligence database. Bannerman had to wonder whether leaving the spotlight solely on Ames wasn't his intention all along, to make sure no one looked anywhere else.

Everyone I've talked to agrees the Ames hunt was deliberately run along the lines of a blinkered legal prosecution rather than a proper counterintelligence investigation, omitting obvious contradictions and doubts in order to strengthen the case against Ames. It's ironic, given that Redmond, who sat on the Hanssen Damage Assessment Team said it was crystal clear to him the FBI deliberately led Hanssen in the questioning in an attempt to minimize the damage Hanssen had caused. For the FBI, it's standard practice, known as a "selective intelligence investigation," to expedite an investigation by focusing on its best, most compelling evidence rather than getting hung up by potentially exculpatory facts. The motivation is to arrive at a confession and plea deal as quickly as possible rather than producing a complete and detailed account of an espionage case. The senior Directorate of Operations representative on the Ames Damage Assessment Team told me no one who objectively looked at the evidence believed for a moment Ames first betrayed Gordievsky and the other two. He added that when years later he went back and reread the report, he recognized it for the "crummy damage assessment" it was. Gordievsky and the other two should have been clearly flagged as unexplained compromises. But, as he told me, there'd been implicit pressure "to posit all the compromises" on Ames. "You simply couldn't win," he said. When he privately approached Redmond about it, Redmond was forced to agree, saying to him more than once, "We didn't catch them all." But Redmond didn't care to explain his suspicions or why he hadn't acted on them.

For the SIU-in-exile, the list kept getting longer. Another

thing Redmond never did was take a serious look at was what cases survived Ames and why. For instance, in the early nineties the FBI had recruited the Washington KGB deputy rezident, but made the decision not to inform the CIA, including Redmond. Was that the reason the agent was never compromised? They came across other anomalies like this, but without being in contact with the FBI, there was no way for them to put them in context. They could only note them in the in-case memo.

Bannerman had no illusions that any of this, even added up and put in the worst light, constituted evidence of espionage. But she held on to her hope that one day it would all come together when the right Russian volunteer showed up, one who knew enough about the Fourth Man to identify him. Until then, all she, Worthen, and Hough could do was assemble their case and wait.

Bannerman would eventually find her footing when Lofgren moved her from South Group to become number two in Russia Group. Knowing Lofgren's temperament and the fact that Lofgren still had the ear of CIA director John Deutch, there was nothing Redmond or anyone else could do about it. It left Bannerman to freely go through the Russian files, but inasmuch as professional validation mattered to her, it was some recognition that the career she'd built with years of dedication and loyalty hadn't been completely destroyed. Even if Redmond was innocent, he could have only been anxious what she might now dig up on him. It was all the worse because Worthen was also now in Russia Group. The best Redmond could do was put up passive resistance. For meetings he was scheduled to attend with Russia Group, he'd promise to be there but then find a last-minute excuse not to.

Meanwhile, now in direct charge of the Fourth Man hunt, Redmond chased one red herring after another. From their perches in Russia Group, Bannerman and Worthen could only stand by silently watching the chutzpah of it all. His intent, as far as they were concerned, was to distract the FBI giving it shiny objects to chase. Bannerman couldn't prove it, but she was convinced it was to divert the FBI's attention from the November 1994 profile, the one that had made Redmond a suspect. He seemed to have the full support of the FBI, although it was apparent some at the FBI were starting to have their doubts about Redmond.

Aside from Milburn, one person at the FBI who had doubts was John Lewis, who would rise to assistant FBI director in charge of the intelligence division. He outranked Curran but wasn't in a position to directly intervene in Curran's work at the CIA. Lewis had little doubt there was a Fourth Man. He obviously didn't know who it was but always harbored his suspicions about Bearden. One time when Lewis interviewed Bearden in Bearden's office, there was a desk light between the two of them. Lewis was sure Bearden positioned it there to intimidate whoever was sitting in that chair. Without saying a word, Lewis got up and, to Bearden's shock, moved the light out of the way. Still, it was Redmond that Lewis trusted least. Once when Lewis offered Worthen a ride from FBI headquarters to Langley, they happened to spot Redmond walking in front of the Original Headquarters Building. Thinking on his feet, Lewis told Worthen to crouch down on the floor so Redmond wouldn't see them together. Lewis didn't want Redmond to know that he and Worthen were friends.

What all Redmond's red herrings shared in common was, like him, they'd been on the USSR Branch or in Soviet counterintelligence around the times the unexplained compromises occurred. Among them were Cold War veterans like Fran Smith, John O'Reilly, and Bill Deardorff. Their names aren't known to the public, but friends in counterintelligence told Bannerman and Worthen they thought Redmond was offering these people up as mole suspects.

Smith was a convenient target because she took over the USSR Branch after Redmond, then in 1986 moved over to the Special Task Force in counterintelligence, the group that first started to look into the '85–'86 losses. She was read into many of the unexplained compromises of agents and technical operations on the matrix, including Gordievsky and the other two intelligence officers lost in May 1985. So it's understandable why the FBI would seriously consider her. But as SIU looked deeper into Smith, there were large parts of her story that didn't fit the profile. O'Reilly was easy prey because he had some of the same access to the lost agents but also had a drinking problem and a topped-out career. The FBI duly pulled his personnel file and checked things like travel and credit, but discarded him as a suspect because he couldn't account for all the unexplained losses. Nonetheless, the unwanted attention didn't help his career. The investigation destroyed Deardorff's career when his plum overseas assignment was pulled. Deardorff would retire never knowing what had happened.

One whose career was more obviously wrecked was counterintelligence officer Brian Kelley. He was suspected of compromising the investigation into an alleged Russian spy in the State Department, Felix Bloch, to the Russians. The CIA and FBI would eventually acknowledge they had made a mistake, but Kelley's life in the meantime was destroyed. He went public, describing how he and his family had been aggressively pursued by the CIA and FBI, and how with scant evidence he was suspended from his job. His daughter lost her job at the CIA thanks to the investigation into her father. But what few knew was that Kelley was collateral damage in the hunt for the Fourth Man. Bannerman, who was read into the investigation, knew Kelley only fit the Fourth Man profile if you didn't understand the mechanics of CIA Russian operations and counterintelligence (as the FBI didn't). For that matter, she and others didn't believe it was possible that Kelley had betrayed the Bloch investigation to the Russians. Even knowing that intuition shouldn't be involved, they felt they knew him well and didn't think it was in him. Bannerman was also certain that it had been Redmond who'd first fingered Kelley to the FBI. She wondered if he'd done it because Kelley vaguely fit the Fourth Man profile and had access to most of the unexplained compromises on SIU's matrix.

Redmond disputes this. He told me there was some preliminary evidence that suggested it was Kelley who tipped off the Russians about the Bloch investigation, but that he quickly figured out it wasn't Kelley and dropped the angle. Then, he said, the FBI decided without evidence that Kelley was the Fourth Man, putting blanket coverage on him, from telephone taps to physical surveillance. According to Redmond, it got worse when the FBI started cooking the books. When there were gaps in the vehicular coverage of Kelley, the FBI would falsely claim the gaps were longer than they actually were, to make it look as if Kelley had an opportunity to pick up or put down a dead drop. Bannerman agrees the FBI manipulated the evidence against Kelley. But as merely a deputy in Russia Group, Bannerman didn't have the authority to put up a fight against either Redmond or the FBI. (She didn't know it at the time, but it would turn out that it was Hanssen who'd told the KGB about Bloch.)

Another Redmond red herring to come down the road was yet again one of his back-pocket cases, a Russian of murky antecedents. The CIA has asked me not to identify him, so I'll call him Sergei. As with Alex, Redmond personally oversaw the running of Sergei. Meetings with Sergei occurred in Germany and Britain, sometimes with headquarters officers tagging along like when Rolph flew to Berlin to meet Alex with no idea what was going on. But Bannerman's suspicion is they were only at the meetings as window dressing, to make it look as if it were part of a larger, organized counterintelligence investigation. Another thing that drew the women's suspicions about Sergei was that instead of running him out of headquarters, meetings related to him took place in the Northern Virginia residence of two CIA officers. Operating out of private residences rather than at Langley is about as unorthodox as you can get (for whatever it's worth, I never heard of it happening in my time at the CIA), though it makes sense if Redmond worried that Langley was bugged.

Another thing that drew Bannerman's suspicions is that Sergei had initially been introduced to Redmond by retired KGB general Viktor Budanov, the same First Chief Directorate officer who'd interrogated Gordievsky. It set off all sorts of alarm bells.

Not only was Budanov an unreconstructed hard-liner, but his last job before he retired in 1992 was as the deputy of Directorate K, the First Chief Directorate counterintelligence arm. Overseeing Line KR officers in the field, he was in the same directorate Max worked for, the one that ran Ames and Hanssen. Like most KGB retirees, he was in its active reserve, which meant while he wasn't paid, he was subject to the same draconian security as when he'd been active. For the SIU-in-exile, it made absolutely no sense then that a man this trusted and high up would cross lines to help the CIA hunt for a mole in his former service. It was as inherently suspect as approaching the Czech triple agent Koecher. But no one wanted Bannerman's opinion, and as she predicted, Sergei proved to be a wash—or worse.

At a meeting in late 1996, Sergei implicated a senior CIA officer named Joe Hayes as the Fourth Man. Hayes specialized in Russian cryptology and was a highly regarded officer. But none of this stopped Redmond's acolytes from going after him. As soon as CIA field officer Debby Fitzgerald got the tip from Sergei about Hayes, she ran up to the seventh floor in a panic demanding Hayes be immediately removed from the building. The FBI had to be informed right away, she said. The seventh floor did call the FBI to alert it to Sergei's accusation, but by now the FBI was done with Redmond's double agent hunting. It concluded Hayes was framed by Budanov, little doubt at the behest of his former employer. Throwing up its hands for now, the FBI effectively parted company with Redmond.

The way Bannerman saw things, Budanov and Sergei nicely fit Redmond's long-standing practice of running off-the-books agents, with zero accountability to anyone other than himself.

They were never encrypted or assigned 201 file numbers, no cable traffic related to them was ever generated, and nothing they reported was entered in databases or put in memos. It meant only Redmond possessed the full details about these agents. Who could know other than Redmond what the likes of Alex and Sergei had reported about CIA moles? In the view of SIU-in-exile, Redmond's back-pocket cases misshaped the Fourth Man narrative, drawing attention away from the rigorous counterintelligence work SIU had done. But Redmond was a master of the game, and there was no way to prove it.

Bannerman kept reminding herself over and over again that it amounted to conjecture rather than proof of treason. But at the same time, the evidence was irrefutable that the Russians enjoyed a high-level penetration of the CIA, and for some reason the careful work SIU had done to investigate what should have been a matter of utmost importance was being ignored. Other than a handful of allies like Lewis, Milburn, and Lofgren, no one was listening. She'd just have to wait until a new Russian volunteer came out to fill in the story.

But in the end, it was another CIA Russian double agent other than the Fourth Man who threw a spanner into the works.

SEVENTEEN

check·mate / ˈtʃɛkˌmeɪt / *n.* When someone is completely cornered, having no possibility of escape.

Former Soviet Union; 1995–96

AFTER THE MEETING between Max and Corbin in South America, there were two more meetings with Max. Both took place in a city in the former Soviet Union, a place Max could travel on short notice and without rousing the suspicions of his employer. The other advantage was the local intelligence service cared a lot less than the Russians did about what the CIA was up to within its borders. With some basic precautions, a meeting with a Russian intelligence officer could safely be made there. It helped that Max finally agreed to regularize his contact with the CIA.

As the first meeting with Max came together, Bannerman fervently prayed that Max would have something new on the Fourth Man. In the best of all possible worlds, he would flag an upcoming meeting between him and his handler, like he had with Karetkin and Ames in Caracas. It would all depend on how much networking Max had done since his meeting with Corbin in South

America. But like so much in this story, it took a turn Bannerman should have anticipated.

Accounts vary, but likely at Max's first sit-down with his case officer, he dropped the terrible news that he'd come under suspicion by his service and was completely cut off from all secrets. He had no idea why, but knew they were on to him. Bannerman's high hopes now dashed, the meeting was worse than a bust: In all likelihood, the CIA had lost its best Russian counterintelligence source.

But then, almost as an afterthought, Max said he'd heard his service, the SVR, was running another double agent in the CIA. As usual, he didn't know the man's name or position, but said he'd first been recruited in Kuala Lumpur and now was assigned to the Farm, the CIA's training facility in Northern Virginia.

Maryann Hough wasn't part of the investigation, but it took her less than an hour after she heard about Max's tip and checking personnel to figure out it had to be Harold "Jim" Nicholson. Having never worked in Soviet or Russian operations, Nicholson definitely wasn't the Fourth Man. But Bannerman and company knew without a doubt that a full-fledged FBI and CIA investigation into Nicholson would completely derail the Fourth Man hunt.

Which is precisely what happened. The FBI got completely tied up making an airtight legal case against Nicholson. The case drew in scores of agents from the Washington field office, including techs installing concealed cameras in Nicholson's office and hundreds on an FBI surveillance team following him around for months. The CIA played second fiddle, but dozens on its side took part, with Redmond leading the charge.

Nicholson was arrested on November 16, 1996, tried and convicted for espionage, and is now serving a life sentence in the ADX

Supermax prison in Florence, Colorado. The arrest was another feather in Redmond's cap. Having caught two Russian moles, he was a bona fide counterintelligence legend at the CIA, more untouchable than ever. Bannerman's hope of someone going back to the November 1994 matrix and profile was dead and buried.

There was absolutely no way to prove it, but SIU-in-exile was tempted to believe that the Russians had given up Nicholson in order to protect the Fourth Man. Another bright shining object for the FBI to chase. Max, they speculated, was likely the unwitting vehicle to accomplish it. The school that believed Russian intelligence would give up an agent to protect a more valuable one was no bigger than it had ever been, but the way Bannerman and company saw it, with Nicholson having no access to anything of burning interest to the Russians—like Russian operations or counterintelligence—they would have looked at him as a convenient throwaway.

And there was some urgency to it. At this point there's little doubt the Russians likely knew a Fourth Man investigation was seriously underway. There was the Russian liaison operative who approached the Moscow chief of station in 1994 all but admitting to it. Plus the Russians almost certainly knew about Phil and Michele's Moscow probe. The chances are, then, that someone in Moscow at the very least would have considered giving up Nicholson in a pawn sacrifice. Then again, the truth is lost somewhere in the wilderness of mirrors. But if just maybe SIU-in-exile was right about sacrificing Nicholson, the Fourth Man and the Russians once again outplayed both the CIA and the FBI.

The way Bannerman, Hough, and Worthen saw things, Redmond had created a kaleidoscope lined with mirrors of his own manufacture, turning the Fourth Man into his own private hunt.

Operating his personal stable of Russian agents, he alone got to decide which counterintelligence leads were taken seriously and which weren't. And he'd been at it for a long time. It was Redmond in 1986 who'd first arranged to remove Soviet counterintelligence from official cable traffic and finished analysis, then eventually off paper altogether. It was Redmond who finagled himself into a position where he alone got to pick and choose what evidence would be used to unearth the Fourth Man. It was Redmond who shut down SIU. Guilty or not, as they saw it, there just wasn't any other way to look at this side of the story.

None of this is to suggest that the victims Redmond dished up to the FBI weren't plausible suspects. They'd all at one time or another had access to the USSR Branch and Soviet counterintelligence. But none of them completely fit the profile or accounted for all the matrix's unexplained compromises. As for any help from Lofgren, their only real remaining ally with any power, he at one point considered taking it to John Deutsch, the CIA director after Woolsey. If Deutsch were to grasp the implications of the matrix and reopen the investigation, it might at least have "taken the shine off Redmond," as Lofgren put it. But instead, Lofgren decided he had had enough with the CIA and took his retirement. As Lofgren would tell me years later, he also seriously wondered whether the CIA would survive another Russian spy scandal.

Bannerman and her team would continue to hold out hope, but for now the case was as good as closed. Redmond—Fourth Man or not—was the victor. The real losers weren't the three spy catchers, though; it was the CIA, which had given up perhaps its best opportunity to make sure its house was in order and was now blind to a world on the verge of drastic change.

EIGHTEEN

fly·ing blind / ˈflaɪ ɪŋ blaɪnd/ *v.* Acting or traveling without the aid of a map.

Moscow; 1998–99

IN 1998, TIPPED off by British intelligence that all four of the CIA's remaining Russian agents had been compromised to the Russians, the CIA whisked them away to safety. Max, among them, was exfiltrated out of Moscow. Adolf, who at that point was assigned to the Russian embassy in Ottawa, and his family were woken up in the middle of the night and hustled across the border into the United States. The other two were a counterintelligence officer assigned to Copenhagen and a low-level agent in Moscow. Getting those agents out alive was a rare success for the CIA, but the triumphs masked a wider disaster. When it came to Russia, the CIA was now as good as deaf and blind. Just as Putin and his KGB cohorts were making their play to take the Kremlin, the CIA didn't have a single worthwhile Russian agent.

Explanations I've heard for how these agents were compromised vary. One is that the Russians discovered them by hacking the CIA's covert agent communications. Another is that Bob Hanssen betrayed all four. The former deputy director for operations Mike Sulick told me Hanssen in fact gave up Max's and Adolf's names to his handlers. However, MI6 was certain they'd been exposed at least a year or more before Hanssen reconnected with the KGB in 1999. What Hanssen's treachery also doesn't explain is that around the same time, Russia Group concluded that every advanced CIA Russian developmental around the world had started to feed the CIA disinformation in a clearly coordinated fashion. (Developmentals and informal contacts aren't agents, but rather people the CIA hopes to turn into full-fledged agents.) Russia Group decided that a Russian agent at Langley almost certainly had tipped off the Russians that the CIA was making a run at these people. A problem at the FBI was ruled out because it knew nothing about CIA developmentals. With the Fourth Man investigation dormant—or deliberately run off the rails if SIU-in-exile was right—there was no way to determine if the Fourth Man was responsible.

Deflated and at the end of her tether, Bannerman retired in 1998. However, every once in a while someone from Russia Group would pass by her house to ask her one thing or another about the Fourth Man. On one occasion, there was a question about Tsymbal and his mysterious trips to Washington. In 2002, she was asked to reinterview Adolf. But he had nothing more to say about the KGB penetration of the CIA. No one gave any explanation for the renewed interest in Adolf or Tsymbal, but she assumed the Fourth Man investigation was still active, perhaps a sign all their work and fighting wasn't for naught. Worthen also retired in 1998. Hough soon retired but stayed working at the CIA under contract. One day, in 2007, the deputy director of operations, Mike Sulick, told her he'd destroyed SIU's in-case memo. It was the only copy. He didn't tell her why.

Bannerman, Hough, and Worthen met Redmond for the last time in 1999 at a Langley memorial service for General Dmitri Polyakov, the one who alerted the United States to the Sino-Soviet split before Ames gave him up. Redmond was pleasant enough, but before they parted ways, he said, apropos of nothing, that he was on his way to London and then to Moscow to meet Viktor Budanov and do some business with him.

Bannerman and the other two had no idea how to respond to Redmond saying he was going to work with Budanov, nor did they know whether it was true or not. He could have been lying, and it was nothing more than a taunt: *I won, you lost.*

I asked Redmond about Budanov. He told me after he retired from the CIA in 1997, he went into consulting and traveled to Moscow on behalf of a London law firm to seek Budanov's services. By that time Budanov was out of the KGB and running a security company. It was hoped Budanov could recover money the firm's clients had lost to a Russian crook. Before traveling, Redmond said he called Mike Sulick, then the chief of the division overseeing Russian operations, to ask if it would be okay, and Sulick said it was fine. But in Moscow, Budanov turned out to be a "preening asshole." He snarled at Redmond, accusing him of being nasty and disrespectful to the KGB. In the end, he said, Budanov was of no help.

Either way, here the story leads to a narrative crossroads between Putin and the Fourth Man. After retiring from the KGB in 1992, Budanov went into the private security business. Among other ventures, he was involved in a security consulting firm in Maryland called Parvus International. His partner was a former NSA official. Parvus and an offshoot hired a number of former American intelligence officials, including a retired FBI agent who'd been an investigator in the Ames hunt and the acting chief of station in Athens when Bokhan was run there. Throw Redmond somehow in the mix, and a Cold War spy catcher starts to break out in a cold sweat. But at the same time, this was before Putin, when Russia was still considered good company. Going into business with the former deputy head of Directorate K, the bunch responsible for running double agents around the world, traitors like Ames and Hanssen, was given a pass. Working with Budanov didn't mean they'd gone to work for Russian intelligence. Yet there were those who did wonder if there was more to it than the Russians tapping their raw talent.

At one point, some ex-MI6 officers took a close look at Budanov and whether he was acting under the direction of Russian intelligence. What made them wonder was an interview to an obscure website in which he talked about his connections with Putin when he, Budanov, was head of Line KR in East Germany. The MI6 officers also wondered about the American intelligence officers working in Moscow with Budanov. One time, an ex-MI6 officer visited Budanov's Moscow office to see what was going on. He met a "senior American" there, but never got a name for him.

In 1997, Budanov cofounded Elite Security, a Russian private security firm. It became the subject of controversy in 2017, when the Trump administration awarded it a contract to protect the American embassy and consulates in Russia after Putin ordered the American diplomatic presence in Russia downsized. According to the State Department, they were the only suitable choice. It's not hard to see why many felt uncomfortable with the notion of an ex-KGB general like Budanov guarding the American embassy.

If indeed a former head of CIA counterintelligence considered or actually did end up working with a former KGB counterintelligence officer who targeted Americans, a man in Putin's inner circle, the irony isn't lost on anyone who remembers the Cold War. And especially someone like Bannerman, who knew the history between Redmond, Budanov, and the dangle Sergei. Or as Jim Olson, another former CIA head of counterintelligence, told me, "If indeed Redmond went into business with Budanov, it bears looking into." There could be no possible "benign" explanation for it, he said.

In 2001, against the CIA's forceful advice, Max returned to Russia on what was supposed to be a short trip. The CIA actually considered having him detained to prevent him from making the trip. He was arrested upon landing in Moscow by the faux Second Chief Directorate spy Zhomov, who was now a senior officer in the FSB. In June 2003, a Moscow military court found him guilty of spying for the CIA and sentenced him to eighteen years of hard labor. His wife died while he was in prison.

In 2010, the FBI arrested ten KGB Russian operatives living in the United States under assumed identities. In a stinging humiliation for Putin, Russia was forced to trade them for Max and three other accused spies. But before Max boarded a plane for Vienna, the KGB made it clear to him it wasn't done with him yet. They showed him grainy pictures of his house in Maryland and his family. They'd clearly been taken with a telephoto lens. Max was warned that if he helped American intelligence ever again, they'd kill him. When in 2018 Putin's agents made an attempt on the life of Sergei Skripal, a former Russian military officer who'd been traded along with Max in 2010 and was living in the British city of Salisbury, Max understood just how serious the threat against him is. You can understand why he won't talk to me, and as I'm told, he's had nothing to do with either the CIA or FBI since.

NINETEEN

glim·mer / ˈglɪm ər/ *n.* A flash of dim light.

Washington, DC; February 2006

THERE'S ONE THING in the espionage business you rarely get, and that's closure. You can work on an account for decades and never find the answers to the important questions. Then, after you retire, it's unusual to hear from your colleagues. When you're out, you're out, as the saying goes. But there are the exceptions.

In February 2006, the spy catchers who hunted the Fourth Man in the nineties were rewarded with a bit of closure when the new iteration of SIU started calling around to retired CIA employees who'd been active in Soviet/Russian operations to ask if the FBI could stop by their residences to ask a few questions about an old case. Among those who got calls were Bannerman, Worthen, and Lofgren. The reason the request came through SIU was thanks to an informal agreement between the FBI and CIA that the FBI wouldn't approach retired CIA employees without first getting a green light from Langley.

Jim Milburn attended the meetings, along with an FBI special agent. Their interest cut right to the chase: Was there any reason Paul Redmond would have made a visit to Moscow in the mid-eighties without Langley's permission? Neither Milburn nor the agent said why the FBI thought Redmond had, but the way they asked the question, it was clear they were fairly certain of it.

Bannerman's immediate reaction was "Well, it's about time."

She could only wonder why after twelve years the FBI had finally taken an interest in Redmond. She had no idea if it had anything to do with the 1994 matrix and profile. But knowing the FBI the way she did, and all the hoops it has to jump through to open a full-fledged espionage investigation on someone like Redmond, she now was convinced the FBI considered Redmond a spy.

After the meeting, Milburn pulled Bannerman aside to thank her for all the work she'd done. I can't speak for Milburn, but he must have looked around her home, the same modest Northern Virginia midcentury modern ranch house she'd always lived in, and recognized her for the dedicated, selfless public servant she'd always been, someone very much like himself. More to the point, they saw in each other a quarter-century-old obsession with trying to catch the Fourth Man.

Milburn was too professional to name Redmond, but he did say, "Laine, I'm pretty sure the person you were interested in was in it for the game."

The meaning wasn't quite clear. Bannerman took it to mean either revenge or outplaying the spy catchers.

Jim Olson was asked that same question about Redmond during a visit by the FBI. His response was the same: A CIA officer doesn't wake up one morning and decide on a lark to go to Moscow to meet the KGB. He added: If the CIA had found out about it, it would have immediately fired him and recommended the FBI investigate him for possible treason. As everyone in the CIA knew, an unauthorized and unreported meeting with the KGB behind the Iron Curtain was prima facie evidence of espionage.

John MacGaffin, Redmond's friend and number two in the Directorate of Operations during the initial stages of the Fourth Man investigation, told me Redmond had heard about the FBI investigation and was unsurprisingly downcast about the whole thing. MacGaffin said he was certain the FBI had to be misinformed, and the story about the Moscow trip couldn't be right. For a start, as he told me, anyone with street smarts wouldn't risk traveling to Moscow; you could spy for the Russians and never visit Moscow. When I offered MacGaffin the out that the Russians may have set Redmond up, he took it.

I have no idea what was behind the FBI visits in 2006, or what led them to suspect Redmond had gone to Moscow to meet the KGB. But I did hear about one Russian defector who passed on a similar story. Although the defector didn't have a perfect track record, he was generally reliable. I've omitted and blurred many of the details the defector relayed to make him unidentifiable.

According to the defector, in 1984, after completing a European tour and before returning to Langley, a CIA case officer took leave ostensibly to go on vacation, but instead traveled to a European capital. There, he made contact with a member of a visiting Soviet delegation. He specifically sought out the Second Chief Directorate operative riding shotgun on the delegation. Somehow, the CIA officer knew the Second officer's name and the dates he would be in the European capital.

The CIA volunteer told the Second officer he'd agree to spy for the KGB, but steadfastly refused to deal with the First. As the CIA volunteer put it, it was too riddled with CIA spies to be trusted. Right off the bat, it was clear to the KGB officer that this mysterious American visitor knew his way around the KGB, if for no other reason than he knew his true affiliation and how to find him. Just as this CIA volunteer knew it would be a lot safer putting his life in the hands of a Second Chief Directorate true believer rather than someone from the untrustworthy First. It also surprised the Second operative that the CIA officer was aware that there was a cadre of Second operatives who never left the Soviet Union. When the CIA walk-in said he'd worked on the USSR account and was returning to Langley to do so again, it made sense.

The CIA volunteer wasn't without his demands. He said he alone would call the shots rather than the KGB. He wouldn't pass documents, and on top of it, he would decide which secrets he'd pass and which he wouldn't. He also refused to meet the KGB in the United States, instead only overseas when he happened to be there on CIA business. He'd agree to take some cash, but not enough to draw the FBI's attention.

From their conversations, the Second Chief Directorate officer gleaned that the walk-in had been passed over for promotion, and his motivation for volunteering to the KGB was to teach Langley it had made a grave mistake overlooking his talents. Along with that, the walk-in was absolutely convinced he could outplay both the CIA and FBI, and parry every conceivable investigative tool they might bring to bear. None of this came as a surprise to the KGB operative: Some of the best spies in history are driven not by money but by resentment and a burning desire to even the score with their employer. And like Max, they pride themselves in knowing more about spy tradecraft than their handlers.

Normally, the KGB would have been reluctant to play by the volunteer's rules. But because he would be working on the USSR account when he returned to Langley, it had no choice other than to accept them. The KGB then facilitated the volunteer's travel to Moscow, where he was met and debriefed by two Second Chief Directorate operatives who henceforth would manage the case from Lubyanka.

According to the defector, after the volunteer returned to Langley, dead drops and covert electronic communications served as the means of communication in between face-to-face meetings in Europe. Second Chief Directorate travelers serviced dead drops for the volunteer, but they were never clued in to his identity or position. Nor did the First Chief Directorate bosses in Moscow or Washington know anything about him.

It's a tidy, intriguing story, but one with more than a few holes in it. For one, it lacks the extraordinary proof you need for an extraordinary claim. Like a picture of the Fourth Man on his secret trip to Moscow in 1984. I also have my suspicions about the sourcing and timing of the story. For a start, how was it that the defector had heard about such a sensitive case? Sure, rumors float freely around Russian intelligence, but I would have thought this particular one would be locked up tight and the key thrown away. It's more understandable that Max, working in counterintelligence, would have picked up the rumor about Ames's trip to Caracas, but this particular defector was not in counterintelligence and did not have the same sort of access to the KGB's running of double agents. As for problems with timing, the defector relayed the story out of Russia after the FBI in 2006 started asking about Redmond's alleged visit to Moscow to meet the KGB. By this time, it's almost certain the Russians knew all about the Fourth Man investigation, and maybe even that Redmond had been a suspect.

So you see why I'd have my doubts about the defector's story, why it's a little too convenient for my liking. Frankly, when you look at the KGB with a skeptical eye, it stinks of Russian disinformation, of a piece with the KGB's same tired campaign of trying to lure the CIA into a new Angletonian mole-hunting frenzy.

I'm not sure if the FBI relied on this defector's story to an important degree. I also don't know if the FBI used the November 1994 matrix and profile to come to the conclusion Redmond might be a Russian spy. But in either case, I was told by a former colleague seconded to FBI counterintelligence at the time that the FBI would never go around the country asking by name about a renowned former CIA officer without good evidence against him and a green light from high up in the Department of Justice. Almost invariably, when investigating Americans for espionage, the FBI takes a strictly by-the-books approach. In other words, without the kind of smoking gun I've been writing about—something more concrete than the matrix or the defector's story—the FBI would never have pursued the Redmond lead so aggressively.

I mentioned this story to Redmond. He said indeed the FBI had asked him about an unauthorized Moscow trip. He told the FBI "the dates didn't work." He couldn't possibly have gotten away to visit Moscow during that time frame. He added that he didn't visit Moscow until after he was appointed USSR Branch chief, which was in 1984.

Then I asked him if he thought the Russians might have framed him as a spy, acting on some old grudge and in the bargain tying the CIA up in knots. Redmond said he didn't know that to be a fact, but thought it possible. As for the FBI's motivations, he said that it had always distrusted and hated him—and consequently was prepared to believe the worst about him. "They would welcome anything they could use against me," he said. Redmond said another explanation for the FBI's interest in him could be because the FBI runs its own stable of Russian sources in Moscow, and that one of them could have falsely accused him of spying for the Russians. (John Lewis confirmed to me that while he was at the FBI, it did "operate" independently of the CIA in Moscow.) But Redmond says the bottom line is that to the FBI, "he was the enemy." No one I talked to has a satisfactory explanation for what got the FBI interested in Redmond and the Fourth Man again. The FBI wouldn't tell me when I queried it in an email. I suspect it was another defector with some sort of plausible evidence establishing his existence, but I certainly don't know that to be a fact. Those who chased the Fourth Man in the nineties are largely out of the picture. Maryann Hough has passed away. She was buried in her tennis togs. Max is living in exile, but like every Russian in the world knows, he isn't beyond Putin's reach. Laine Bannerman and Diana Worthen, the two surviving women of SIU, have not been able to put the Fourth Man hunt out of their minds. The FBI's visit in 2006 was small consolation, but better than nothing.

For now, with the Fourth Man still an open case, it remains the most compelling espionage mystery of modern times.

EPILOGUE

AFTER LIVING INSIDE this story for several years as a reporter, an outsider obsessed with getting the whole story, I don't know who the Fourth Man was. Redmond's getting involved with an ex–Russian intelligence officer of Budanov's reputation is proof of bad judgment but not espionage. His vendetta against SIU is also proof of nothing. It could have been simply a matter of defending himself at a time when the FBI was on the warpath against the CIA. There was no way Redmond could have known what Curran would do with the November 1994 briefing; a full-fledged FBI investigation on Redmond would have destroyed his career. I also don't know whether the Russians framed Redmond. They certainly had cause, if for no other reason than his helming the Ames and Nicholson investigations. As the old saying goes, the KGB doesn't have an eraser on its pencil.

And there's this I can't let go: Why weren't there more clear-cut compromises tied to the Fourth Man? If he'd been a fully recruited and responsive agent, why wasn't the damage more demonstrable? Howard and Ames left wide, undeniable paths of destruction; there's no obvious reason the Fourth Man wouldn't have, too. It indeed could have been that he was such a valuable agent Moscow decided not to act on all his intelligence. Maybe he betrayed the same agents as Ames, but it wasn't until Ames passed along their names that the KGB felt it could act against them. No doubt I'm overthinking this. With a story so complex, and all the more so because it involves Russian intelligence, I suppose it's inevitable.

Then there are questions about the credibility of Max and Adolf. Neither of them came up with a name for the Fourth Man or for that matter any lead that could be corroborated. The 3×5 cards and the compromise of Michele and Phil's probe are intriguing but far from a smoking gun. Further, if the Fourth Man was as well-placed in CIA Soviet operations as suspected, chances are excellent that he would have very early on informed his handler about both Max and Adolf. It keeps coming back to the possibility the two were vehicles for disinformation, again wittingly or unwittingly. Or alternatively, it could be the KGB decided not to act against them in order to protect the Fourth Man. With all this in mind, I asked Mike Sulick about Max's claims of a post-Ames mole in the CIA. His response was unequivocal: Max in the end started exaggerating in an effort to make himself relevant.

As for Redmond's outburst at the November 1994 briefing, I don't know why he reacted in the way he did. It could have been because he was guilty, as SIU was convinced, or maybe it was as simple as he was furious anyone would challenge his reputation as the CIA's preeminent spy catcher. He'd been lionized for catching Ames, but now SIU effectively accused him of having lost two very big fish, a KGB spy in the FBI (Hanssen) and the Fourth Man. Finally, there's Redmond's off-the-books mole hunt. Perhaps Redmond truly had been tracking the Fourth Man and didn't trust anyone other than his own people to help him, but then the

November 1994 briefing revealed how the KGB had suckered and framed him—ensnared him in the KGB's Monster Plot. It would certainly have been enough to make him lose his cool.

I asked a recent head of Russian operations whether it's possible the Russians had framed Redmond. He said he wouldn't put it past them. "The truth is disinformation is the only thing the Russians are still good at," he said. "It's not like they use their brains to invent the iPhone or something." Another CIA Russian hand told me the Russians often build "offensive counterintelligence" into the handling of agents. In other words, it's not inconceivable they framed Redmond in order to protect the real Fourth Man.

Be that as it may, the deeper I dug into the Fourth Man story, the more evidence I came across substantiating the Fourth Man's existence. One set of anomalies particularly caught my attention. A case officer assigned to the USSR Branch in the early eighties told me that around 1984 the Pentagon sent the CIA a list of detailed questions it wanted answered about Soviet advanced weapons, things like the glacis composition of its latest main battle tank, the T-80; the hull designs of its new submarines; and so on. The list was named Priority Collection Programs. To the surprise of the CIA, not long after receiving the list, Soviet volunteers started showing up at its door with top secret documents that seemed to answer the Pentagon's questions.

Initially the CIA was jubilant. But its military analysts quickly caught on that it was a setup from the start, all the volunteers little doubt dangles run into the CIA by the KGB. The documents mirrored genuine documents, but many details were off by enough to make them useless. It was a slick, elaborate KGB disinformation campaign intended to skew the Pentagon's understanding of new

Soviet weaponry and in the bargain lure the United States into building worthless weapons in response.

The point for the Fourth Man story is that a CIA double agent circa 1984 almost certainly passed the Pentagon's questions to the KGB—and it wasn't Howard or Ames. It's the only explanation for how the KGB was able to tailor its disinformation with such precision. SIU was unaware of this disinformation campaign and the suspicion that someone passed the Pentagon's questions to the KGB. I'd have to imagine it would've been great assistance helping fill in the matrix and profile, maybe even pinpointing who on the USSR Branch passed it to the KGB.

Even if the Fourth Man hunt hasn't yet caught its mole, it changed the lives of everyone involved. For Redmond, a man who devoted his life to catching moles, it's a stain on a stellar reputation he feels he has well earned. I was surprised when Redmond called me back a couple of weeks after I emailed him. He'd obviously taken his time thinking about what he'd say to me. We set up time to talk. I didn't entirely know what to expect after spending so much time learning about the man's career, what some believe he did, what others believe he didn't. I thought it might be a terse phone call full of denials. I expected him to deny that he was the Fourth Man, which he emphatically did. But to my surprise, we spent a long time talking convivially.

It surprised me all the more so when he freely offered me his version of the FBI's ongoing investigation into him. It was as if he wanted to rebut the FBI's suspicions point by point, from his contacts with Budanov to the accusations he'd made an unauthorized trip to Moscow in the mid-eighties. He insisted that the FBI was plain wrong about his having made an unauthorized trip to Moscow on the dates it mentioned. He was more than willing to go on about his problems with the FBI, but his bottom line was that the FBI was pursuing him for no other reason than it hated him.

He volunteered a strange story about the time he bought an expensive but broken Rolex watch from a KGB officer and then had it fixed, receiving a considerable windfall. He also told me that when he was on a private visit to Moscow after retirement, he was given a tour of the Lubyanka KGB museum, where he met the notorious Aleksandr Zhomov, still a serving KGB official. Redmond said he later had dinner with Zhomov, during which the Russian told him he knew who Redmond had bought the watch from. The implication was that the watch was some sort of bribe. I have to wonder if this is what caught the FBI's attention, though Redmond denied the watch represented some sort of KGB compensation. Either way, the watch was something I'd never heard about before, but the way he told the story, it sounded like something he wanted to get off his chest. For now, it remains another question mark in this enduring mystery.

As I was finishing this book I caught up with Jim Milburn. I told him what Redmond had told me, how he, Redmond, had no idea what drew the FBI's attention to him other than that he believes the FBI detests him. I threw in Redmond's accusation that the FBI has a habit of fudging evidence in order to justify keeping an investigation open. Milburn scoffed: "He knows exactly what the FBI has on him. And you don't know a quarter of it."

Milburn wasn't in a position to offer me the evidence the FBI has against Redmond. Most frustratingly, he didn't say why in 2006 the FBI went around the country asking retired CIA officers why Redmond had made an unauthorized visit to Moscow in the mid-eighties. Not that I needed it, but what Milburn's comments did do is remind me is I'm still missing a big piece of the Fourth Man hunt.

As for Alexander Zaporozhsky, aka Max, the preponderance of evidence suggests he was the real thing, if erratic. Redmond believes he was. From everything I've heard, he truly detested the KGB and did his part to aid its adversary the United States. But as with so many Russian defectors and spies, it didn't end well. He paid for his beliefs at a price most of us can't comprehend.

For Laine Bannerman, Diana Worthen, and Maryann Hough, the Fourth Man hunt was the culmination of several lifetimes devoted to counterintelligence and the CIA. They put their careers on the line for what they believed was the truth, and salvaged an institution they'd never lost faith in. Lofgren risked his career by throwing in his lot with hard-boiled spy catchers brazen enough to suggest one of the CIA's best and brightest could have been a mole.

Or, perhaps, they all fell hook, line, and sinker for a cunning KGB trap—the world's best intelligence organization doing what it does best: deceive and disrupt.

The story of the Russian double agent in the CIA who got away may sound like some unfinished piece of business from the Cold War. But with Russia reverting to form, turning back into the implacable enemy it was during the Cold War, it's starting to look more like the mystery of the Fourth Man is a lot more historically significant than an old-school spy tale. It's part of the much larger

story of how America completely missed Putin and the KGB's res-
urrection, and how it happened Putin's Russia inflicted more political sabotage on the West than the Soviet Union could have only
dreamed about. Russia's irredentist wars in Ukraine and Georgia,
undermining the United States in the Middle East, and, not least,
meddling in American elections promise to be just the start of it.

At the risk of one too many superlatives, it's not much of an
exaggeration to say Putin's mysterious appointment is turning out
to be the most consequential, nonviolent handover of power since
Paul von Hindenburg appointed Adolf Hitler chancellor in 1933.
The fact that we didn't see it coming can only be described as an
intelligence failure on par with Pearl Harbor. When the American ambassador to Moscow in 1999 told me that Moscow taxi
drivers were better informed about Putin's rise than the CIA, I
finally understood just how bad it was.

As a former intelligence officer, what amazes me is that
although Putin has become one of the most powerful men in the
world, to this day we still don't have an authoritative, firsthand
account of how he got to where he did. There have been all sorts
of rumors about his rise, but none have ever been substantiated by
uncontested fact or eyewitnesses who don't come with baggage.
Take, for instance, the suspicion that Putin blackmailed Boris
Yeltsin into resigning and appointing him interim president. To
make a long story short, Yeltsin's family was caught in flagrante
with its hand in the cookie jar, but then skated thanks to Putin's
stepping in to publicly discredit the prosecutor with salacious
kompromat. That much is definitely true. But one reasonable suspicion is that Putin and ex-KGB co-conspirators lured the Yeltsin
family into the corrupt deal in the first place, playing both arsonist

and fireman. Even if that's true, what definitely hasn't been nailed down is Putin's precise agency in the affair, whether it was a carpe diem moment, his seizing history by the horns, or perhaps he was the beneficiary of a labyrinthine Russian intelligence plot.

Another plausible rumor has it that Putin was behind the bombing of four apartment buildings in 1999, slaughtering more than three hundred innocent Russians. In framing Muslim terrorists for the attacks, Putin's supposed intent was to terrorize Russians into voting for him, a sort of "either me or the deluge" offer. That's also plausible enough, yet one can't help but wonder how it's possible no one's come forward to back up the accusation with hard evidence. Somebody planted the explosives on somebody's orders, but neither somebody has been identified by what could be considered court-admissible evidence.

According to one senior Clinton administration official responsible for Russia I spoke to, American ignorance about the mechanics of Putin's rise was nearly complete. The only thing the White House knew is that when Yeltsin was considering changing prime ministers in 1999, he was intercepted on a phone call with the Duma head. Yeltsin told him the new prime minister would be the minister of railways. The minister wasn't a star in the Russian political firmament, but on the other hand, he didn't represent a political threat to Yeltsin. However, less than twenty-four hours later, Yeltsin's daughter Tatiana was on the phone pressing her father to name Putin instead. Yeltsin sounded confused. "Who?" he asked, sounding as if he genuinely didn't know who Putin was.

It makes absolutely no sense Yeltsin wouldn't know Putin's name, because at the time Putin headed the powerful Federal

Security Service (FSB), roughly the equivalent of the FBI or Britain's MI5. Who knows, Yeltsin's memory lapse about Putin may have been thanks to his failing health and mind. Some even wondered if Yeltsin wasn't being incrementally poisoned. Either way, Tatiana patiently reminded her father that Putin was the one who'd saved the reformist ex-mayor of St. Petersburg from arrest. The upshot of Tatiana's call was that Yeltsin called back the Duma head to inform him he'd changed his mind about his new prime minister: Instead of the minister of railways, it would be Vladimir Putin. In other words, he traded in a nonthreat for a threat.

These intercepted calls between Tatiana and her father go some way in substantiating rumors Yeltsin's daughter Tatiana played an instrumental influence in Putin's replacing her father. They do the same for rumors that Putin kept the former mayor of St. Petersburg out of jail by spiriting him out of the country. But what they don't do is explain Tatiana's underlying motivations. The benign interpretation is that she and her father's inner circle genuinely misread Putin, fell for the deceit he was one of them, a reformist. With seeming candor, they've consistently insisted that Putin had always exhibited the fealty of a compass, and certainly never betrayed any sign of his later authoritarian streak. But is it possible they truly forgot the KGB's a nest of vipers that knows all about biding its time and striking when the iron's hot? Or for that matter, did they forget the old Soviet aphorism "Once a spy, always a spy"? Anyhow, who knew better than a KGB operative how to feign loyalty?

The closest the Clinton administration would come to clarity about Putin's rise didn't come from intercepts but rather a human source—Yeltsin's wife, Naina. It happened in 2000 when Clinton made a visit to Moscow to see Putin but set aside time to see his old friend Boris Yeltsin.

As Yeltsin and Clinton met behind closed doors, Ambassador Collins took a seat next to Naina to keep her company.

Decidedly in a glum mood, out of nowhere and almost to herself, Mrs. Yeltsin blurted out, "They're back."

Collins didn't need Mrs. Yeltsin to elaborate on who she was talking about: KGB revanchists, with Putin as their front man. Collins sensed there was no way he was going to get anything more out of her and didn't try.

As Collins found out, with Clinton, her husband, Boris, had been neither more forthcoming nor more optimistic about Putin. The only thing Yeltsin would say about Putin was "He's no democrat. But I hope he becomes one."

One has to wonder whether these guarded asides aren't tantamount to an admission Putin got to where he did thanks to a bona fide coup. But with Russia the blank slate it had become for America and the CIA, who can say for sure.

What's more certain is that without agents in Russian intelligence, the CIA didn't stand a chance of understanding the forces and mechanics behind Putin's KGB-backed takeover, or even very well the country in which it took place. What it comes down to is that if you don't understand the KGB, you can't understand contemporary Russia. Or, for that matter, how it's possible the KGB could have perhaps run an agent at the top of American intelligence for so long and not get caught.

Another way to look at the Fourth Man is if we're unable to nail down the intelligence career of one of the most powerful men in the world, it's not difficult to understand why SIU never was able to determine whether the Fourth Man reported to the First or Second Chief Directorate. Or for that matter whether he existed at all.

The Fourth Man hunt is a spy story for the ages, perhaps one of the best the Cold War has to offer. But when we stand back, it's so much more. It's a story of how the CIA failed its principal mission, how self-serving bureaucrats chose survival over the truth, and how the United States forfeited any hope of understanding Russia at a pivotal moment in its history. It also goes a long way in explaining why the world so confounds America and why contemporary events so often take it by complete surprise.

Spies, then, do matter, and the spy catchers catching them all the more so.

WHO'S WHO:
CRYPTONYMS, ALIASES, AND OTHER SPY ARCANA

"Adolf": Line KR KGB officer.

"Alex": KGB Second Chief Directorate officer who volunteered to the CIA and was first met in Berlin by CIA case officers David Rolf and Mike Sulick.

Angleton, James Jesus: An OSS veteran, appointed chief of CIA counterintelligence in 1954 and fired by CIA director Bill Colby in 1974.

Bannerman, Laine: Chief, Special Investigations Unit, 1994–95.

Bearden, Milt: Chief, Central Eurasia Division, CIA's Directorate of Operations.

Budanov, Viktor: From remote Altai region. Headed Line KR in the KGB's East Berlin residency when Putin was assigned to Dresden in the eighties. In 2007, he gave an interview on an obscure Russian website in which he talked about his association with Putin. In 2017, under the Trump administration, he landed a contract to provide security for the American embassy in Moscow.

Central Eurasia Division: New name for Soviet–Eastern European Division in the CIA's Directorate of Operations.

Cherkashin, Victor Ivanovich: Chief of Line KR in the Washington, DC, rezidentura in 1985. Ames's first case officer.

CIC, or Counterintelligence Center: Formed in 1988 from old CI staff and other CIA counterintelligence components. As the first chief of CIC, Gus Hathaway had two titles: associate deputy director for operations for counterintelligence, and chief of the Counterintelligence Center. Ted Price, his deputy, also wore two hats: deputy chief of the Center, and chief of operations for the Center.

CIC/SIU, or Counterintelligence Center/Special Investigations Unit: Formed by Paul Redmond, the deputy of CIC, in 1991 to reopen the investigation into the '85–'86 losses of Soviet agents. It answered directly to Redmond.

Curran, Ed: FBI special agent. Headed CIA counterespionage in the mid-nineties.

Directorate K: KGB's First Chief Directorate arm responsible for counterintelligence.

Felfe, Heinz: The Bundesnachrichtendienst's (BND) chief of Soviet counterintelligence operations. He was arrested in 1961, tried, and sentenced to fourteen years hard labor for spying for the KGB.

First Chief Directorate: Russia's equivalent to the CIA or Britain's MI6.

Gerber, Burton: CIA chief of station in Moscow, then later chief of Soviet–Eastern European Division. Retired in 1995.

Gordievsky, Oleg: KGB colonel and acting rezident recalled to Moscow in May 1985, nearly a month before Ames's fateful meeting with his Soviet handler at Chadwicks on June 13, 1985. Neither Howard nor Hanssen knew about Gordievsky.

"Gray Mouse": FBI investigation of Jeanne Vertefeuille.

Grimes, Sandy: CIA Ames investigator.

GTPROLOGUE: CIA cryptonym for Aleksandr "Sasha" Zhomov, a Second Chief Directorate officer long a thorn in the CIA's side.

Hall, John: Chief, CIA's Counterintelligence Center.

Hanssen, Robert: FBI agent who spied for the GRU and KGB. First volunteered in New York for the GRU in November 1979, and in October 1985 established contact with the KGB, broke it off in the early nineties, and then reestablished it in 1999. He was arrested in 2001.

Hathaway, Gardner ("Gus"): CIA chief of counterintelligence, 1985–90.

Hayes, Joseph: Senior CIA officer who fell under suspicion as a Russian spy.

Hough, Maryann: Fourth Man investigator, 1994–95.

Howard, Edward Lee: CIA case officer who defected to the Soviet Union. Howard died in Moscow on July 12, 2002, of an accidental fall.

Klimenko, Valentin: Second Chief Directorate officer who rose to head the FSB.

Line KR: The counterintelligence section in a KGB overseas rezidentura.

Lofgren, Bill: Chief of Central Eurasia Division.

MacGaffin, John: Chief of Central Eurasia Division and associate deputy director for operations.

"Max": Alexander Zaporozhsky. First Chief Directorate Line KR officer.

Milburn, James: The FBI's best analyst on the Soviet "target." In 1991, he was assigned to the CIA's SIU to help investigate the 1985–86 losses.

NKVD: People's Commissariat for Internal Affairs. The main Soviet intelligence service between 1933 and 1946.

Price, Hugh "Ted": CIA deputy director of operations who ordered the Fourth Man investigation. Price retired in 1995.

Redmond, Paul: Chief of the CIA's Counterintelligence Center and associate deputy director for counterintelligence. Retired from the CIA in 1997, but brought back in 2001 as part of the Hanssen Damage Assessment.

Rolph, David: CIA chief of station, Moscow.

Second Chief Directorate: KGB division in charge of internal Soviet counterespionage. Roughly equivalent to America's FBI or Britain's MI5.

SIU: Special Investigations Unit in the CIA's Counterintelligence Center (CIC).

Smith, Fran: Chief of Soviet Branch of SE Division, which ran operations inside the Soviet Union. Was brought into CI/STF under Hathaway in 1986. Moved into newly created Investigations Branch of CIC as chief of the Soviet Section in 1988.

Soviet–Eastern European Division: A division under the CIA's deputy director of operations.

Sulick, Mike: Director of the CIA's National Collection Division (2007–10), chief of CIA counterintelligence (2002–4), chief of Central Eurasia Division (1999–2002).

Twetten, Tom: CIA deputy director of operations, 1991–93.

Vertefeuille, Jeanne: Head of SIU/Ames hunt.

Vetrov, Vladimir: Codename FAREWELL. KGB S&T officer working for French intelligence. Arrested in 1982 for murder. While in prison, he was uncovered as a spy and executed in 1983. It is suspected he was betrayed by an American spy other than Howard, Ames, or Hanssen, probably in 1983.

Worthen, Diana: Investigator, Special Investigations Unit.

Yurchenko, Vitaly: KGB colonel who defected to the CIA in Rome on August 1, 1985, then re-defected back to the Soviet Union in October 1985. He was never arrested.

Zaporozhsky, Alexander ("Max"): First Chief Directorate counterintelligence officer.

Zhomov, Aleksandr "Sasha": Second Chief Directorate officer. Encrypted by CIA as GTPROLOGUE. Head of FSB's Americas department.

ACKNOWLEDGMENTS

This book could not have been written without the help of former FBI and CIA investigators who spent their working lives hunting Russian spies in the American government. They were all circumspect to one degree or another, but their experience and advice were indispensable. The book also couldn't have been written without the deep edit and advice of Sam Raim at Hachette. Spending incalculable hours on the manuscript and research, he turned what otherwise would have been a dry counterintelligence investigation into a fast-paced mystery, treating the reader to all the details needed, but not losing them in too much inside baseball. Thanks as well to everyone at Hachette who contributed to the making and publication of this book. Finally, the book would never have come about without the encouragement and vision of my agent Paul Lucas.

NOTES

While this book mainly relies on firsthand reporting, where possible I have included textual sources that corroborate my sources or, in some cases, diverge from what I have learned.

Author's Note

vii **several agencies:** Yevgenia Albats, *The State within a State* (New York: Farrar, Straus and Giroux, 1994), p. 298: "On October 24, 1991, two months before the Soviet Union ceased to exist, Mikhail Gorbachev signed into law the formal end of the KGB. But instead of 'abolition,' the official term for the action was *dezintegratsiya*, dismantling."

Chapter One

2 **Alexander Ivanovich Zaporozhsky:** Gordon Corera, *Russians Among Us* (New York: William Morrow, 2020), p. 57: "In 1993, Zaporozhsky, even though he did not know the traitor's name, passed on a piece of information that helped identify the mole that the KGB and SVR had inside the U.S. intelligence community." Also, while Max appears in both Bryan Denson's *The Spy's Son* (New York: Atlantic Monthly Press, 2015) and Gus Russo and Eric Dezenhall's *Best of Enemies* (New York: Twelve, 2018), both books contain errors about his identity. Denson, for example, notes that he was in the "first department [United States] of the SVR's counterintelligence directorate," but in fact he never worked in that department or had direct access to American cases, namely Ames, Hanssen, and the Fourth Man. Russo misidentifies Max as Avenger, another agent who will appear later in this book.

2 **KGB double agents:** Although I use the term "double agent," Paul Redmond noted to me that the CIA never called them "double agents" but rather

"penetrations." This was also my experience at the CIA, but I have employed common parlance throughout.

2 **known as Max:** Interview with Diana Worthen.

2 **where Sparkman worked, the CIA:** Interview with Mark Sparkman.

4 **get his hands on it:** Interview with Laine Bannerman.

4 **two agents in American intelligence:** Denson, *The Spy's Son*, p. 296: "Zaporozhsky gave up information that helped point U.S. authorities toward Robert Hanssen and other Russian moles inside U.S. intelligence circles, including Aldrich Ames, according to published accounts."

5 **never knew when to trust him:** Interview with CIA officer.

6 **list of suspects:** Interview with Sandy Grimes.

6 **more than two hundred suspects:** Interview with retired FBI Special Agent Dell Spry.

6 **contact with Russian intelligence:** Sandra Grimes and Jeanne Vertefeuille, *Circle of Treason* (Annapolis: Naval Institute Press, 2012), p. 144: "Luckily in 1993 additional information became available. This new information, while it did not identify Ames, pointed in his direction. It added to the comfort level of those who had not been convinced by the results of our analytic efforts and forced the FBI to open a full-scale investigation of Ames."

7 **worthwhile intelligence:** Rolf Mowatt-Larssen, *A State of Mind* (Township, NJ: BookBaby, 2020), p. 145: "All hopes of productive liaison cooperation were dashed."

7 **the charade continued:** Kimberly Dozier, "How Moscow's Spies Keep Duping America—Over and Over Again," *Daily Beast*, June 25, 2017.

7 **Max there as a notetaker:** Tim Weiner, David Johnston, and Neil A. Lewis, *Betrayal* (New York: Random House, 2014), p. 217: "Investigators were bogged down trying to write a final report. Then, in late January 1993, the CIA received an intriguing report from a highly placed intelligence source in Moscow. The source, who is still in place and working for the CIA, did not identify a mole by name or provide the Agency with a smoking gun. But what he had to say closely matched the conclusions of the investigators."

7 **only pocketing it:** Interview with David Rolph.

8 **hotel where they were staying:** Call with Yuri Koshkin, former Russian intelligence officer.

8 **hallways and stairwells:** Interview with Laine Bannerman.

9 **Corbin took Max fishing:** Interview with Laine Bannerman. Paul Redmond also told me that Corbin and Max went fly-fishing early one morning.

9 **one rainy, cold morning:** Interview with John MacGaffin, then CE chief who headed the CIA side of meetings with the Russians. He remembers

Max dropped the Ames/Bogotá/Caracas lead when he went fishing with Corbin.

9 **Yuri Karetkin:** Grimes/Vertefeuille, *Circle of Treason*, p. 132: "The KGB, and later SVR, officers who traveled to meet Ames generally did so in alias, but for some reason one of them used his true name on a trip to Bogotá. We were able to ascertain that he was there at the same time as Rick because Rick had not tried to conceal his travel, merely providing an innocuous explanation."

9 **traveled to Caracas:** Interview with Dick Corbin.

9 **possibly could be corroborated:** Grimes/Vertefeuille, *Circle of Treason*, p. 144. See above.

9 **with those of Ames:** Tennent Bagley, *Spy Wars* (New Haven: Yale University Press, 2008), p. 225: "Then Langley's guardian angel woke up, saw their plight, and sent a miracle from heaven in the form of a new, genuine source from inside the KGB. He pointed them toward a KGB mole inside CIA's ranks."

9 **and search it:** Grimes/Vertefeuille, *Circle of Treason*, p. 145: "On 12 May 1993, the FBI opened a full investigation of Ames." Public accounts about what evidence moved the FBI to seek legal authority to tap Ames's phones, install a concealed camera in his office, and search his house vary. None of my sources remember the exact sequence. One FBI agent at the center of the Ames investigation told me he knew nothing about Max and his Caracas lead.

9 **Ames behind bars:** Grimes/Vertefeuille, *Circle of Treason*, p. 144. See above. Also: Russo/Dezenhall, *Best of Enemies*, p. 8: "Aleksandr Zaporozhsky, possibly AVENGER (b. 1951)—Zaporozhsky was convicted in Russia of having been paid $1 million *each* by the FBI and the CIA in 1993 for the information that may have led to the arrest of Aldrich Ames. . . . Zaporozhsky was arrested by the KGB in 2001 and sentenced to eighteen years in prison. Released in the 2010 spy swap, he flew back to the U.S. . . . Today, he lives in the eastern U.S." As previously noted, Avenger was not Zaporozhsky's cryptonym.

10 **some came to call him the Fourth Man:** Milt Bearden and James Risen, *The Main Enemy* (New York: Random House, 2003), p. 529: "The conclusion is almost inescapable that there was a fourth man—an as yet unidentified traitor who may have left Langley or simply stopped spying by 1986." Also, Milt Bearden, "No Letup in Search for 'the 4th Man,'" *Los Angeles Times*, June 15, 2003.

Chapter Two

14 **Russia operations beyond Ames:** One prominent example: David Wise, "Thirty Years Later We Still Don't Truly Know Who Betrayed These Spies," *Smithsonian Magazine*, November 2015.

14 **sobriquet the Fourth Man:** Bearden, "No Letup in Search for 'the 4th Man.'"

17 **There'd been an investigation:** Interview with Mike Sulick.

17 **Max in the beginning:** Interview with the chief of station of the East African country where Max was met.

17 **Max's story better than he did:** Interviews with CIA case officers who handled Max.

17 **search for the Fourth Man:** Interview with Russia Group head.

18 **London one Saturday night:** Emails with former MI6 officer who worked in Russian operations.

19 **a mole in CIA Soviet operations:** Michael J. Sulick, *American Spies* (Washington, DC: Georgetown University Press, 2020), p. 195: "the CIA suffered from the same disbelief that had plagued counterintelligence in the past, a disbelief that one of its own could spy for the enemy. Still haunted by the legacy of Angleton's witch hunt in the 1970s, the CIA was even less disposed than its sister agencies to suspect a spy in its midst."

19 **brought him back into operations:** Interview with former head of CIA Russian operations.

19 **briefed on the Fourth Man:** Interview with Gina Haspel, who said she'd been briefed on a Russian mole in CIA operations by her heads of counterintelligence (Mark Kelton and Cindy Webb). She did not use the term "Fourth Man," nor did she mention a suspect. She said she was unaware of the current FBI investigation into Redmond.

20 **active FBI investigation:** Multiple sources confirm this. An interview with Redmond confirmed that there was, at least at one point, an investigation. Redmond told me he was well aware the FBI would like to nab him as a Russian spy. He said their main problem is they're cops rather than spy catchers, not to mention in his view most are completely incompetent. There's no point in getting into the name-calling, but Redmond did have choice insults for the agents who worked on the Ames and Fourth Man investigations.

21 **another mole to believe otherwise:** Corera, *Russians Among Us*, p. 118.

Chapter Three

24 **fixation on the KGB:** Bearden/Risen, *The Main Enemy*, pp. 364–65: "Stolz and Twetten knew that the SE Division had to start thinking more broadly to seek out the kind of political intelligence that policy makers in Washington were hungry for as they tried to grapple with the accelerating pace of change in the Soviet Empire. But they also worried that SE Division

managers were still so focused on obtaining yet another microdot message from a spy inside the KGB that they were missing the big picture. Stolz realized that Burton Gerber and his deputy, Paul Redmond, were both products of the SE Division culture and were not the right people to try to change it."

25 *chasse gardée*: Bearden/Risen, *The Main Enemy*, p. 454: "...the growing rift between me and my deputy. In the year since I had returned to the SE Division, I had begun to worry that Redmond and some others on the division staff were stuck in a time warp. Couldn't they see that the revolutions that had swept across Eastern Europe would inevitably change the CIA's mission? The sad truth was that the SE Division's insular subculture didn't want to let go of the Cold War."

25 **America's new best friend, Russia:** Bearden/Risen, *The Main Enemy*, p. 63: "To some back at Langley, in fact, I was considered too much of a Third World cowboy, better suited to dusty covert operations than quiet 'denied-area' spy cases."

26 **off to counterintelligence:** Bearden/Risen, *The Main Enemy*, pp. 364–65. See above.

26 **shunt him off to Bangkok:** Interview with Paul Redmond.

27 **480,000 officers and troops:** Britannica.com.

32 **lives of Americans:** Bearden/Risen, *The Main Enemy*, p. 203. Re Zhomov: "...he felt he knew them all. He had listened carefully to what they said to one another when they felt they were alone in their apartments. He knew when and how often they made love to their wives, or maybe even the wives of other men. He knew what problems they were having on the job in Moscow or back home when they received telephone calls on the Moscow-Washington tie-line. Zhomov and his people knew almost everything you'd want to know about the Americans."

32 **shoulders to cry on:** Bearden/Risen, *The Main Enemy*, p. 201: "As Clayton Lonetree talked, it became clear to Olson that he had fallen into the oldest KGB trap in the business. While serving as a Marine guard at the U.S. embassy in Moscow, Lonetree . . . had met a beautiful Soviet embassy employee."

32 **one former KGB operative:** Interview with Yuri Shvets, a former First Chief Directorate officer assigned to the Washington, DC, rezidentura.

33 **with another million:** Interview with former FSB officer.

34 **recruited him in Moscow:** Interview with former Russia Group chief.

34 **through Congress:** Interviews with Clinton official responsible for Russia.

36 **during the Cold War:** Interview with Laine Bannerman.

NOTES

Chapter Four

41 lackluster tour in Burma: Pete Earley, *Confessions of a Spy* (New York: Berkley, 1998), p. 29: Carleton Ames Burma evaluation: "He has no redeeming values. I don't see any hope for him to improve. I don't blame him as much as I blame our headquarters for sending him out here." P. 32: "He had started drinking heavily in Rangoon and, back home, his family soon began witnessing the degeneration that comes with chronic alcoholism."

42 got into the University of Chicago: Earley, *Confessions of a Spy*, p. 35: "In August 1959, Rick enrolled at the University of Chicago . . . spending all of his time in the theatre. . . . He flunked out his second. . . . Rick stayed in Chicago, performing bit parts in a few plays at night."

42 thanks to his father: Earley, *Confessions of a Spy*, p. 35: "Carleton told Rick not to worry. He would help him get a job at the CIA."

42 "intelligence analysis": https://www.cia.gov/about/organization/.

42 Notoriously lazy: Interview with Sandy Grimes.

42 assigned to Langley: Earley, *Confessions of a Spy*, and Weiner et al., *Betrayal*.

43 modest ambitions: James Olson, *To Catch a Spy* (Washington, DC: Georgetown University Press, 2019), p. 43: "CI professionals have not been favored to the extent they deserved with promotions, assignments, awards, praise, esteem, or other recognition. The truth is CI officers are not popular. They are not welcome when they walk in. They are the skunk of the garden party."

43 hunt that caught him: Dina Temple-Raston and Adelina Lancianese, "Can a Computer Catch a Spy?," NPR, December 8, 2019.

45 with a drunk: Weiner, *Betrayal*, p. 41: "Ames's sworn account of this list, the recollection of a man whose memory has been blunted by alcohol and shaped by self-interest, is flawed on two points. He has sworn that the two Soviets he gave up in April were dangles and that he betrayed no one else until June. But it is indisputable that he also sold out two men who were recalled on pain of death by the KGB in May 1985—Oleg Gordievsky and Sergei Bokhan." This of course has been incessantly disputed.

45 his meetings with the Russians: Interview with Paul Redmond. Redmond told me there was a lot more to it than that. For instance, he had no obvious way to get Ames's travel records, especially when he traveled under State Department order. The story is involved, but basically what Redmond did was enlist an FBI special agent to quietly confront a CIA IT guy in a Langley stairwell. They told the IT guy they needed to do a "spin search" on Ames. Redmond warned the IT guy that if he told anyone about it, including his boss, he would be arrested. The FBI agent made sure the IT guy got a good look at his badge.

46 **right from the beginning:** Weiner, *Betrayal*, p. 145: "Worthen knew Rosario Ames well enough to know that her family was not rich."

47 **unexplained international travel, and so on:** Olson, *To Catch a Spy*, p. 68: "US law severely limited intrusive surveillance of suspects without probable cause, a warrant, and Foreign Intelligence Surveillance Court (FISA Court) approval. The CI investigators, therefore, despite their desire to do so, could not go willy-nilly into the banking, credit card, tax, and travel tax records of the 200 plus candidates."

47 **palace coup:** Catherine Belton, *Putin's People* (New York: Farrar, Straus and Giroux, 2020), p. 118: "Turover refused to disclose the names in the group plotting to remove Yeltsin from power. But it was clear they were angling to replace him with Primakov, who as a former spymaster was one of their number. From the start, the group was looking for evidence directly linking Yeltsin to financial corruption for something that would taint the president irredeemably…'Because he'd been praised as the great democrat, no one knew how to get rid of him,' said Turover. 'The only clear path was a legal path.'"

47 **how many more there were in its ranks:** James M. Olson, "The Ten Commandments of Counterintelligence," *American Intelligence Journal* 21, no. 1/2 (Spring 2002): pp. 21–26.

48 **an NKVD mole:** Roger Hollis.

Chapter Five

49 **former FBI special agent:** Bearden/Risen, *The Main Enemy*, p. 7.

50 **Russian or otherwise:** Bearden/Risen, *The Main Enemy*, p. 6: "The CIA's most important spy in twenty-five years."

50 **missiles and radar:** Sulick, *American Spies*, p. 115: "Tolkachev was an electronic engineer at the Moscow Aviation Institute, which was engaged in the highly classified research and development of the USSR's most advanced weapons systems. Institute researchers like Tolkachev worked on projects so secret that they were not permitted to travel outside the USSR."

50 **intelligence victory:** David E. Hoffman, *The Billion Dollar Spy: A True Story of Cold War Espionage and Betrayal* (New York: Doubleday, 2016).

51 **reported to the KGB:** Interview with former FSB officer.

52 **August 1, 1985:** Bearden/Risen, *The Main Enemy*, p. 73.

52 **handling of Tolkachev:** David Wise, *The Spy Who Got Away* (New York: Random House, 1988), p. 68: "Howard consistently sought to minimize the extent of his knowledge about the CIA's operations in Moscow. He said he

did not know the true names of Soviet agents, since they were encoded [*sic*], or the locations of the operational sites, also coded."

52 **FBI in time:** Bearden/Risen, *The Main Enemy*, p. 87: "the CIA had still not warned the FBI that Edward Howard now might be a threat to national security."

53 **Ronald Pelton:** Bearden/Risen, *The Main Enemy*, pp. 123–24. Re mug books: "The FBI widened the net to include a photo of a former NSA employee. It didn't take long for Yurchenko to identify Ronald Pelton."

53 **intelligence bonanza:** Bearden/Risen, *The Main Enemy*, p. 75: "the biggest counterintelligence catch in the history of the CIA."

54 **spying for the KGB:** Bagley, *Spy Wars*, p. 228: "Pelton and Howard had one disturbing characteristic in common. From the KGB viewpoint, both cases were stone cold dead. Pelton had already left NSA under a cloud and could never return. Howard had gone to the Soviets only after being fired from the CIA, and he had told the KGB all he knew by the time Yurchenko fingered him."

54 **sensitive cases:** Bearden/Risen, *The Main Enemy*, p. 80: "the KGB bureaucracy was filled with dozens of 'deputies' with small areas of responsibility, and few ever knew what their bosses were doing."

54 **valuable agents:** Sulick, *American Spies*, p. 111: "The two major spies whom Yurchenko compromised, Edward Lee Howard and Ronald Pelton, were considered throwaways by some because both were former employees without current access to secrets."

55 **Tolkachev's arrest:** Interview with Joe Wippl, DO rep to the Ames Damage Assessment Team.

55 **stop wondering:** Sulick, *American Spies*, p. 111: "Yurchenko was no more a double agent than Yuri Nosenko had been twenty years earlier."

55 **nothing about Ames:** Bearden/Risen, *The Main Enemy*, p. 81: "But then Yurchenko passed on some KGB gossip that sent a chill through Ames....It seems likely that Yurchenko told Ames that he had heard of a sudden and unexplained trip home to Moscow by the KGB's Washington *Rezident* Stanislov Androsov. Androsov (along with his counterintelligence chief, Viktor Cherkashin) had turned up in Moscow in April or May, so the speculation along the corridors in the First Chief Directorate's headquarters was that something big had happened in Washington at about that time."

55 **water defeats mics:** Bearden/Risen, *The Main Enemy*, p. 14: "...such things could be learned only over time from the 'wall talkers' lined up at the urinals used by senior KGB officers."

56 **position at his institute:** Bearden/Risen, *The Main Enemy*, p. 85: "While most of the case files revealed only the cryptonyms of the Soviets working for the CIA in Moscow, Howard could have gained access to files with their true names."

56 **timing was way too tight:** Interviews with Bannerman and Worthen.

56 **information from his institute:** Hoffman, *The Billion Dollar Spy*, p. 260:
"We share your profound dismay and can only imagine the agony with
which CKSPHERE has lived since late April 1983." CKSPHERE was the
cryptonym for Tolkachev.

57 **somewhere in the institute:** Bearden/Risen, *The Main Enemy*, p. 92: "Rem
Krassilnikov later insisted that the KGB's Second Chief Directorate was
already investigating Tolkachev before the First Chief Directorate provided information about Tolkachev from a source. But while the Second
Chief Directorate had conducted a security probe of Tolkachev's institute in
1983—before receiving Howard's information—the KGB had not focused
on Tolkachev specifically until Howard betrayed him."

57 **allow it to run its course:** Interview with former FSB officer.

58 **as soon as he was caught:** Interview with former FSB officer.

59 **Soviet counterintelligence, which Ames headed:** Interview with Sandy
Grimes, who told me everyone working in Soviet operations in those days
knew about Tolkachev, and even if Ames wasn't read into it he would have
known something about him. Also: Grimes/Vertefeuille, *Circle of Treason*,
p. 77: "Ames knew almost nothing about the case, certainly not enough
to pinpoint Tolkachev before the latter's arrest... it was the most carefully
compartmentalized of all SE operations."

59 **a British agent:** Gordievsky.

59 **June 13 meeting:** Interview with Ames Damage Assessment operations
head Joe Wippl.

60 **Mikhailovich Vasilyev:** GTACCORD. Grimes/Vertefeuille, *Circle of Treason*, p. 84: "Vasilyev was compromised in two stages. His first betrayer was
Edward Lee Howard. According to Yurchenko, during Howard's first meeting with the KGB, which took place in Vienna in late 1984, he reported on
an unnamed 'angry colonel' who was being run by the CIA in Budapest . . .
this report unleashed an investigation of all of the KGB colonels in Budapest. . . . Ames would have had his facts straight because much of the case
was handled by SE CI. . . . The most probable date for Ames' initial betrayal
is 13 June 1985."

60 **in the fall of 1985, Vasilyev:** Grimes/Vertefeuille, *Circle of Treason*, p. 113:
"Vladimir Mikhaylovich Vasilyev, the GRU who had worked with us in
Budapest."

60 **make contact with him in Moscow:** Bearden/Risen, *The Main Enemy*,
p. 151: "In mid-September, Moscow reported that GTACCORD [Vasily-
ev's crypt] had signaled that he had information to pass. But now the SE

Division was worried that the KGB had identified GTACCORD as GRU Colonel Vladimir Mikhailovich Vasilliev. There was a good chance of an ambush if the CIA responded to GTACCORD's request for a meeting in Moscow. So before Moscow was given the green light to meet with GTAC-CORD, I was asked to talk with Yurchenko to try to determine how much progress the KGB had made in identifying the 'angry colonel' whom How-ard had mentioned."

61 **East European operations:** SE/EE/PCH. With PCH standing for Poland, Czechoslovakia, and Hungary.

Chapter Seven

71 **got under way in May 1994:** Interviews with Laine Bannerman and Paul Redmond.

72 **ordered the investigation:** Interview with Paul Redmond.

72 **Ames and Howard:** Olson, "The Ten Commandments of Counterintelligence."

72 **were now legion:** Interview with Diana Worthen.

73 **solitary confinement for almost four years:** www.cia.gov/open/Family. Yuri Ivanovich Nosenko defected in 1964.

73 **Stalin's intelligence services:** NKVD and military intelligence, the GRU.

74 **chalk marks on walls:** Victor Cherkashin, *Spy Handler* (New York: Basic Books, 2004), p. 2: "There was no need to mention our old habit of never saying anything of importance over the telephone, even three years after the collapse of communism."

74 **possibly be bugged:** Cherkashin, *Spy Handler*, p. 22. Re Ames visiting the Soviet embassy on 16th Street: "Deciding to communicate on paper to avoid the risk of wiretaps, we drafted a letter to hand to Wells (the alias Ames first used with the Russians)....I assured the Center we'd hold the meeting in a secure place in the embassy, where we could prevent Wells from recording our conversation."

75 **betraying them:** Cherkashin, *Spy Handler*, p. 8: "In the highly compart-mentalized world of intelligence, our commodity—information—was sacred. Only those who had to know were informed. To have spoken to Kalugin—my former boss and friend—would have amounted to treason." (Refers to Oleg Kalugin, who was unavailable to talk because of ill health.)

75 **sensitive Russian secrets:** Bearden/Risen, *The Main Enemy*, p. 106: "I went to Gerber's four-drawer safe in his outer office and retrieved a small two-ring notebook with a thick red stripe running diagonally across the black cover. I was one of five people in the division with access to the notebook,

which contained the case histories of all SE Division operations going back more than a dozen years."

76 New Headquarters Building: Grimes/Vertefeuille, *Circle of Treason*, p. 117: "The office space itself was a vault within a vault, consisting of a maze of small rooms in a far corner of the basement of the new headquarters building."

76 trusted officers: Bearden/Risen, *The Main Enemy*, p. 166: "Sandy Grimes and Diana Worthen, two trusted and experienced SE Division officials, were put in charge of making the new system work in early 1986."

76 all above suspicion: Grimes/Vertefeuille, *Circle of Treason*, p. 116: "Due to the increase in new assets, the back room added personnel, each handpicked by Sandy and Redmond. In addition to Worthen, two more luminaries were brought in—Sue Eckstein, a retired senior division officer on contract, and Myrna Fitzgerald, a superstar intelligence officer and Sandy's alter ego from their days in the Africa Branch."

77 face-to-face with their boss: Bearden/Risen, *The Main Enemy*, p. 160: "Initially, that meant handling agents without any cable correspondence between Langley and the field. When a new agent was identified and recruited, CIA officers would fly back and forth to Washington to discuss the case. The word went out to senior officers in the field that if they got a potentially important Soviet intelligence source, they were not to send any cables about the case. They should get on a plane and tell Gerber in person."

77 recruitment of a Russian official: Bearden/Risen, *The Main Enemy*, p. 198: "The phony recruitments in Nairobi and Moscow had been painstakingly played out for months without any sign of the bait being taken. Both Soviet intelligence officers set up in the fake operations remained in place, and Redmond concluded the two probes had failed. But why? he wondered."

78 cottage industry in Russian operations: Interview with former CIA officer.

78 when they retired: Interview with former Russia Group chief.

78 When he was first met in East Africa: Interview with Mike Sulick.

79 simply Max: Interview with Diana Worthen.

80 including in China: Bearden/Risen, *The Main Enemy*, p. 371: "Price was not a Soviet expert—he had learned the craft of intelligence along the streets of Hong Kong and Beijing and in Third World postings like Addis Ababa."

80 Price ran counterintelligence: Weiner, *Betrayal*, p. 149: "Webster named Ted Price as the new chief of the Counterintelligence Center."

81 Price knew better: Weiner, *Betrayal*, p. 165: "Ted Price, the center's director, was starting to develop an idea that someone somewhere in the CIA had sold the Soviets secrets in the mid-1980s and then retired."

81 **"With all the unexplained losses":** Interview with Joe Wippl.

82 **piece about him in the *Los Angeles Times*:** Bearden, "No Letup in Search for 'the 4th Man.'"

82 **CIA polygraph operators:** Interview with Mike Sulick. The CIA's problem was lifestyle polygraphs, like digging down into a question of whether someone took a government pen home for personal use. While the FBI, on the other hand, asked one question on a polygraph: "Are you a spy?"

82 **cloud of suspicion:** Interview with former CIA officer.

82 **"holding pens":** Interview with former CIA officer.

83 **White House orders:** Sulick, *American Spies*, pp. 202–3: "The White House introduced its own reforms. In May 1994 President Bill Clinton issued a presidential directive establishing the National Counterintelligence Center to coordinate activities more effectively among agencies involved in counterintelligence, particularly the FBI and CIA."

83 **An FBI agent:** Wise, *Spy*, p. 172: "In August 1994, Curran came from the FBI to CIA headquarters in Langley, Virginia, and took over the Counterespionage Group. In that post he supervised SIU, which was first located on the fourth floor of the new CIA headquarters building."

83 **spies in its own ranks:** Christopher Lynch, *The C.I. Desk* (Indianapolis: Dog Ear Publishing, 2010), p. 305: "Ed Curran was not terribly adaptable, and heading a CIA office was very frustrating to him. He was also having health problems that led to dizzy spells, and he was occasionally blowing up in anger."

84 **Department of Justice:** Lynch, *The C.I. Desk*, p. 306: "With the new rules that were imposed after Rick Ames was arrested, even the slightest hint of a possible crime was now enough to require passing the lead to the FBI."

85 **it never notified CIA management:** Interviews with a retired FBI agent who worked on the Ames hunt, Sandy Grimes, and John MacGaffin, the ADDO at the time of Vertefeuille's investigation.

85 **sensitive counterintelligence cases:** Jack Devine, *Good Hunting: An American Spymaster's Story* (New York: Picador, 2015).

85 **how toxic things were at the CIA:** Interview with Diana Worthen.

86 **executive suites:** Interview with Paul Redmond.

86 **warrants on CIA officers:** Interview with former CIA officer.

86 **"each other's laundry":** Bearden, *The Main Enemy*, p. 470. Richard Kerr to Bearden.

87 **"too paranoid and in love with detail":** Interview with Joe Wippl.

Chapter Eight

91 Laine Bannerman: Wise, *Spy*, p. 173: "Laine Bannerman, whose father had headed CIA security a generation early, was the first, albeit short-lived, head of SIU. 'She was very friendly, a DO person from the Russian side,' Curran said, 'but very protective of the CIA. She thought she was in charge and would decide what the FBI got. We had to resolve that right away. We immediately had conflicts. She's trying to protect the agency's jewels, and we're trying to investigate.'"

91 call from Paul Redmond: Grimes/Vertefeuille, *Circle of Treason*, p. 127: "Paul Redmond joined CIC in April 1991, as deputy to Olson. On one of his first days in the center, he and Jeanne went down to the FBI to deliver a sensitive memorandum to Ray Mislock. . . . Paul mentioned that Jeanne was planning to revisit the 1985 problem."

92 "I want Diana Worthen": Wise, *Spy*, p. 172: "Only Diana Worthen, a midwesterner who had been Ames's intelligence assistant in Mexico City, was a holdover from Jeanne Vertefeuille's task force. She had good qualifications for the job—it was Worthen who was the first to raise the alarm about her old boss when she saw his affluent lifestyle and large house in Arlington, Virginia. But Worthen stayed with the new mole hunt unit less than two years."

93 "knew her stuff": Interview with Paul Redmond.

93 CIA's founders: cia.gov: Robert L. Bannerman, deputy director for support.

94 at larger stations: Interview with Laine Bannerman.

95 kept in the dark: Interview with Sandy Grimes, in which she said there was a case when she and Redmond kept Bearden out of the loop although Bearden, the Russian division chief, was Redmond's boss.

96 shown the door: Interview with John MacGaffin.

96 as a coffin: Bearden/Risen, *The Main Enemy*, p. 62: "SE Division . . . the most insular subculture in the CIA's Directorate of Operations."

97 none the wiser: Olson, "The Ten Commandments of Counterintelligence": "It has been true for years—to varying degrees through the IC—that CI professionals have not been favored, to the extent they deserved, with promotions, assignments, awards, praise, esteem, or other recognition. The truth is CI officers are not popular. They are not always welcome when they walk in. They usually bring bad news. They are easy marks to criticize when things go wrong. Their successes are their failure."

101 named Jim Milburn: Grimes/Vertefeuille, *Circle of Treason*, p. 128: "Jim Milburn was the FBI's top analyst on the Soviet target. Unfortunately, while he was respected for his knowledge, his system did not adequately reward him because he was an analyst, not a special agent, and therefore a second-class citizen."

101 **second-class citizen:** Grimes/Vertefeuille, *Circle of Treason*, p. 107.

Chapter Nine

103 **counterintelligence entity, SIU:** Grimes/Vertefeuille, *Circle of Treason*, p. 128: "…which we named the Special Investigations Unit of the Counterintelligence Center, or CIC/SIU, which reported to the CIC front office, specifically Paul Redmond."

104 **large utility closet:** Wise, *Spy*, p. 172: "…SIU, which was first located on the fourth floor of the new CIA headquarters building and then hidden undercover behind an unmarked door on the first floor of the adjoining older headquarters building. About seven CIA and three or four FBI specialists staffed the SIU. So secret was the mole hunt unit that very few of the 125 employees of the CIA's Counterespionage Group knew what it was doing or even where it was. Only a handful of CIA people were allowed into the SIU office, although dozens of FBI agents had free access."

106 **full-fledged investigation:** Olson, *To Catch a Spy*, p. 68: "US law severely limited intrusive surveillance of suspects without probable cause, a warrant, and Foreign Intelligence Surveillance Court (FISA Court) approval. The CI investigators, therefore, despite their desire to do so, could not go willy-nilly into the banking, credit card, tax, and travel tax records of the 200 plus candidates."

109 **taking over counterintelligence:** James Risen, "David H. Blee, 83, C.I.A. Spy Who Revised Defector Policy," *New York Times*, August 17, 2000.

109 **a typewriter:** Grimes/Vertefeuille, *Circle of Treason*, p. 105.

109 **rank or reputation:** Grimes/Vertefeuille, *Circle of Treason*, p. 129: "Because it is of course impossible to investigate 160 people without an army to do the job, it was necessary to effect some stringent prioritization. The method Jeanne developed has received a substantial amount of criticism, although no one has been able to articulate a better solution."

110 **Ames in jail:** Corera, *Russians Among Us*, p. 57. Re Zaporozhsky: "But he had been hard to handle, sometimes feeding erratic information to his handlers and disappearing for long periods."

110 **annotated chronology:** Weiner, *Betrayal*, p. 166.

111 **'85–'86 losses:** Interview with former counterintelligence analyst.

112 **get sidetracked:** Interview with Joe Wippl, who headed the Ames Damage Assessment for the Directorate of Operations.

114 **compromised him:** Interview with former head of Russia Group.

116 **"most dangerous man in the KGB":** Ben Macintyre, *The Spy and the Traitor* (New York: Crown, 2019), p. 213: "Colonel Viktor Budanov of Directorate K, the counterintelligence branch, was by general agreement the 'most dangerous man in the KGB.' In the 1980s he had served in East Germany, where one of the KGB officers under his command was the young Vladimir Putin. Within Directorate K, his role was to investigate 'abnormal developments,' maintain security within the various intelligence branches of the First Chief Directorate, eliminate corruption in the ranks, and root out spies. A dedicated communist, spare and desiccated, he had the face of a fox and the mind of a highly trained lawyer. His approach to his work was methodical and fastidious. He saw himself as a detective, working to uphold the rules, not an agent of retribution."

116 **rather than British:** Interview with former head of Russia Group.

117 **remains a mystery:** Grimes/Vertefeuille, *Circle of Treason*, p. 170.

118 **didn't mean much:** Bearden/Risen, *The Main Enemy*, p. 528: "Oleg Gordievsky was another unresolved case. He was recalled to Moscow in May 1985, before Hanssen went to the KGB and before Ames's fateful meeting at Chadwicks. The fact that the KGB questioned but did not immediately arrest Gordievsky suggests that they lacked the hard evidence that they had against the other compromised agents. Ames has been held responsible for betraying Gordievsky, and there is no doubt that he identified him to the KGB. But he did so on June 13, by which time Gordievsky was already back in Moscow and under hostile interrogation."

118 **Sergei Ivanovich Bokhan:** Grimes/Vertefeuille, *Circle of Treason*, p. 72: "Sergei Ivanovich Bokhan . . . his fear in late May 1985 that he was being recalled to Moscow on a ruse."

118 **June 13 meeting:** Interview with Laine Bannerman.

118 **went to jail:** Interview with Dick Corbin.

120 **never seen the document:** I've heard varying and contradictory accounts about which classified CIA documents (or summaries of them) showed up in Moscow in the eighties. But what matters for this story is that SIU was certain neither Howard nor Ames was responsible for passing them to the KGB.

120 **Nikolai Chernov:** Grimes/Vertefeuille, *Circle of Treason*, p. 64: "In the early 1990s some twenty years after his last contact with the FBI, Chernov was arrested in Moscow. In the more permissive post–Cold War atmosphere, he was sentenced to eight years but amnestied after less than a year. He was known to Ames and, presumably, Hanssen. One or both of them no doubt fingered him to the KGB."

121 **FBI and CIA:** Lynch, *The C.I. Desk*, p. 373. Yuzhin, unbeknownst to SIU, had also been betrayed by Hanssen.

121 **Soviet consulate offices:** Grimes/Vertefeuille, *Circle of Treason*, p. 71: "In 1982, Yuzhin returned to Moscow for a new assignment. His FBI handlers did not want the CIA to run him in the Soviet Union, and he had not been issued any means of internal communication. We heard nothing about him until the defection of KGB CI officer Vitaliy Sergeyevich Yurchenko at the beginning of August 1985. Yurchenko reported that the KGB had found the spy camera in a recreation room in the Soviet consulate and launched an extensive CI investigation. This inquiry was later bolstered by some vague reporting from Edward Lee Howard, the former CIA officer who volunteered to the KGB in 1984. Eventually, the field of suspects had been narrowed to a very few. One of those was Yuzhin."

121 **anomalies column:** Bearden/Risen, *The Main Enemy*, p. 126. Hanssen sent a letter to the KGB outing Yuzhin, as well as Sergei Motorin and Valery Martynov, both KGB operatives.

121 **Vladimir Ippolitovich Vetrov:** Public sources differ on when Vetrov was arrested and executed, but Vertefeuille and Grimes report he was executed in early 1983 (*Circle of Treason*, p. 82).

121 **FAREWELL reportedly:** Interview with Bearden, who said he didn't believe a word about the murder and confession stuff related to FAREWELL's arrest. Rather, Bearden believes it's a concocted story to protect the agent who truly betrayed FAREWELL.

121 **executed in 1983:** Grimes/Vertefeuille, *Circle of Treason*, pp. 80–82.

129 **gales of laughter:** Interview with Laine Bannerman.

130 **double agent was active:** Interview with Laine Bannerman.

130 **operation run there:** Bearden/Risen, *The Main Enemy*, pp. 327–28: "Vladimir Tsymbal had been sent from Moscow to visit the Washington Rezidentura in 1985 and again in 1987. Tsymbal . . . was a covert communications specialist in the First Chief Directorates Line KR. The CIA knew from past experience that Tsymbal was used by the KGB to arrange the delicate covert agent communications details for highly sensitive operations. He was one of the KGB's top technical experts, and when Tsymbal showed up somewhere, the CIA's first instincts were to start looking for a spy. So why had Tsymbal been sent to Washington in 1985 and again two years later? What agent operations in Washington were so important that they required Moscow's best covert communications tech?"

131 **"covert communications tech":** Bearden/Risen, *The Main Enemy*, p. 327. Hanssen wasn't in touch with Russian intelligence when Tsymbal visited Washington, so he wasn't the double agent being serviced.

270

NOTES

Chapter Ten

136 Langley and the FBI: Interview with Laine Bannerman.

137 The Monster Plot: Grimes/Vertefeuille, *Circle of Treason*, p. 21: "Within the CIA a maze of double- and triple-think developed toward all operational activity against the Soviet Union. It was later dubbed the 'Monster Plot' and its subscribers were known as the 'Back Hats.'"

138 back into Russian operations: Interview with Bill Lofgren. In coordination with the FBI, Lofgren told Ames he'd make him chief of Russia Group, giving him the impression he wasn't under investigation.

140 foreign intelligence service: Ludwig Albert. See Bagley, *Spy Wars*, p. 138.

140 if the story ever came out: Interview with Yuri Shvets.

140 Aleksandr Vasilyevich Zhomov: Bearden/Risen, *The Main Enemy*, p. 202: "Valentin Klimenko was Rem Krassilnikov's deputy, and Aleksandr Zhomov directly supervised the people who watched the Americans twenty-four hours a day, seven days a week."

141 beyond Ames: Mowatt-Larssen, *A State of Mind*, p. 150. Klimenko: "Who's the other mole?"

141 genuine double agent: Interview with Rolf Mowatt-Larssen.

141 beyond Ames: Cherkashin, *Spy Handler*, p. 253.

142 "Gray Mouse": Interview with Dell Spry.

Chapter Eleven

146 British embassy: James Risen, "A Frantic Call, a Fifth of Bourbon," *Los Angeles Times*, December 29, 1997. Also: Grimes/Vertefeuille, *Circle of Treason*, p. 137: "...received some misleading reporting from Sergei Papushin, the defector from the KGB's internal CI component, to the effect that this component was running a CIA officer who had been assigned to Moscow."

147 untrustworthy elite: Andrei Soldatov and Irina Borogan, *The New Nobility* (New York: PublicAffairs, 2010), p. 11: "The KGB was rife with internal rivalries. The foreign intelligence directorate, the First Chief Directorate, a powerful agency arm, looked down upon counterintelligence officers. The directorate felt it was more enlightened because of its exposure to the outside world, and it felt the counterintelligence agents were narrow-minded and inward looking."

147 defect to the CIA: Corera, *Russians Among Us*, p. 286: "...FSB to press their case that the SVR could not be trusted to look after its own internal security."

147 **only four Second Chief Directorate officers:** Interviews with former CIA officers.

147 **espionage than the First:** Interview with Laine Bannerman.

148 **anything about them:** Message on LinkedIn from Mike Rochford.

150 **a CIA apartment in Maryland:** Risen, "A Frantic Call, a Fifth of Bourbon."

151 **before he was found dead:** Interview with Diana Worthen.

151 **point a finger at him:** As highly improbable as it was, SIU couldn't categorically exclude the possibility that Ames had tipped off the KGB to Papushin's location and a KGB-hired assassin forced a bottle of bourbon down his throat, fast and in enough quantity to kill him. There's a term for it: forced alcohol intoxication. The intent presumably would have been to punish Papushin for defecting or, for the truly conspiratorially minded, seal his lips for good about a Russian double agent in the CIA. The FBI dismisses this possibility because, according to the medical examiner's report, Papushin was already about one bottle of scotch away from the grave.

152 **independently in Washington:** Andrei Soldatov, "Inside Vladimir Putin's Shadowy Army of Global Spies," *Daily Beast*, August 30, 2021.

152 **independently of the First:** LinkedIn message.

152 **Vladislav Kovshuk:** Bagley, *Spy Wars*, p. 282: "KGB counterintelligence officer, head of its section working against the American embassy in Moscow."

153 **CIA Russian operations:** Interview with former head of Russia Group.

154 **not the Soviet embassy:** Interview with former FSB officer.

Chapter Twelve

159 **at one point Sue Eckstein:** Grimes/Vertefeuille, *Circle of Treason*, pp. 116–17.

159 **"breeds disaster":** Interview with Laine Bannerman.

160 **Gus Hathaway:** Grimes/Vertefeuille, *Circle of Treason*, p. 112: formation of Counterintelligence Center: "Gus Hathaway would now wear two hats: Associate Deputy Director for Operations for Counterintelligence, and Chief of the Counterintelligence Center. Senior DO officer Ted Price was brought in and also wore two hats: Deputy Chief of the Center, and Chief of Operations for the Center."

161 **Redmond also was on the list:** Interview with Sandy Grimes.

161 **on a dark night:** The Redmond character, portrayed by Stuart Milligan, is named Arthur O'Neill. Redmond is credited as a consultant.

162 **"not abandoned":** Interview with Milt Bearden.

162 **"would give a fuck":** Weiner, *Betrayal*, p. 165: "'Paul's an intelligent guy with an abrasive manner that he cultivates,' Ames said."

163 **the bottom of the '85–'86 losses:** Bearden/Risen, *The Main Enemy*, p. 378: "The Vertefeuille investigation continued for years, but it was crippled from the start by the fact that Hathaway had made it clear that he didn't want a full-fledged mole hunt, one that would have included polygraph examinations of all those who had access to the blown cases."

163 **lascivious behavior:** Interview with Milt Bearden.

164 **most of the Soviet agents:** Bearden/Risen, *The Main Enemy*, p. 48: "Jim Olson, the taciturn chief of the SE Division's operations group, which oversaw all activities inside the Soviet Union and the Warsaw Pact countries."

165 **in Mexico City:** Weiner, *Betrayal*, p. 145: "A CIA officer named Diana Worthen first stumbled onto this stage set of suburban splendor in November 1989. She knew Rick and Rosario from Mexico City, where she had worked side by side with Rick as a reports officer focused on the KGB residency. . . . Worthen was a good CIA officer, trained to notice details and discrepancies."

165 **spying on the KGB:** Interview with Bill Lofgren. Also: Grimes/Vertefeuille, *Circle of Treason*, p. 175: "[Ames] was assigned to the 'KGB Working Group,' and worked closely with the new division chief, Milt Bearden. His job was to think strategically about how the CIA should manage its dealing with the KGB in the future. This effort has been described as 'placing the stake in the heart of the KGB,' but the evidence does not support that view . . . the KGB was no longer considered a major adversary and Ames, as instructed by Bearden, wrote short conceptual reports about the new outlook."

166 **subject to it themselves:** Interview with former CIA case officer.

166 **beloved Soviet division:** Interview with John Lewis. Lewis was seconded to the station in Vienna when Corbin was there as chief. Corbin told Lewis he was worried Bearden was off seeing the Russians when Bearden was on visits. Lewis took this to mean Corbin suspected Bearden was a Russian spy. It's neither here nor there, but it gives you an idea about the paranoia.

168 **including Bearden:** Interview with Sandy Grimes.

169 **took place, Berlin:** Call with former head of Russia Group.

169 **Second Chief Directorate:** Interview with Laine Bannerman.

170 **volunteer or a dangle:** Interview with Dave Rolph.

170 **Sulick debriefed Alex:** Interview with Mike Sulick.

171 **CIA cable traffic:** Interview with Sandy Grimes.

Chapter Thirteen

174 documents mentioned by Yurchenko: Benjamin B. Fischer, "My Two Moles: A Memoir," *International Journal of Intelligence and CounterIntelligence* 35, no. 1: pp. 147–63.

177 from CIA security: The account of this briefing comes from interviews with multiple former CIA officers. In a phone call, Gina Haspel said that she'd heard about an SIU confrontation with Redmond. She did not say anyone had implicated him in espionage. Nor did anyone in the CIA brief her that Redmond might be a KGB spy.

178 betrayed all three, period: Redmond told me he still believes Ames betrayed Gordievsky.

179 Ames never had access: Fischer, "My Two Moles." Fischer writes that Hanssen passed the counterintelligence to the KGB.

Chapter Fourteen

182 interview the CIA director had just given: Tim Weiner, "Man in the News: John Mark Deutch; Reluctant Helmsman for a Troubled Agency," *New York Times Magazine*, March 11, 1995.

182 "don't bother asking": Lofgren now doesn't remember ever mentioning to me his "special project" or hinting about a seventh-floor mole when I worked for him in CE Division. But it doesn't matter because this story depends on the memories of dozens of spy catchers who hunted the Fourth Man rather than ours. Also: Lynch, *The C.I. Desk*, p. 306: "A good chunk of another counterespionage office was purged at nearly the same time I was. Laine Bannerman, Diana Worthen, and Maryann were all kicked out together, and most of the remaining unit members angrily left the Center as soon as they could find jobs."

183 women of World War II fame: Interview with Milt Bearden.

184 special project staff meeting: Lynch, *The C.I. Desk*, p. 306: "Laine, Diana, and Maryann all ended up back in CE Division, and I frequently saw them together. We had become a small subculture of the purged, and they supported me as I kept them posted on what was happening with me. We joked among ourselves, wondering how long it would take them to change the locks now that they had removed us. A week and a half. . . . The unit members were closemouthed about why they had been purged, but when I talked to them, it was obvious that mentioning referrals of cases to the FBI touched a raw nerve. With the new rules that were imposed after Rick Ames was arrested, even the slightest hint of a possible crime was now enough to require passing the lead to the FBI. Despite promising discretion, the FBI would swoop down in force, and reputations were ruined even before any real 'probable cause' was established."

186 **in the hundreds:** Wise, *Spy*, p. 176: "...the CIA and the FBI were slowly working their way through a bureaucratic maze known inside the CIA as 'the-A-to-Z list.' The list was a direct fallout from the Ames case. The Counterespionage Group and CIA's Office of Security (OS) were reviewing a huge backlog of polygraph tests to make sure another mole was not lurking somewhere inside Langley. It was a tedious, time-consuming job. . . . 'The A-to-Z list had about three hundred people who had SPRs,' said one CIA official. 'Significant Physiological Responses on the polygraph. Some of those on the list had nothing to do with CI. Some had contacts with foreign nationals. Several dozen were referred to the bureau, as required by law. The vast majority were sorted out by the Office of Security.' "

188 **taken against them:** Interview with Laine Bannerman.

189 **"caught the Fourth Man":** Interview with Laine Bannerman.

189 **it was in fact the FBI:** Interview with Paul Redmond.

190 **a CIA analyst:** Wise, *Spy*, p. 173: "Soon, Mary Sommer, a CIA reports officer from the Central Eurasia (CE) division, was brought in to run the unit, although Bannerman remained a member."

190 **most importantly Max's:** Interview with Laine Bannerman.

190 **Max's intelligence:** Interview with Laine Bannerman.

190 **heart-wrenching for her:** Interview with Laine Bannerman.

Chapter Fifteen

193 **FBI to his side:** Lynch, *The C.I. Desk*, p. 307: "It wasn't until David Wise's *Spy: The Inside Story of How the FBI's Robert Hanssen Betrayed America* that I saw confirmation that the FBI referrals was indeed the driving force behind the purge."

194 **"I'll kill you":** Interview with Laine Bannerman.

194 **"gruff personality":** Lynch, *The C.I. Desk*, p. 192: "Paul had a reputation for flying off the handle...It seemed to be the standard DO management style at the time."

195 **withholding evidence:** Lynch, *The C.I. Desk*, p. 306: "The unit members were closemouthed about why they had been purged, but when I talked with them, it was obvious that mentioning referrals of cases to the FBI touched a raw nerve."

196 **Department of Justice for prosecution:** Interview with Laine Bannerman.

196 **"we're trying to investigate":** Wise, *Spy*, p. 173.

Chapter Sixteen

203 **being a double agent:** Bearden/Risen, *The Main Enemy*, p. 197.

204 **the Ames scent:** Interview with Mike Sulick.

204 **counterintelligence databases:** Interviews with Laine Bannerman and Diana Worthen.

205 **MI6 disputed this:** Interviews with Laine Bannerman and Diana Worthen.

205 **called his CIA contact:** Interview with Dave Manners.

206 **people had met Koecher:** Grimes/Vertefeuille, *Circle of Treason*, p. 124: "After the Czech Velvet Revolution in 1989, he [Koecher] visited the West. Dan contacted him and talked to him at some length. Dan's interest in Koecher revolved around the period that Koecher had been assigned to SE Division. Although he worked in a building outside CIA headquarters, he interacted with his fellow transcribers at the same outlying location."

208 **ones Redmond ignored:** Interview with Laine Bannerman.

208 **Ames knew about:** Interview with Laine Bannerman.

208 **favorite suspect:** Earley, *Confessions of a Spy*, p. 294: "Milburn and Holt didn't like the idea. Relying on a poll to whittle down a suspect list ran against everything they had been trained to do at the FBI."

208 **unpopularity contest:** Grimes/Vertefeuille, *Circle of Treason*, p. 129: "Jeanne and Sandy did some further paring, removing from the list a few people whom they subjectively believed were unlikely to betray their country. Then they submitted the new, smaller list to a vote. Those who voted included Sandy, Jeanne, the two Jims, Paul Redmond, Jim Olson, Fran Smith, John O'Reilly (who at the time was CI chief in SE Division), and Wade and Mislock."

209 **damage Hanssen had caused:** Interview with Paul Redmond.

209 **Ames Damage Assessment:** Interview with Joe Wippl.

209 **"You simply couldn't win":** Interview with Joe Wippl.

210 **including Redmond:** Interview with Laine Bannerman.

212 **veterans like Fran Smith:** Grimes/Vertefeuille, *Circle of Treason*, p. 104: "Fran Smith, who transferred from her job as chief of the Branch in SE Division that ran our operations inside the Soviet Union. . . . Fran was the best prepared, possessing up-to-date and in-depth familiarity with the operations that SE had been running in recent years."

212 **access to the lost agents:** Lynch, *The C.I. Desk*, p. 228. Names O'Reilly meeting Gordievsky. Redmond and Grimes attended the meeting, too.

213 **Redmond disputes this:** Interview with Paul Redmond.
214 **Rolph flew to Berlin:** Interview with former Russia Group chief.
214 **Langley was bugged:** Interview with Paul Redmond.

Chapter Seventeen

218 **Harold "Jim" Nicholson:** Denson, *The Spy's Son*, p. 296: "It was Zaporozhsky, counterintelligence experts would later confirm to me, whose assistance to the U.S. government helped put Jim Nicholson behind bars in 1996."

Chapter Eighteen

221 **out of Moscow:** Denson, *The Spy's Son*, p. 296: "Getting Zaporozhsky back to the U.S. was a major victory for the CIA."
221 **into the United States:** Interview with Mike Sulick.
221 **a low-level agent in Moscow:** Interview with Laine Bannerman.
222 **coordinated fashion:** Interview with Laine Bannerman.
223 **wasn't for naught:** Interview with Laine Bannerman.
223 **SIU's in-case memo:** Interview with Laine Bannerman, who was told this by Maryann Hough. I asked Sulick about the in-case memo and he never answered. Various sources tell me the memo never made its way to the FBI.
223 **out of the KGB:** From everything I know about the KGB, it's unlikely Budanov was completely out and was no doubt at this point in the active reserve.
223 **Sulick said it was fine:** By the time Redmond told me this story, Sulick had stopped speaking to me.
223 **Budanov was of no help:** Interview with Paul Redmond. Redmond was suspiciously vague about his American partner who initially set up the meeting with the London lawyers who represented Budanov. He first said he was dead, and then said he'd never talk to me. Oddly, he couldn't remember his name.
224 **former NSA official:** Leslie Wayne, "The Nation: Rent-a-Spy; Cold War Foes Join as Capitalist Tools," *New York Times*, February 7, 1999.
225 **prevent him from making the trip:** Interview with Mike Sulick.
225 **eighteen years of hard labor:** Denson, *The Spy's Son*, p. 297: "The district's military court later found Zaporozhsky guilty of betraying Hanssen—the greatest mole Moscow ever ran inside the KGB—and sentenced him to eighteen years for high treason."

226 **the threat against him:** Adam Goldman, Julian E. Barnes, Michael S. Schmidt, and Matt Apuzzo, "U.S. Spies Rush to Protect Defectors After Skripal Poisoning," *New York Times*, September 13, 2018.

Chapter Nineteen

228 **fairly certain of it:** Interview with Milt Bearden. The only CIA officers in those years allowed to make official (liaison) contact with the KGB were Chief/CE Burton Gerber and head of counterintelligence Gus Hathaway. It was called the Gavrilov channel. It started in Vienna in 1984. See Bearden/Risen, *The Main Enemy*, p. 189.

229 **possible criminal prosecution:** Interview with Jim Olson.

229 **visiting Soviet delegation:** Cherkashin, *Spy Handler*, p. 54: "The SCD was tasked with monitoring Soviet delegations abroad."

232 **by-the-books approach:** The FBI has been known to cut corners. One recent example is Carter Page. The FBI used the Steele dossier, far from hard evidence, to reopen their investigation.

Epilogue

236 **off-the-books mole hunt:** Interview with Paul Redmond. Redmond told me that he made a practice of conducting extremely compartmented counterintelligence investigations.

237 **"to invent the iPhone or something":** Interview with Tom Rakusan.

237 **answer the Pentagon's questions:** Interview with Dave Manners, who was on Soviet Branch when the Pentagon sent over the list.

238 **passed the Pentagon's questions to the KGB:** Interview with Milt Bearden, who confirmed Pentagon wish list. Said list had to do with things like clocking submarine acoustics. He said that when he was number two in the Soviet division in the mid-eighties the Pentagon queries related to advanced Soviet weapons was never sent up to the front office, and agreed it would have been held by USSR reports. After Islamabad, when he came back as C/SE in 1989, they were starting to figure out the Russian walk-ins were dangles, part of a systemic KGB disinformation campaign. He has no idea who might have given the Pentagon list to the KGB.

239 **Redmond believes he was:** Interview with Paul Redmond.

240 **just the start of it:** Corera, *Russians Among Us*, p. 45: "The end of the Cold War had not been a moment to relax for Directorate S. Rather it was a time to double down. The world was fluid and uncertain and that meant intelligence was more important than ever."

NOTES

241 **hand in the cookie jar:** Belton, *Putin's People*, p. 119.

241 **salacious kompromat:** Belton, *Putin's People*, p. 130: "Yumashev and the little known Vladimir Putin took matters into their own hands....They gave the copy of the tape [of Skuratov with prostitutes] to a federal TV channel....Putin gave a press conference...at which he vowed that the tape was authentic."

241 **definitely true:** Belton, *Putin's People*, p. 127: "...a tape would be the ultimate kompromat, powerful enough to cost Skuratov his job and close down the Mabetex case." But Belton doesn't apparently know who made the tape. She implicates Nazir Khapsirokov, head of the prosecutor's property department.

241 **in the first place:** For a summary of the Mabetex scandal, see: Sharon LaFraniere, "Yeltsin Linked to Bribe Scheme," *Washington Post*, September 8, 1999.

242 **Putin's rise was nearly complete:** Interview with senior Clinton NSC official working on Russia.

242 **minister of railways:** Belton, *Putin's People*, p. 137: "Until late June, part of Yeltsin's family had been toying with the idea of another candidate, Nikolai Aksenenko, the railways minister, who they believed would more strongly defend their interests, but Yeltsin soon took a strong dislike to him."

242 **incrementally poisoned:** Interview with senior Clinton NSC official working on Russia.

242 **patiently reminded her father:** Steven Lee Myers, *The New Tsar: The Rise and Reign of Vladimir Putin* (New York: Vintage, 2016), p. 62: "After Sobchak's election, Putin ended his work at the university, and in June 1991 he joined the mayor's staff as the director of the city's committee on foreign relations."

242 **ex-mayor of St. Petersburg:** Anatoly Alexandrovich Sobchak.

243 **spiriting him out of the country:** Belton, *Putin's People*, p. 140. Re Yumashev: "What struck him most, he said, was his dogged loyalty to his former mentor and boss, Anatoly Sobchak, the former St. Petersburg mayor...He'd [Putin] whisked him off on a private jet."

243 **one of them, a reformist:** Corera, *Russians Among Us*, p. 110: "Berezovsky soon learned he had underestimated the man he had sponsored. His TV station had criticized the new president when the *Kursk* submarine sank, with the loss of 118 lives, in August 2000. Putin was lacerated for vacationing while the sailors perished. Putin summoned Berezovsky to the Kremlin and told him to hand over his TV channel. Berezovsky refused. He fled to the United Kingdom and claimed asylum."

243 **when the iron's hot:** Masha Gessen, *The Man Without a Face* (New York: Riverhead, 2013), p. 94. Re KGB chairman Vadim Bakatin, who was appointed by Gorbachev to dismantle the KGB: "The KGB, as it existed, could not be

termed a secret service. It was an organization formed to control and sup-
press everything and anything. It seemed to be created especially for orga-
nizing conspiracies and coups, and it possessed everything necessary to
carry them out: its own specially trained armed forces, the capacity to track
and control communications, its own people inside all essential organizations, a monopoly on information, and many other things."

243 **It happened in 2000:** "Vladimir Putin and Bill Clinton had their first meeting as the US president visited Moscow," Kremlin news service, June 3,
2020, http://en.kremlin.ru/events/president/news/38511.

244 **"I hope he becomes one":** Interview with Ambassador Collins.

244 **who can say for sure:** Belton, *Putin's People*, p. 153: "'The institutions the
security men worked in did not break down,' said Thomas Graham, the former senior director for Russia on the US National Security Council. 'The
personal networks did not disappear. What they needed simply was an individual who could bring these networks back together. That was the future. If
it hadn't been Putin, it would have been someone else like him.'"

Who's Who

246 **knew about Gordievsky:** Bearden/Risen, *The Main Enemy*, p. 528.

247 **Retired in 1995:** Bearden/Risen, *The Main Enemy*, p. 536.

247 **head the FSB:** Bearden/Risen, *The Main Enemy*, p. 534.

248 **investigate the '85–'86 losses:** Grimes/Vertefeuille, *Circle of Treason*, p. 128.

248 **Price retired in 1995:** Bearden/Risen, *The Main Enemy*, p. 536. The book
has him retiring in 1996, but my reporting clearly contradicts this.

248 **Hanssen Damage Assessment:** Bearden/Risen, *The Main Enemy*, p. 536.

248 **chief of station, Moscow:** Bearden/Risen, *The Main Enemy*, p. 536.

249 **probably in 1983:** Bearden/Risen, *The Main Enemy*, p. 528: "Viewed against
the pattern of betrayal and misdirection, it is possible, if not probable, that
Vetrov was betrayed—like Bokhan, Polyshchuk, and possibly Gordievsky—
by an American who has still not been identified."

249 **He was never arrested:** Bearden/Risen, *The Main Enemy*, p. 533.

249 **Head of FSB's Americas department:** Bearden/Risen, *The Main Enemy*, p. 534.

INDEX

INDEX